CW01213574

Rider & Horse
Back to Back

Susanne von Dietze
Isabelle von Neumann-Cosel

Translated by Julia Welling

TS

TRAFALGAR SQUARE
North Pomfret, Vermont

First published in 2011 by
Trafalgar Square Books
North Pomfret, Vermont 05053

Printed in China

Originally published in the German language as *Rücksicht auf den Reiterücken* by FNverlag der Deutschen Reiterlichen Vereinigung GmbH, Warendorf

Copyright © 2009 FNverlag der Deutschen Reiterlichen Vereinigung GmbH, Warendorf
English translation © 2011 Trafalgar Square Books

All rights reserved. No part of this book may be reproduced, by any means, without written permission of the publisher, except by a reviewer quoting brief excerpts for a review in a magazine, newspaper, or website.

Disclaimer of Liability
The authors and publisher shall have neither liability nor responsibility to any person or entity with respect to any loss or damage caused or alleged to be caused directly or indirectly by the information contained in this book. While the book is as accurate as the author can make it, there may be errors, omissions, and inaccuracies.

Library of Congress Cataloging-in-Publication Data
Dietze, Susanne von
  Rider and horse-- back to back : establishing a mobile, stable core in the saddle / Susanne von Dietze and Isabelle von Neumann-Cosel ; translation by Julia Welling.
    p. cm.
  Includes index.
   ISBN 978-1-57076-465-3 (hardback)
  1. Horsemanship. 2. Horses. I. Neumann-Cosel-Nebe, Isabelle von. II. Title.
  SF309.D468 2011
  798.2'3--dc23
                                    2011020991

Photographs by Jean Christen, Mannheim: ix, 4 *left* (2), 8, 10 (3), 11 (6), 16, 24; 26 (2), 161 (3) from the book *Reiten kann man tatsächlich lernen* by Isabelle von Neumann-Cosel, FNverlag, Warendorf 2003; 29, 32; 34, 35 *right*, 36 from the book *Das Pferdebuch für junge Reiter* by Isabelle von Neumann-Cosel, FNverlag, Warendorf 2006; 38 *bottom*, 53, 99, 109 (2), 114 (2), 115 (3), 118, 144 (2), 145 *bottom* (2), 149 (2); Tammo Ernst, Ganderkesee: vii from the book *Olympia der Reiter—Hongkong 2008*, FNverlag, Warendorf, 2008; Thoms Lehmann, Warendorf: 4 *right* from the book *Balance in der Bewegung* by Susanne von Dietze, FNverlag, Warendorf, 2007; Mary Mc Kenna, Silver Spring, Maryland: viii, ix, 3, 13 *top left*, 15, 19, 20 *top* (2), 44, 47, 56, 59 *bottom* (3), 65 *right* (2), 68, 69, 71 *bottom*, 75 (3), 86 (2), 89 *top*, 96 (6), 97, 98, 105, 107, 108, 113, 120 (2), 121, 122 (3), 123 (3), 124, 125 *top*, 126 (2), 127, 128 (2), 129, 130, 131, 132, 133, 135, 141 *top*, 142, 143 (2), 145 *top*, 147, 148, 150 (2), 151, 154 (2), 156 (2), 157 (2), 158, 159 (2), 163 (4), 164 (3), 165, 166 (2), 167 (4), 168 (4), 169 (4), 171 (2); Ricarda Mertens, Mannheim: 17, 18, 61 (2), 136, 137 (7), 138 (5), 172 *top*; Julia Rau, Mainz: v, 7 from the book *Olympia der Reiter—Hongkong 2008*, FNverlag, Warendorf, 2008; Carl Thomas Nebe, Ladenburg: 35 *left* from the book *Reiten kann man tatsächlich lernen* by Isabelle von Neumann-Cosel, FNverlag, Warendorf, 2003; Barbara Schnell, Krefeld: 1 (4), 9 (6), 12 *right* (4), 13 (3), 20 *bottom*, 23, 25 (2), 38 *top*, 51, 58, 59 *top*, 63, 64 (4), 65 *bottom*, 70 (2), 71 *top* (3), 73 (3), 78 *left*, 79, 81 (3), 82 (2), 83 (4), 84 (2), 85 (2), 87 (6), 89 *bottom*, 91 (3), 92, 93, 100, 102, 104 (4), 106 (2), 111, 112, 116 (2), 125 *bottom*, 140, 141 *bottom* (2), 146 (3); Shira Yeger, Givat Haim Ichud, Israel: 12 *top left*, 23 *bottom right*, 41, 43, 46, 48, 49, 55, 60 (3), 76, 77 (2), 78 *right*, 80 (3), 94 (3); private collection: 101, 134, 172 *left*. Illustrations by Jeanne Kloepfer, Lindenfels

Cover design by RM Didier
Typefaces: Rotis Sans Serif, Rotis Semi Serif, Tekton Pro

10 9 8 7 6 5 4 3 2 1

Table of Contents

FOREWORD BY INGRID KLIMKE vii

INTRODUCTION
Ride as far as the back can carry you viii

PART 1
The Back—the Center of the Body and All Movement x

1.1 The Back's Function 1
Contradiction: mobile yet stable
Try it yourself: dynamic stability
The function of each individual body part
The spine's function
Anatomy: understanding back function
Curvature of the spine
Anatomy of the vertebrae
Function
Back muscles
Subconscious motion patterns of the back
Individual characteristics and differences

1.2 Everybody Is Different—Nobody Is Perfect 8
The individuality of height and built
Reference lines to measure proportions
Individual proportions
Every horse is different

1.3 The Importance of the Senses and Perception 14
Perception before motion
Five senses are not enough
Coordination and perception training
Taste
Smell
Hearing
Sight
Feeling
Sense of balance
A sixth sense

1.4 Awareness and Motion 25
Be aware of your own back
Every form of perception is subjective
The instructor as a "medium" for your perception
Develop a feel for movement
What you feel versus what others see
Body awareness and seat corrections

1.5 Pain—A Challenge to Your Perception 30
Feeling pain
Riding with back pain
Take care of your back

1.6 Learning How to Move 34
Different ways to start riding
Life is motion
Is age an issue?

Back stability is paramount
Shifting weight—rider
Shifting weight—horse
Developing dynamic stability—rider and horse
Executing a movement
Planning a movement
Train your sense of body motion
Compensation
Improve incorrect posture
Recognize the problem
Analyze—find the cause
Go back to the basics
Eradicate bad habits and compensations
Train correctly by using less demanding movements
First, visualize the movement
Improve awareness
Reciprocal movement

1.7 Sense and Nonsense about Exercises 48
Practice makes perfect
Patterns of evasion and compensation
The importance of a schoolmaster
Fitness and cross-training
Adolescents: growing tall and becoming lanky
Recognizing, understanding, and influencing motion
Your individual motion pattern
The key factor

PART 2
Practice Strengthens the Back—Go Easy on It to Protect It 56

2.1 Plan and Organize Your Own Schedule 57
Take responsibility for your back
Plan your riding sessions
Riding equipment
The importance of the saddle
Correct stirrup length
Mounting and dismounting
Tips for riding instructors

2.2 Versatile Basic Training 62
Varied movement experiences
Forward seat—back-friendly?
How much strain does jumping put on your back?
Riding on the trail

2.3 Back to Back 66
The horse's spine
The swinging back
What happens in the horse's back
The pelvis as the joint between horse and rider
The neck: mobility and the ability to compensate
Movement control starts from the head
Controlling the horse's poll
Sequence of footfalls in the basic gaits

Table of Contents

2.4 Letting Go, Feeling, and Going with the Flow of the Horse's Movements 76
- Get to know your own back a little bit better
- Feel the position of your pelvis
- Center your upper body
- Let your horse move you
- Stretch your hip muscles
- Move your thighs away from the saddle
- Riding a bicycle
- Stretching exercise: lower back
- Stretching exercises: upper back
- Mobility of the hips during rising trot
- Upper body balance in rising trot
- Improve your balance and rhythm during rising trot
- Follow the horse's movements

2.5 Improve Flexibility, Stability, and Dexterity 90
- Rotating the spine increases stability
- Diagonal patting
- Turning toward the horse's rear end
- Stretching and turning combined
- The independence of the pelvis and shoulder girdle
- Imagine you are a juggler
- The game of mobile and stable body segments
- Mobility of shoulder girdle, neck, and head
- Turning your shoulder girdle and pelvis in opposite directions

PART 3
Putting Riding Theory into Practice— The Back-Friendly Way 98

3.1 Training without Overstraining 99
- Recognize your own limits
- Below-the-limit training—and with variety
- Recovery phase for muscles

3.2 The Training Scale: Its Connection to the Rider's Back 103
- The principles of classical riding
- Training in a back-friendly manner

3.3 Taking Up the Reins—Shortening the Reins 109
- Taking up the reins as a basic exercise
- Problems with taking up the reins
- Shortening the reins
- Learning how to shorten the reins—step by step

3.4 Danger to Your Back 114
- Preventing risks
- Leaning on the reins
- Horses with a stiff back
- Lazy horses
- Unpredictable events

3.5 Transitions and Half-Halts—Basic Work Presented in a Different Way 119
- Rising trot and transitions
- Smooth transitions—in rising trot
- Walk-trot transitions
- Transitions between rising trot and canter
- Trot-canter transitions in sitting trot
- Canter-trot transitions
- Rising trot during transitions between walk and trot
- Sitting trot during transitions between walk and trot
- Walk-canter transitions
- Transitions from canter to walk
- Shortening intervals between transitions
- Halt

3.6 Sitting Trot—the Standard Criterion of Correct Posture and Influence 135
- Quality over quantity
- Walking on the spot
- Being aware of walking
- Walking backward
- Lifting and lowering your hips
- Practicing sitting trot in multiple ways
- Stretching and toning your muscles at the same time
- Riding without stirrups
- Mini biking
- Transitions between forward and dressage seat
- Being flexible with your weight
- Subtle weight shifts

3.7 Naturally Crooked 147
- "Crooked" is normal
- The difficulty of riding straight
- Bending and collecting
- The horse in a turn

3.8 Tools for Back-Friendly Collection 152
- Basic training: gymnastics for rider and horse
- Circle: set cones as marker points
- Circle: counting
- Circle: using counting to influence the horse's movement
- Riding through a corner: triangle
- Counting corners
- Corner: a quarter of a circle
- Circle: diamond or square
- Circle: control of the forehand
- Influencing bend with your seat
- Slalom on a straight line
- Slalom on a circle
- Controlling the forehand on a circle
- The value of flexion and counter flexion on a straight line
- The basis of all lateral movements: shoulder-in
- Diagonally and straight
- Lengthening and shortening the stride
- Crescendo, decrescendo, and a musical scale

Acknowledgments 172

Foreword by Ingrid Klimke

Among riders, we have a saying: "A horse can only be as good as his weakest leg." Applying this piece of wisdom to the rider, the saying could go as follows: "A rider can only be as fit as her back."

Being a professional athlete myself, I know how important a healthy and fit body is in order to achieve top performances in the various disciplines of equestrian sports. Your back plays a central role: Even the most insignificant problems can have serious consequences. You might even put yourself and your horse in danger if your back fails you during highly demanding sport of eventing, for example.

Even high-performance athletes are not immune to back problems. The secret is to get to know your own body with all its strengths and weaknesses and use it accordingly—not only during competition, but also in everyday training.

I recommend this book to all riders—it will help you become more aware of your back, be more considerate of its weaknesses, and make use of its strengths.

The authors of this book have succeeded in showing how "back-friendly" riding is part of classical riding's principles and how it can be achieved based on "feel" and delicacy rather than with strength. I would be delighted to see them get this clear message out to as many riders as possible.

Ingrid Klimke

Introduction

Ride as far as the back can carry you

Is riding good or bad for the back?

More than any other part of the human body, the back has become an indicator of health. According to statistics, back pain is the most common physical problem afflicting people in industrialized countries. We see it not only in adults (women are slightly more affected than men) but also in children and adolescents.

Essential for stabilizing the body in an upright position, the human back is having to "cope" with humans becoming taller with each generation, and their changes in lifestyle: limited space for children and adolescents to move and play; an increased amount of time spent in front of computer and TV screens; more sitting at school; jobs that commonly require us to be seated all day; less time spent on exercise decreasing as we age—all of these examples show what the human back has to deal with today.

Improved screening methods have enabled us to diagnose people with degenerative spinal conditions who, in the past, probably would not have known about their affliction. However, treatment possibilities have not been able to keep up with improved diagnostics. Hardly any other clinical picture requires you as a patient to take as much responsibility for yourself: back exercises; physical therapy; improved posture; fitness training; and cross-training.

People have come to realize that a healthy, pain-free back tremendously contributes to the quality of their life, and consider back pain extremely stressful—both physically and psychologically.

The image of a rider is defined by a straight back, whether upright as in dressage or forward in show jumping. Even without understanding the various functions of the spine in all their detail, you can immediately see how sitting on a horse has a direct and important influence on your back.

Three contradictory opinions

- Riding—like few other sports—helps to keep your back strong and healthy.
- Riding puts additional strain on your back and leads to premature and excessive wear and tear.
- As far as the effect on your back is concerned riding is as good or as bad as any other sport.

The question of whether riding helps or harms the back has been grounds for heated debate among doctors and physical therapists.

In addition, riders of all disciplines and performance levels engage in discussions about the positive and negative effects of riding on the back. There are pleasure riders, for example, who believe their weekly riding lesson to be a form of physical therapy for their back, and others who consider the pain they experience after every lesson the price they have to pay for a lifestyle that includes a job that requires them to sit most of the day. Show jumping is now widely believed to be detrimental to the back so is avoided by some. As an example, in Germany, there are medals given out for riding a test designed to judge riding skills: dressage, show jumping (cross country, if desired), and theory. However, in recent years, in order to accommodate riders frightened of jumping because of potential damage to their back—and armed with a medical certificate—an alternative test has been offered that excludes the jumping part, requiring them to pass a test at a more difficult level of dressage instead. But then these same riders can often be seen riding a stiff horse in sitting trot—for a whole lesson!—and this poses the question: Won't this put more stress on their back than jumping?

Introduction

Among young professional riders, it is expected that they should ignore pain and be willing to expose themselves to situations that are potentially harmful to their back—without thinking twice about it. In this way, "motion patterns" start to manifest which, in many cases, lead to premature wear and tear. A back problem is the number-one reason why professional riders and high-performance athletes have to retire from their active careers.

Similar to running and swimming, riding is, nevertheless, considered a lifetime sport, routinely done professionally by riders in their seventies. And, there are more than a few examples of people continuing to ride on a regular basis up to the ripe old age of eighty while proving to still be in astonishing shape.

Based on the varied functions of the back, the purpose of this book is to investigate the actual strain the rider's back is exposed to during riding. However, the fascinating diversity and individuality of both human and equine bodies make it impossible to come up with a definitive answer about whether or not riding helps or harms the back.

Studying the back's requirements—according to classical riding theory—offers an amazing conclusion: Not only is this theoretical ideal of the rider's posture or seat perfectly tailored to human anatomy, it also equips you with the tools to dynamically stabilize your back and keep it healthy. You simply need to understand and know how to use these tools.

Unfortunately, there are no standardized exercises—with or without the horse—to relieve you of the responsibility you have for your back. In order to obtain a "back-friendly" style of riding, you need to open up to your body and learn to focus part of your senses and awareness on what the Germans call "*Reitergefühl*," which is a special "feel" for the horse, yourself, and all the movements you as a rider have to learn.

This way, it is possible to learn how to ride sensitively, with feeling, and in tune with the demands on both your body and your horse's at all times. In this regard, suppleness acts as the common denominator for a healthy back—for both horse and rider.

By taking your back into consideration, you are not only tending to your own health but also the health of your horse. When you have finished this book you will find it's a "message" full of hope directed to all riders, but in particular those afflicted with back problems. A back-friendly style of riding can be correct, effortless, and effective at the same time. It might also be the key to achieving a harmonious understanding between horse and rider.

1

The Back—
The Center of
The Body and
All Movement

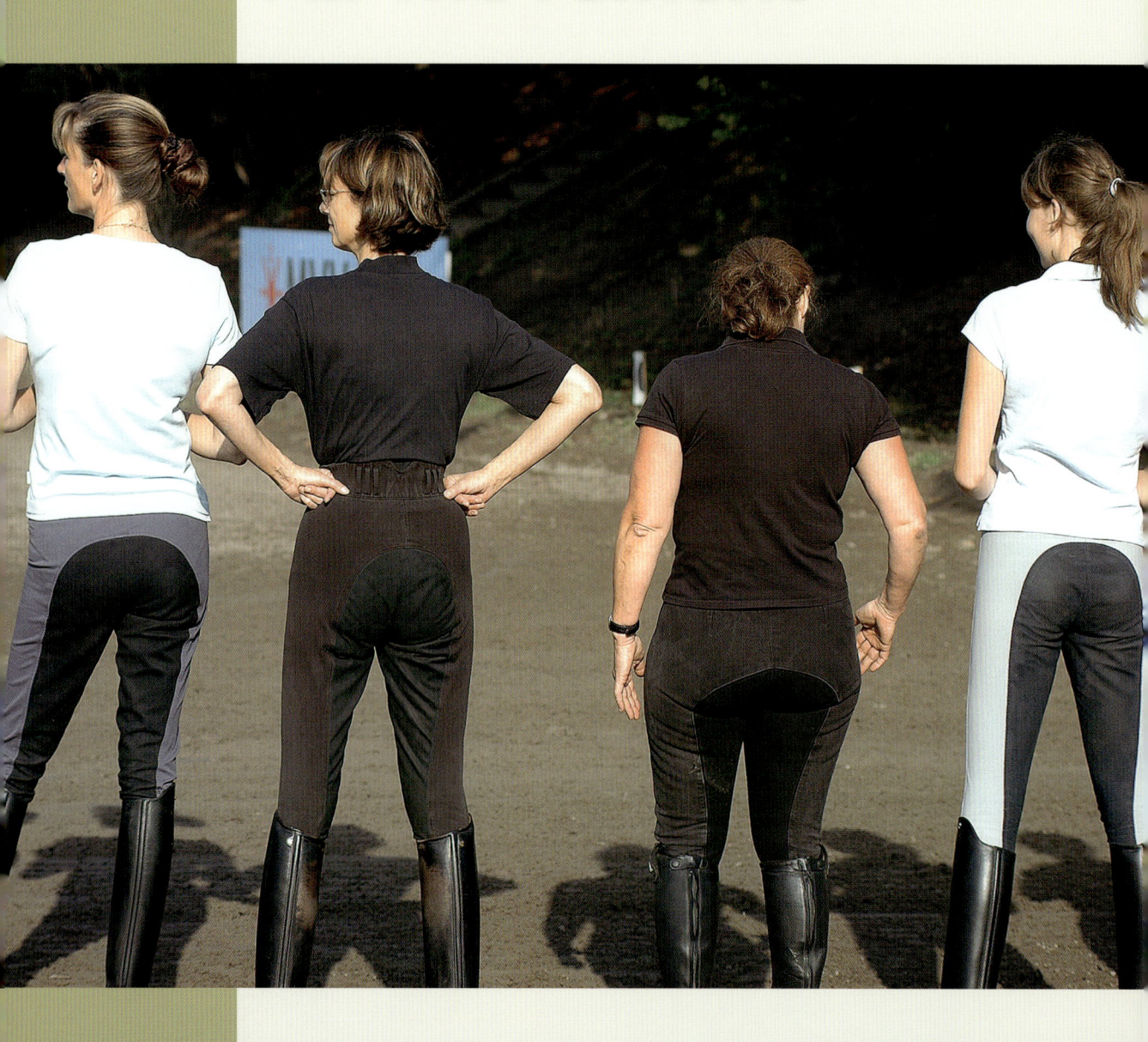

The Back—The Center of the Body and All Movement

1.1 The Back's Function

Contradiction: mobile yet stable

A healthy back is a back you do not even know you have! Every rider will probably agree with this piece of wisdom dispensed by physical therapists: As long as your back is doing what it is supposed to do, you do not even notice it. But the slightest pain or mere notion of stiffness makes you aware of it immediately. The back is the central part that is responsible for the body operating smoothly in everyday life: Walking, standing and sitting are possible only when your back is stable. You could say that walking (and sitting) upright is a process "organized" by the back itself: The back's stability is genetically programmed and happens automatically like many of the functions your back fulfills. The back is significantly more automated than hands or feet, for example.

Only when you fully understand the functions of a human back, can you make informed decisions about what is good or bad for yours. Two of its characteristics seem to contradict each other, however: It is both mobile and stable at the same time. Its scope of motion is three-dimensional, which means you can bend and stretch your back forward, backward, and sideways, and rotate it. The body's trunk (also known as the "core") stabilizes your whole "movement system" and is responsible for coordinating motion of your arms and legs. The spine is the central part within the upper body and it's only with good stability in this area that refined coordination and control of movement can be attained. When the core lacks dynamic stability, you are not able to keep your balance while walking, for example. Core stability is of paramount importance to riders and lack of core development can result in a predisposition to injury.

The back can only fulfill its tasks if it is stable yet mobile. There are forces from all directions threatening to upset its stability. When the back is flexible, it can protect itself against these "attacks," that is, it can move in all directions to keep its stability. Physical therapists call this the "dynamic stability of the back." The main function of your back is to reestablish stability and maintain your balance.

Try it yourself: dynamic stability

Dynamic stability is "alive"—strength is built up by mobile, elastic interaction of small back muscles and vertebrae, whereas *passive* stability is secured through "outside" support of tendons and ligaments acting like a brace or corset, and very vulnerable to injury.

When you stand on tiptoe trying to find—and maintain—your balance, you do not stand still, but use effortless and seemingly invisible movements to balance your body above your feet. Even when you are just standing normally with your weight evenly distributed over the soles of your feet, your body is always occupied with these small balancing motions. To improve your awareness of these, close your eyes while standing and you will be able to precisely feel the movement of your spine around an imaginary center line. Without your being aware of it, your spine also engages in "swinging" motions when you are seated. Straightening your back, even when subconsciously executed, strengthens all the muscles involved. So, knowing this, don't just think of having to sit upright as pure "torture," but look at it as a valuable workout of the deep muscles around your spine. Any posture that inhibits the spine from this "refined" movement is a position that puts a strain on your back!

Dynamic stability serves as the basis for you to *allow* and *control* movement. To clarify the importance of this statement, stand on one leg: Only when you are in a stable position, will you be able to control exactly where you would like to place your other foot. When the leg you are standing on is unstable, you will not be able to control where your free foot touches the ground because your body is too busy trying to keep its balance.

A proper seat enhances the spine's ability to move freely.

Rider & Horse Back to Back

The function of each individual body part

The body can be divided into several parts: arms, legs, head, trunk and pelvis. By looking at these as building blocks, it becomes clear that the trunk serves as the center of stability. On all sides, other body parts connect to it. Arms, legs, and head are fixed to the trunk at one place only—giving them a lot of mobility. The pelvis is different in this regard as it is connected to the trunk at one end and to the legs at the other. This does allow a certain potential for mobility—not as much as that of arms and legs, but significant nonetheless.

If you could assign tasks to individual body parts, you would say that the legs are designed for forward motion and the arms for freedom of movement and "conscious" action. The pelvis serves as a "switch" that converts the leg movements into small muscle movements that build up the stability in your spine (i.e. *mobility* into *stability*). This dynamic stability enables the trunk to build up balance to coordinate movement of your limbs. Your head should be free to do the thinking.

*Stability of the trunk—the body's "center"—is a fundamental necessity for good balance and controlled movement of arms and legs.

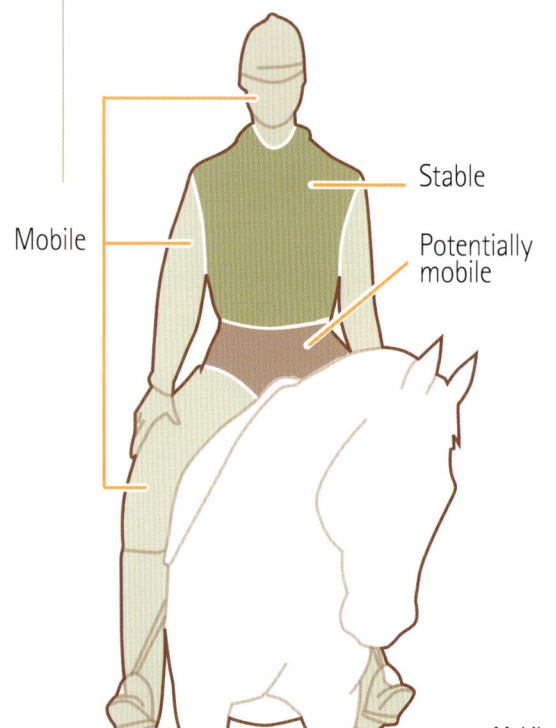

spine's function

Especially when riding, the dynamic stability of the spine is essential so you are able to independently use your lower legs and hands to apply aids. There are other sports that require your back to work in a comparable fashion: For example, in most forms of dancing (especially ballroom, but also tap), the back needs to remain motionless while the legs, pelvis, and arms move a great deal. In slalom skiing, it is interesting to note that only those skiers who can keep their trunk stable and quiet are able to ski through all the poles at high speed. In cross-country skiing, the trunk is very still while the arms and legs are moving—however the more tired a skier becomes, the more his trunk starts to move.*

Anatomy: understanding back function

In order to get a better understanding of how the back works you need to take a closer look at its anatomy. It is not important to know the names of bones, muscles and joints by heart but to understand the functional setup of the back as a system. This will help you realize why, where, and how back problems occur, and with the help of which particular movements and exercises they could be prevented—or even cured.

The spinal column is made up of a "chain" of individual parts: the vertebrae. Vertebrae are placed on top of each other like a tower—hence the term "spinal column." Similar to a skyscraper, the spine is both mobile and flexible in all directions, and stable and strong enough not to topple down.

Mobile and stable sections of the rider's body.

The Back—The Center of the Body and All Movement

Basically, the spine is constructed like a chain linking lots of little individual pieces. This way, it is better able to withstand shock and vibration than a solid piece of wood or metal. Think of that desktop ornament with a row of metal suspended balls. When you knock against a ball at one end, you don't move the ball next to it, but the one at the opposite end of the row; it appears as though the balls in the middle remain still—even though they have passed on or transmitted the energy of the starting ball.

The spine transmits kinetic energy by following the same principle. All motion passed on through the spine ends up in the sub-occipital joints, which is why they can have a significant influence on our well-being. Back problems are often connected to headaches.

Riding influences not only your lumbar spine but every single part of the back.*

Curvature of the spine

The spine is divided into three segments: cervical, thoracic, and lumbar.

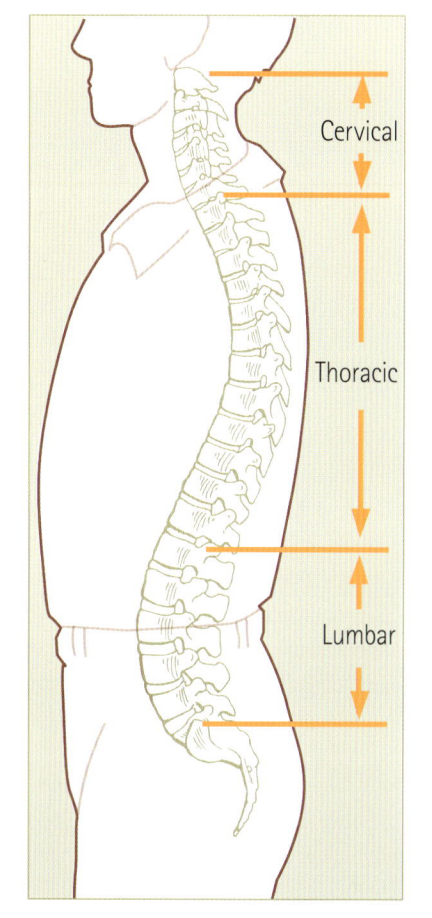

Spinal segments.

*A good supple seat is defined by its ability to let the horse's motion pass through the rider's entire spine.

The horse's motion is transmitted through the rider's back all the way to the head.

1.1 The Back's Function

Rider & Horse Back to Back

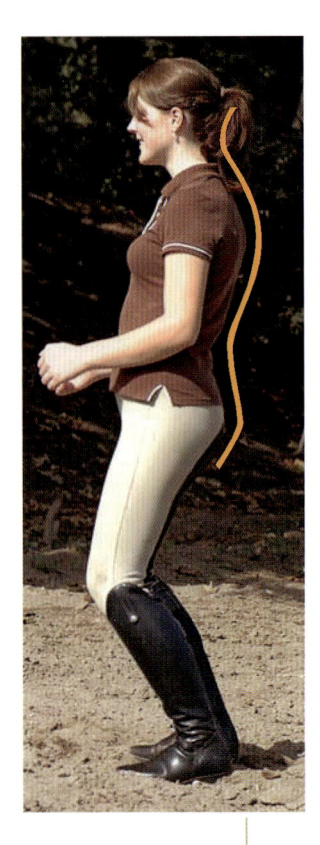

A pronounced S curvature.

The spine is characterized by its S shape, which functions like a shock absorber, cushioning the spine from various forces. Depending on the person, the S is more or less pronounced. In the photos, there are two riders with very different shapes to their spine.

Within the S shape notice that both the cervical and lumbar parts of the spine are bent toward the front of the body in a slightly "hollow" position, while the thoracic spine is more "rounded" backward. In conclusion, you could say that a hollow back is to some degree natural and healthy. (This is why you should not try to keep your back straight like a rod.) Instead, adjust to its S curvature. It is only harmful when the hollow position becomes exaggerated, thus putting strain on the lower back and possibly causing disc injury, for example.

Considering how shock is transmitted through the "wavy" chain, that is, the spine, some parallels between the cervical and lumbar spine become apparent. Movements in the lumbar spine are mirrored in the cervical spine and vice versa. (This explains the phenomenon of back pain moving up and down the back.)

An example of a very long, straight back.

Anatomy of the vertebrae

There are other ways to distinguish the individual segments of the spine than just their characteristic curvature and direction of bend. Every segment has a different degree of mobility and is equipped to do certain movements because each vertebra making up the segment is shaped differently.

The most flexible segment is the *cervical* spine where movement is possible in every direction (that is, three dimensional: bending forward and backward, laterally bending right and left, and rotating right and left). The mobility of the *thoracic* spine is significantly restricted by the ribs and the rib cage: Bending backward, forward, and sideways is possible only to a certain degree; turning works best. With regard to the *lumbar* spine, turning is almost impossible; bending sideways is restricted; but bending backward and forward is easily done.

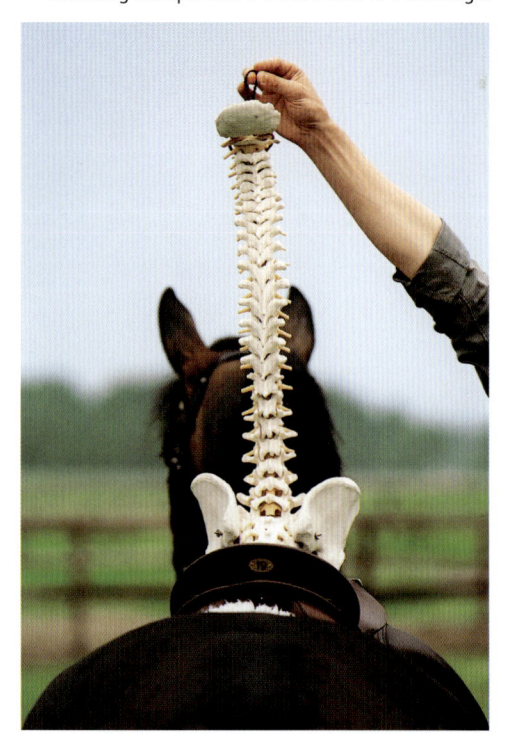

Balancing the spine on a horse's back is a challenge.

The Back—The Center of the Body and All Movement

The reason for these differences in mobility is the manner in which the individual vertebrae are constructed. Each vertebra comes equipped with joints (known as *facet joints*) that connect it to the vertebra above and the one beneath. For the most part, the facet joints determine the mobility of the spine. This construction is as brilliant as it is complicated. The shape of the joint can differ and thus define the direction of the spine's mobility. In between the vertebrae, you can find the discs that the vertebrae rest and move on—like a gel pad—and these discs act like buffers or sponges to cushion all movement.

You can imagine the number of individual joints that have to work together in harmony in order to stabilize your back. In the photo on page 4 you can see an attempt to stack all the vertebrae in the most anatomically correct way. It was successful only to a certain degree. However, the lack of perfection mirrors reality quite well—there are no perfectly formed spines in real life. Each back is constructed as uniquely as the human being it belongs to. Similar to the little piles of wooden building blocks children like to play with, the decisive factor of stability is balance.

By the way, horses do not care whether their rider's back is straight or crooked—what matters is *how* your weight is distributed on your seat bones. It makes sense, however, that the closer your back comes to meeting the ideal, the better your chances are at symmetrically distributing your weight. Even though good posture is desirable, it needs to be accompanied by the ability to correctly distribute and constantly shift your weight when in motion. What matters most is the rider's ability to align his own center of gravity with the horse's center—at all times.

Function

In order to grasp the entire functional anatomy of the back, just concentrating on the movements of the spine is not enough. When you think of the back, you need to connect it to the entire body. You will notice that the parts of the back serve different purposes—similar to the three segments of the spine.

The *cervical* spine supports the windpipe and esophagus while allowing for the highest degree of mobility without restricting the ability to breathe, swallow, or speak.

The *thoracic* spine is part of the trunk. Within the trunk's cavity are situated the lungs and the heart. Its bottom end is closed off by the diaphragm—the most important muscle for breathing. On the one hand, the trunk is stable, while on the other hand, it is elastic and flexible enough to allow you to breathe in and out. The ribs and the breastbone stabilize and support the thoracic spine.

The *lumbar* spine is also located in the back part of a cavity containing numerous organs. In contrast to the trunk with its breastbone and ribs, this part of the back does not have an all-surrounding bone structure to support its stability. The front and sides of the lower cavity are made up of muscles (oblique and straight abdominal muscles). This is why the lumbar spine is closely connected to the function of the abdominal muscles.*

Back muscles

All of the functions described above are made possible by a complex system of muscles. Looking at back function, it is more important to understand the setup of the muscular system than learn the names of individual muscles.

*Many problems originating in the lower back are caused by insufficiently developed (not properly toned) abdominal muscles.

1.1 The Back's Function

Rider & Horse Back to Back

The function of the back muscles can only be explained through their connection to other muscle groups. Take the abdominals, for example, which are built differently from the muscles of the arms and legs. Since they are not needed for moving the body forward but are designed for support and stability, the abdominal muscles cannot contract or extend as much as arm and leg muscles. Instead, they contain a higher amount of elastic and sinewy fibers that are designed for support. Understanding these facts is important for you to exercise correctly. If you are trying to build up your abdominal muscles by doing sit ups and jackknives, you are not taking the actual purpose of these muscles into consideration. Think about it. When in everyday life would abdominals have to contract or extend this much? Instead, they need to build up a stable "wall" for the organs within the abdomen, and react elastically with every breath you take as the diaphragm pushes. Stability along with elasticity needs coordination of the deep muscles, thus a different kind of strength from what you achieve by lifting weights.

The trunk's muscles are characterized by:

- A diagonal structure
- Short muscles making up the deeper layer
- Long muscles in the superficial layer

The superficial and deep muscles of the back.

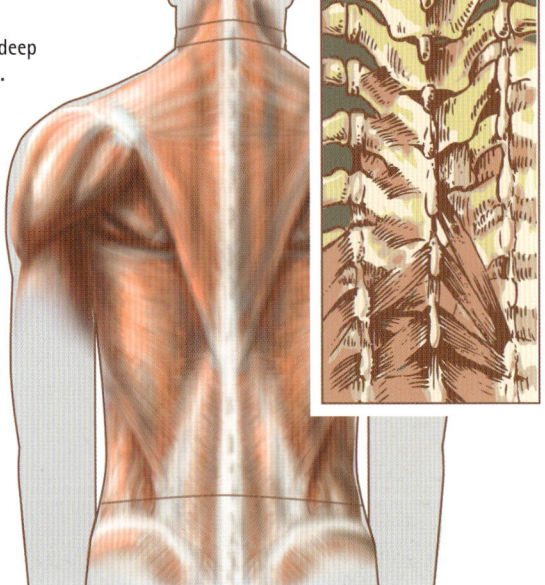

The diagonal structure of the muscles significantly increases the stability of the upper body without obstructing its mobility. If you have ever put a bookshelf together, you know how important diagonal struts are to the stability of the shelf. The entire spinal column is secured by diagonal muscles. These fan out on both sides of the vertebrae like the branches of a pine tree.

The muscles along the spine are systematically organized in layers, which allow them to work more efficiently. The deepest layer contains the shortest muscles able to almost invisibly execute the smallest and most accurate movements. They are responsible for balance and dynamic stability of the body. Visible movements are usually carried out by the superficial, longer muscles, which stretch over more than just one joint of the spine. This means that every time they work they are influencing more than just one part of the spine and move many joints at a time.

Subconscious motion patterns of the back

To keep your balance, you mainly need the invisible muscle work done "underground." Just as a spectacular stage show would not be possible without an incredible amount of work backstage, the mobility you can actually see depends on many little invisible movements you usually do not even feel.

This is why you sometimes get the impression mentioned at the beginning of the book: A healthy back is a back you do not even know you have. This is because you do not feel the work that the deep muscles do! As mentioned, in your daily life, you are seldom aware your back even exists. When you overdo something, it acts up every now and then, gets tired, or pinches here and there, or overstrained muscles tense up. This kind of back "pain" represents your body's "police" and you should take seriously the "ticket" your back gives you in order to prevent secondary damage.

But it is a common characteristic of humans not to listen to a quiet reprimand—only to a loud protest!

The human's perception and awareness has not evolved to include the back. You cannot see it, you barely feel it, and have even less control over it. You can tell exactly where your left index finger is at any given time, but you have no way of knowing where the left joint of your second lumbar vertebra is and how to move it.

This shortcoming has nothing to do with lack of education, however. Your brain is not built to consciously control movement of your back. For the most part, these movements are controlled by reflexes, some of which do not even get to the brain and only pass through the spinal cord. If at all, the brain has very little control over them.

When you put your hand on your back while walking, you will notice how the muscles to the left and right of your spine alternately contract and relax again without your express order to do so. If in order to walk, you had to think about which muscles to use, when to use them and how strongly, you would never get going.

The subconscious motion patterns described above are what make the back so special. There is a reason why some people think it is a mirror of the soul. It even influences our language and the way we express things: We talk about "upright citizens" and "people with backbone." We also notice when someone is feeling well—or not—by looking at their posture.

Individual characteristics and differences

Backs are not all the same. There are long, short, broad, slender, and crooked ones. Every person's back is individually built and needs to be treated as such! In riding, it is not important to have a perfect back to begin with, but to use the one you have in the most efficient way.

Efficient movement is all about effort equaling the task at hand: Use as much effort as needed, but as little as possible. Such movement looks easy, effortless, and fluent. Onlookers often describe it as beautiful.

In high-performance riding disciplines, you see riders with all types of back shapes (see photo below). In order to ride well, you do not need an ideal figure or back but a precise feeling for and control over your balance as well as good coordination of your strength and power so you can apply them at the right moment and in the right dosage.

Successful eventers have to be ready for three equestrian disciplines—and these riders come in all shapes and sizes!

1.2 Everybody Is Different—Nobody Is Perfect

The individuality of height and build

Everybody is different. The way we move is defined by the length of our limbs and the body itself: the mobility of tendons, ligaments, and joints; and the definition, tone, and strength of muscles combined with learned motion patterns and experience. In contrast to most other sports, there is no ideal figure for riding; in high-level riding, you can find successful riders of every height and stature.

In reality, striving for the perfect body and perfect movement is an unattainable goal. However, the closer you get to the desired form of perfection, the more beautiful your movement will appear to be. Dressage measures your degree of perfection in scores and percentages. Considering that a score of 10 is rare, 80 out of 100 percent in a Grand Prix test usually qualifies you as a candidate for a medal in international championships.

There are mathematical-geometrical reference lines to see if someone has what are considered standard harmonious body proportions. Even though no human body has ever exactly fulfilled these criteria, it is helpful to use these kinds of standards in order to evaluate conformation and movement.

The more symmetrical and "normal" your body is, the easier it is for you to balance yourself. In this regard, however, function is more important than conformation. In order to become a good rider, you need good balance and coordination in everyday life—standing and walking—not only on the horse. First of all, every rider needs to work on her balance while standing or walking before mounting. Only riders who are able to balance themselves will be able to find their balance in the saddle without using muscle strength. Every time, you use your muscles more than you have to, you put unnecessary pressure on your spine.

An unbiased observation of a person's body proportions can help you better understand how her conformation influences her motion pattern. In this way, you can improve awareness of your own body's individual features.

Reference lines to measure proportions

One of the most helpful lines of reference separates the body into an upper and lower half or, simplified, legs and upper body (see photo below). The line runs horizontally through the hip joints and defines whether a person seems tall when she sits or appears to have very long legs. The difference between the two is very important as every person automatically uses their strong points to achieve balance on horseback and apply aids (see top right photo p. 9).

The center of gravity of a rider with a longer trunk, for example, is situated relatively high up. This person will fall off her horse more quickly when her trunk becomes unbalanced. A longer trunk requires you to put more effort into stabilizing the surplus of body mass so your abdominal muscles will be more defined while you'll have more general muscle tone.

A rider with long legs, in contrast, will find it easier to relax her hip joints and follow the horse's movement. In order to properly exert influence on the horse, however, legs, pelvis and trunk need to work together as an inseparable, coordinated whole.

The Back—The Center of the Body and All Movement

Two riders with the same length of leg but different upper body shape and size: The man on the left has a shorter, more square upper body, and the one on the right is longer and more "trapezoid," with broader shoulders.

One rider has long legs, the other, a long upper body—the reasons for one appearing taller when sitting, and the other, when standing.

It is always surprising to see the results obtained by applying the reference lines that help you better understand the individual conformation of different riders. The two riders in the top left picture wear their belt at the same height—but look how the length and width of their backs differ! The two riders in the top right picture vary in how long their trunks are in relation to their legs. As a result, their relative height is exactly opposite when seated and standing. The stirrups of both riders in the pictures below would be exactly the same length. The arrow shows that one balances with the upper body more forward, while the other has a more upright, even a slight backward tendency. Observing these two riders in rising trot shows exactly these two balance tendencies (see photos on p. 87).

Four riding postures where some good riders find their individual balance. Left to right: Showing more hollow posture in lower back and neck; looking for balance by shifting his weight forward; bending more in her knees and keeping the weight back in her pelvis; shifting her weight slightly backward and more onto her left foot.

Left: Even though these two riders appear so different they actually ride with the same length stirrup! Right: The woman has long thighs and the man, long lower legs and a short thigh.

1.2 Everybody Is Different—Nobody Is Perfect

Rider & Horse Back to Back

Individual proportions

Your individual body proportions are important to finding your balance: An especially long body part, for example, trunk, pelvis, or thigh, can act as a powerful lever when it interacts with a shorter—thus weaker—one; it can overpower the shorter body part causing loss of balance and stability. In order to learn about your individual balance, stand while bending your knees in riding position: You will discover whether you have a tendency to bend your upper body forward or backward for balance. Analyzing your own body this way can help you better understand the needs your body structure imposes on your back.

Eventually, however, balancing in motion is the most important thing: The better developed your sense of motion, the quicker you will be able to use the horse's movements as support. Even though balance comes more naturally to riders with mostly "normal" proportions, a "deviation" can turn out to be productive: Riders with a long upper body, in particular, will appear elegant and balanced in the saddle once they have gone through a difficult learning process and mastered their body.

The photos on theses two pages show how different riders can be. Standing in a riding position emphasizes the different lengths of their body parts. Length plays an important role in an individual's balance since the body always uses the strong parts to help our weaker parts.

There is no rule about which type of conformation is good or bad; a rider just needs to understand how her balance can be improved and coordinated.

This "standing-riding" position is balanced, supple, and effortless. As her proportions are well balanced (see photo on p. 8)—she is close to an ideal length of body parts—it is easy for her to stay in balance.

Long arms, long legs and a long upper body—she is able to balance in the correct outline, but it is taking much more effort. A vertical line can be drawn correctly through ear, shoulder, hip, and ankle but she appears tense and not as supple in this position. She will need to learn how to relax in order to regain suppleness in all movement.

With limbs longer than his upper body, it is hard to build up stability in his trunk. He compensates by leaning slightly back—a difficult habit to get rid of. But, knowing this will help him choose the right prevention exercises. This is often seen in adolescent riders whose limbs suddenly get longer, which causes issues with their coordination.

The Back—The Center of the Body and All Movement

This rider automatically bends her long legs so that the proportion between her upper body and legs appears equal, which shows she has good feel for a stable balance. She prefers a shorter stirrup because coordinating and influencing the horse is easier—her legs can react more quickly. Later, with a horse obedient to the leg, she can ride with a more elegant, longer stirrup.

This girl shows a difference within the length of her legs: Her lower leg is significantly longer than her thigh. This causes her to shift her weight forward toward the balls of her feet when bending in her knees. She could ride with a little too much weight on her stirrups or keep her lower legs further back and the stirrups too far forward under her feet.

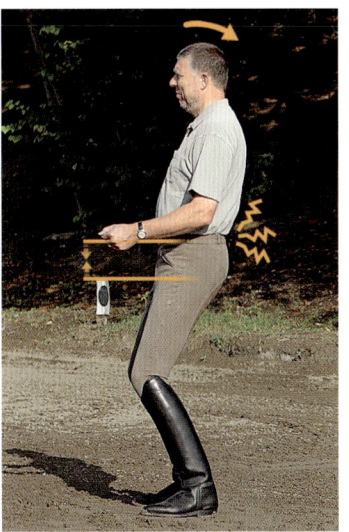

Balancing his upper body by leaning backward: Combined with his long thighs and short pelvis, this position puts a lot of stress onto this man's lumbar spine. To prevent and avoid back problems, he needs to learn to feel a more forward, straight upper-body position—on and off the horse. His trunk appears very solid, so he can use the stronger parts in his body (trunk and thighs) when the situation is challenging.

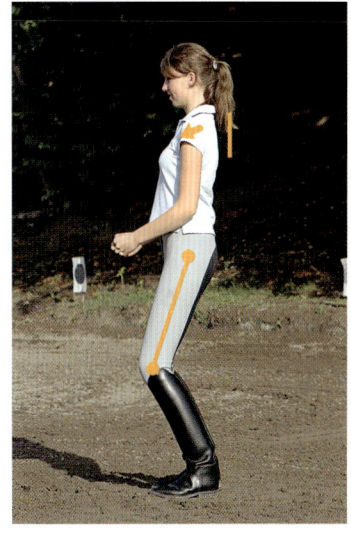

Here we see length in the upper arms and thighs. Along with a very straight back (not a very big S curve) these long limbs will make it difficult for this girl to build up enough stability within her trunk to allow her arms and legs to be independent. Her tendency to bring the shoulders slightly forward is already a sign of instability in her trunk.

This rider has a long upper body with a long pelvis. She balances her body with more weight on her heels so counterbalances by carrying her neck and head slightly more forward. Second, her short upper arms keep the angle of her elbows straighter than someone with longer upper arms (see photos to the right).

This rider has long limbs, a long neck and a long pelvis, but her trunk is short and compact. This causes her difficulty when stabilizing her upper body as well as when controlling and coordinating refined movement of arms and legs. Areas connected to the trunk (for example, the neck) can become tense as a result. She will need to watch out not to become stiff when she lacks stability within her upper body.

1.2 Everybody is different—Nobody is perfect

Rider & Horse Back to Back

A harmoniously proportioned horse.

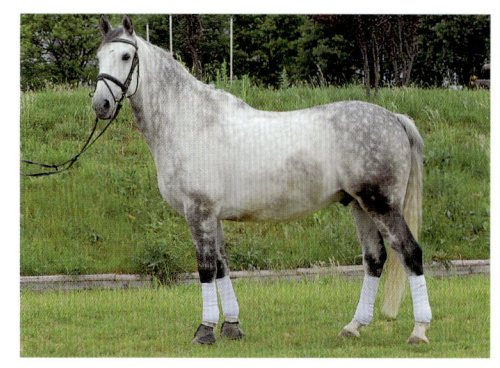

Short back.

Long back.

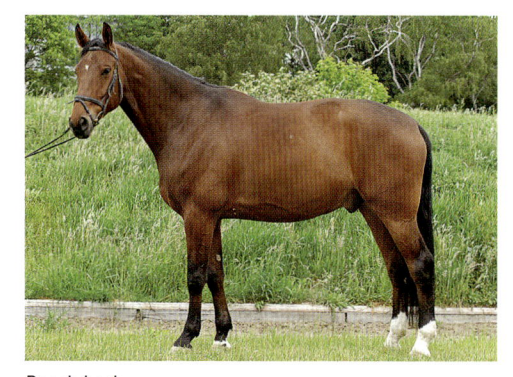

Roach back.

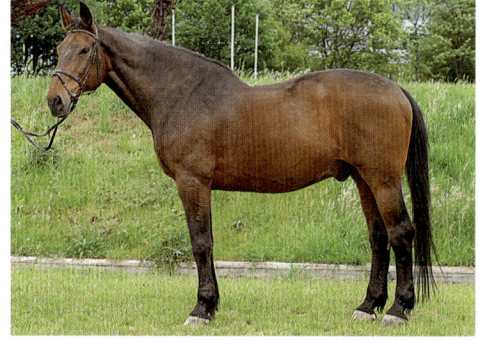

Sway back.

Every horse is different

One of the reasons why riders are fascinated by horses is their individuality. Each horse is different from all others because of a special combination of physical and psychological characteristics. Physique is one of the distinguishing marks. Similar to humans, the way a horse looks—his conformation—is defined by the shape of his spine (see drawing on p. 66) and the length of its three individual segments. In combination with the length and proportions of his limbs, the back defines his range of natural movement.

When looking at a horse from the side, the first thing that draws your attention is his topline (poll to tail). Even though mathematically defining the ideal proportion of the horse's back is not as easy as it is with humans, people have agreed on the ideal topline. Its shape determines the way it operates. In order to be able to "swing" the body as classical riding theory requires, the back needs to be of sufficient length and shaped like an S.

The Back—The Center of the Body and All Movement

"Cresty" neck.

Thin neck.

Short neck.

Long neck.

In order for his daily work to be back-friendly, you need to better understand the way your horse's body is structured. On the following pages, many aspects of the varied interplay between the backs of horse and rider will be discussed. Meanwhile, if you study the pictures on these pages you will increase your awareness of the many possible differences.

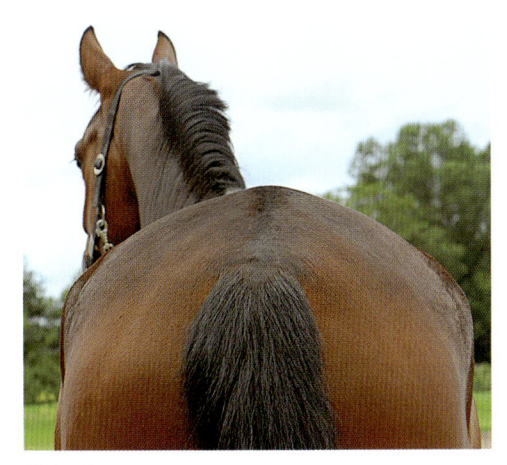

"Pointy" croup.

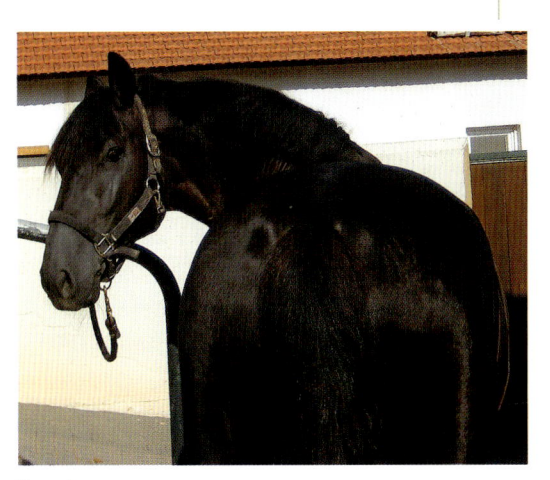

Round croup.

1.2 Everybody is different—Nobody is perfect   13

1.3 The Importance of the Senses and Perception

Perception before motion

To simplify matters, think of your brain like a slot machine that comes to life only when you put in a coin. Your brain controls all of your movements—including consciously controlled and subconsciously experienced reflexes—based on the stimuli it receives prior to triggering a response. Movement is possible only when the brain registers something. In order for you to consciously control your movements, all your senses need to work together in a complex interplay.*

This is why teaching perception and awareness is an essential challenge facing riding instructors: It is not the strongest but the *most sensitive* person who will become the better rider!

The term "perception" combines taking in and processing stimuli sent by your own body—and the world around you. You "perceive" with the help of all your senses in a process of increasing differentiation. What in the beginning is perceived as a confusing "whole" becomes clearly structured as development and training progress. The brain becomes able to sort and process information filtering in through one or more sensory "channels" producing more and more complex physical and emotional reactions. Movement of any kind belongs in this category.**

Five senses are not enough

Ever since Aristotle defined the five senses, people have persistently held on to his classification of them. Five senses, however, are not enough to sufficiently describe all the ways in which we are able to perceive. Body awareness—which is the most important issue in riding—is controlled in a complex manner by the different senses and receptors for such awareness.

*The better you perceive, the better you react!

**Perception is the basis of all learning processes.

Perception can be directed *outward* toward your environment (*far senses*) or *inward* toward your own body (*near senses*).

Functions of the senses

Far senses:
- Ears—Hearing.
- Eyes—Sight.

Near senses:
- Nose—Smell.
- Tongue—Taste (in combination with smell).
- Skin—Touch (ability to feel on the surface of the skin).
- Proprioceptors—Inside the muscles, tendons, and joints these inform the body about the position of the joints and the level of tension in the muscles (see p. 21).
- Equilibrium organ in the inner ear—Sense of balance (influenced by sight and body awareness, among others).

Coordination and perception training

If one or more senses are impaired or no longer work, the remaining senses become more important. They are necessary for the body to compensate for the loss. The ability to sense and perceive cannot be defined in absolute terms even though hearing and sight can be measured. Many ways in which you perceive something require different senses to work together, each one on its own task. In order to find your balance with the help of your equilibrium, for example, you need to be oriented, which is achieved by using your eyes, your sense of smell supporting your sense of taste, and your mouth and hands contributing to your skin's sense of touch.

The brain has to process all incoming perception stimuli at the same time; it does this by setting priorities. Riders are faced with the challenge of being aware of their own body and the horse's at the same time—they need to be able to quickly shift their focus between individual aspects of "perfection" in an organized manner.

The Back—The Center of the Body and All Movement

With regard to the senses, *dynamic* focusing like this requires the highest degree of concentration of mind and body: When you are too tired to concentrate or your mind is busy, you should expect less and adjust your goal for that specific lesson.

It is possible to improve the way your brain receives and processes stimuli, especially with complex combinations of senses such as required for balancing. There is a reason why the demanding coordination of all movement depends on highly developed body awareness. In order to follow the horse's movement, for example, you need to control your pelvis and shoulders independently of each other, and this tests your coordination skills.*

It goes without saying that it is impossible to work on all perception processes at the same time—you need to systematically prioritize. On the following pages, there is a closer look at the respective senses, including a short comparison to the way the horse perceives things.

Taste

You should not underestimate the role that taste plays in riding—even if it's just a subordinate one. Some riders have reported that they had a certain taste in their mouth; a few of them attributing it to the fact that the respective riding lesson had been particularly intense or gone well. I often hear about riders sensing a bitter taste when they work really hard and exert themselves.

Your sense of taste is a combination of the perception that's produced by taste buds on your tongue and the perception of smell. Glands in your mouth produce saliva, which changes in compound and quantity depending on the situation.

Who has not had a dry mouth when getting nervous or excited? Saliva production is controlled by the autonomous nervous system. Your influence on this process is limited—at best.

It is known that the horse's salivary glands are influenced by the position of neck and poll and when the poll is relaxed, the glands produce more saliva. The frothier the horse's mouth, the more relaxed he is. In some cases, this conclusion can be misleading since horses also can chew on the bit when they are nervous and tense. (Horses with a dry or "dead" mouth usually lack correct rein contact and suppleness.)

*Improved perception skills help you use your body in a conscious manner—a basic requirement for a back-friendly, harmonious style of riding.

A horse "frothing" at the mouth.

1.3 The Importance of the Senses and Perception

Rider & Horse Back to Back

The occipital joint at the very top of your cervical spine (neck) should also be relaxed enough so not to impair saliva production. If your mouth tends to be dry a lot, your riding seat might not be relaxed, so pay special attention to your breathing: Breathe in through your nose and breathe out very slowly through your mouth. It sometimes helps to chew "virtual" gum in order to relax your jaw.

Holding your jaw in a clenched manner (for whatever reason) leads to breathing problems and increased tension throughout your whole body; a relaxed seat becomes impossible. This kind of negative tension can lead to tense muscles and headaches as well as a vertebral joint in the lower back becoming "blocked," that is, not moving freely. As your joints are surrounded and kept supple by the interplay of muscles, negative tension can cause a joint to "block" or "freeze" just like a drawer getting stuck in a bureau so you can't pull it out.

Checking your mouth—how dry it is, or whether the taste is bitter, sweet, or neutral—and learning how it is related to your own suppleness can become a tool to help you work on your basic suppleness when riding.*

*Riding is also a matter of good taste!

Smell

Horses stink? This statement can only have come from someone who does not ride. To riders, horses smell nice. Not all horses emanate the same scent, however, which is why some horses and humans get along better than others. Stallions, for example, have a special, different smell than geldings. Instinctively, (and unconsciously) humans react to this smell as other horses do, which is to give stallions more respect than other horses. Analyzing a new horse's smell is part of the horse's social behavior, and the welcoming ritual includes mutual sniffing. By this point, horses decide whether they will like one another or not.

The nose of the horse is far more sensitive than the human's: He can easily differentiate between two people by their individual scent. When a horse does not like your body odor, he might decide not to cooperate. Moreover, a horse is able to smell fear and excitement in a human. (In any case, strong perfume always irritates them.)

When a horse whose body odor you normally like smells bad to you all of a sudden, he might be sick. For example, bad breath can indicate teeth issues and there are diseases that change the body's odor secreted by the sweat glands. Unusual sweating also can be a sign of illness such as colic, and this can be smelled by a rider with a sensitive nose.

At first, your sense of smell might seem to play a subordinate role to perception in general, but as it turns out, just the opposite is true. Smelling sensations often control an entire chain of reaction that can even influence the way you ride. Experience linked to scent has surprising penetration and long-term effects—the memory of specific smells that date back to childhood can last for a lifetime.

The chemistry is working here!

The Back—The Center of the Body and All Movement

For riders, the smell of a barn is inseparably intertwined with their sport so that to them, not even manure stinks! They can even have fond memories of the smell of burned hoof horn from the farrier's work: No one ever forgets this acrid odor lingering in her clothes. People who take up riding again after years of no real contact with horses sometimes relate how the unmistakable smell they experience while sitting on horseback triggers riding experiences they thought they had completely forgotten.

Since smell is connected to breathing, it is easy to imagine how a pleasant scent is kind to your nose and helps you take deeper breaths, resulting in improved oxygen supply to the body. If you do not like a smell, on the other hand, you will definitely not breathe in and out as deeply as possible. Quick, shallow breathing entails a decrease in blood oxygen levels and leads to excessive or accelerated hyperacidity.*

Hearing

Over the last couple of years, dressage freestyles have become more and more of a crowd pleaser. Watching riding and music fit together well is highly enjoyable. However, there are other ways besides external sources of music that can make you aware of the rhythm of the horse's movement. No one is able to resist the sound of a herd galloping in unison and its demonstration of concentrated power. The same herd effect can occur when you are riding in a large group: If all the horses canter together rhythmically (without rushing or pulling as they do during hunting, for example), the movement of horses and riders are united equally to form a rhythm—an unforgettable experience.

People who go on trail rides regularly often learn to listen automatically to be sure that when their horse's shoes touch the ground they heard the same sound—and if not, wonder whether one of the shoes is loose. Listening like this enables you to detect a loose shoe the second your horse steps out of his stall. And, someone with a trained ear is able "hear" when a horse puts more weight on one or more legs as they touch the ground (diagonally during trot, for example) and can then tell if this is the beginning of lameness that only becomes clearly visible later on.

Recently, it has become fashionable to use electronic communication systems or radios in order to communicate during riding lessons (see photo on p. 18). Often used in warm-up rings before a show, these systems are also very helpful during everyday instruction: The fact that the instructor's voice has the same volume at all times keeps a student from turning her head around or focusing all her attention on trying to hear when she is at the opposite end of an arena. Another advantage is that the transmission device enhances the sound of the horse's movement, thus amplifying his rhythm and helping the rider improve her sense of rhythm.

*A horse and rider need to like each other's smell in order to get along well.

When trying to listen, you automatically turn your head toward your instructor. This can disrupt your flow of motion.

1.3 The Importance of the Senses and Perception   17

Rider & Horse Back to Back

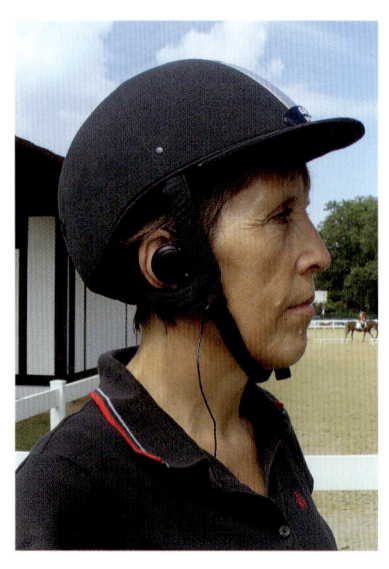

Electronic communication systems make it easy to understand each other during lessons.

The horse's hearing is so acute he is able to hear in frequencies that humans cannot detect. It is amazing how precisely he can distinguish between voices, steps, or the engine of his caretaker's approaching car. Even the dog that accompanies him on trail rides can be recognized by the sounds of tags on his collar. The sound of other horses running off is enough to cause him extreme anxiety. On the other hand, he is well able to adapt his gait to a given rhythm. A good example is a driving team where all horses move in unison, and a freestyle test, in which horses show how well they know their music.

At first, your sense of hearing and your back do not seem to have much in common but once you understand that the dynamic stability of your back is based on the coordinated rhythm of the deep, autonomous muscles in your back and abdomen, the connection between your hearing and back becomes clear. Listening to the horse's movement can help you better adapt to his rhythm and ride in a more back-friendly way.*

*The more stable the rhythm, the more relaxed you become, which results in dynamic stability of both the horse's back and your own!

Sight

The ability to see plays a very important role in perception. The way you balance, in particular, is connected to sight in a special kind of way. Within the cerebellum, there is a point where sight and balance intersect so that various balancing acts can automatically be controlled by optical stimuli. An example that proves this fact is the special-event movie theater where the audience stands instead of sitting. A movie about roller-coasters, for example, can cause the audience suddenly to start making automatic movements to "balance" itself: The people lean backward or dodge sideways even though they are standing on solid ground.

Optical stimuli can be stronger than any other form of sensual perception, which is why it makes sense to sometimes close your eyes when riding in order to get a better and more differentiated feeling for your horse.

There is a close connection between the cervical spine and your eyes. One reason is that the spine reaches up into your head—the first cervical vertebra (the atlas) is at eye height. Whichever way you look, your body automatically activates the respective muscles to move you in that direction. It is crucial to focus your eyes on where you want to go and to aim at a reference point at the end of an imaginary line. Looking down can have negative consequences on your flow of motion.

When your body's position is such that your eyes are not level and horizontal, your body reacts automatically by trying to rebalance you. Keeping your head tilted to one side for example, and purposely working against your line of vision, is stressful for muscles—in particular the cervical and back muscles. Your automatic balance reactions are strongly controlled by visual stimuli.

Your eyes roam around continuously changing depth of focus. When necessary you can intensify this focus onto an object of interest. But staring intensely at something has a tiring effect on the eye muscles and the deep muscle system of the neck. To stay supple when riding, do not stare at your hands or a letter in the arena but allow your gaze to be open and relaxed. (Sally Swift talks about "hard eyes" and "soft eyes" in her book *Centered Riding*.) Just how difficult it is to keep soft eyes is seen in the riding arena when an experienced rider—concentrating very hard—does not "see" other riders and consequently bumps into one.

The Back—The Center of the Body and All Movement

Naturally, you can *consciously* focus on a specific point. Be aware, however, that even a short loss of eye contact to your point of reference requires quite some time for you to reestablish. For example, when riding an extension across the diagonal, do not be tempted to look at the mirror in the ring, because you will lose your focus on the letter at the other end. By the time you refocus, your horse will have felt this minor interruption, incorporated it into "muscle memory," and eventually lose his rhythm and balance.

Look in the direction of movement.

As mentioned, sight and hearing are considered *far senses* and both are closely connected to balance in a neurological sense. Using your far senses for orientation is important for thinking ahead and being ready to improve your balance. When you observe that you will shortly be riding downhill, your body prepares itself accordingly. This way, the first step downhill does not surprise you. When you hear a horse galloping toward you, as a precaution, you will shorten your reins just in case your horse views this as an invitation to join in a race. The *positive body tension* you feel in these scenarios is similar to the type of tension that you need in order to perform a good halt in dressage (as opposed to a horse merely standing still). Looking ahead in the sense of *thinking* ahead is indispensable: It is the only way to correctly prepare for every transition and every exercise.

Far senses are also decisive in horses' instinctive movement and behavior. When a horse sees or hears an unknown, presumably threatening or sense-overwhelming object, a flight response is triggered—shying, for example.*

Feeling

Feeling is the most important sense. Body awareness is the basis for developing a "feel" for riding, which consists of a feeling for the horse's motion *and* control of your own body. Applying the aids evolves like a language—a conversation between horse and rider.**

There are two different kinds of feeling: *superficial* and *deep*. A superficial feeling is the sense of actual touch on the skin; it registers contact and pressure onto the body. A deep sensation, which registers the position of your joints and the tension within your muscles and tendons, "tells" you if your knee is bent or straight—without your looking.

This sense of touch and pressure adapts quickly. This means that although you perceived it strongly at first, when the stimulus remains the same, you will feel it less and less—even becoming nearly unaware of it. Imagine that if all your attention was taken up by feeling what is touching your body, you wouldn't be able to function in everyday life. A classic example to illustrate this fact is when you wear watch: If you have not been wearing one for a while, it almost feels uncomfortably heavy when you first put it on. Once you start wearing it all the time, you don't consider it a "foreign object" anymore and hardly notice it.

This change in feeling from touch also applies to your horse. A horse numb to the rider's leg has usually been desensitized by excessive leg pressure and use of spurs. In order to apply leg aids well, you need to relax your leg *immediately after* giving the aid—just as you yield your hands after giving a rein aid.

*If you want to be able to react in a timely and appropriate manner when sitting on a horse, you need to keep your "far senses" alert.

**Only those riders completely aware of themselves and their horse are able to appropriately react and use body language to make their horse move as intended.

1.3 The Importance of the Senses and Perception

Rider & Horse Back to Back

Contact with the lower leg (left) and no contact (right). Change in contact is easier for the horse to feel (and understand) than constant pressure.

To sum up: Whenever you experience something for the first time, you are very conscious of the stimulus. But when the stimulus remains constant, it is "forwarded" to your subconscious where you hardly notice it anymore.

To "wake up" the feeling of contact with your horse's mouth, try holding the reins in an unfamiliar way like a beginner sometimes tries to do (see photo). This new sensation will help to emphasize how you should follow the horse's movement with your arm acting "independently" as if it were an elastic extension to the rein. This soft contact is very important in riding, and changing the way the reins run through your fingers is a valuable practical exercise—not only for dressage riders but jumpers, too.

Tactile receptors, located all over the body, but which work most intensely in your hands, skin, and mouth, provide you

This rider is holding his two reins differently. Consequently, he will have a completely different feeling of connection between his hands and the horse's mouth.

with information about the world by way of touching and feeling.

Your entire body helps you feel and be aware of horse, saddle, reins, and everything you come in contact with. As mentioned, the longer you are exposed to these stimuli, however, the more their intensity decreases—they are being stored in your subconscious. Many people recommend riding with gloves, for example, which can feel uncomfortable at first (the main argument of riders strongly opposed to them). However, once you have become used to wearing gloves, you start feeling the exact opposite about them: Riding with bare hands feels strange. There are other situations where getting used to tactile stimuli is necessary: If you have not used a double bridle in a while, it takes some time to get reacquainted with four reins and the quality of contact needs practice and time.

The tactile system consists of two functionally different systems: the *defense system* and the *control system*. The defense system acts automatically and reflexively, reacting to pain, temperature and outside stimuli by having you quickly pull back or throw your hands and arms out when you fall. You do both without thinking.

The Back—The Center of the Body and All Movement

The control system, on the other hand, checks and evaluates all your conscious movements—it "feels" pressure—like your weight on a left leg or whether you are touching something that is rough or smooth. It also allows you to suppress a reflex: For example, if you usually look in the direction you are moving, you can choose not to—as long as you consciously think about it. It also allows you to *plan* a movement: It evaluates how much weight there is in a suitcase you are about to pick up so your body automatically prepares to lift it. (When the case is surprisingly light though, you may trip over because you acted faster than your control system.) It registers time and place of all your conscious movements.

To sum up, all movement is a balance between the *defensive reflex system*, and *consciously planned controlled movement* (though in a life-threatening situation, your defense system overrules conscious movement). Your tactile system gets processed through your reflexes and your consciousness and the result makes up the *quality* of movement.

The horse's behavior and movement are also controlled by defense and control systems. His skin contains so many nerve endings and muscle cells that he is able to twitch exactly where an insect lands. Similar to the "far senses," the defense system is connected to the horse's flight response. The rider's aids are tailored in a fascinating way to the horse's tactile system so the horse reacts reflexively (and naturally) to them. One example is the point of contact of the rider's lower leg on the horse's side. It should be situated exactly at a nerve trigger point so your leg stimulates the horse's abdominal muscles to move his hind leg under his belly.

Once you understand that the horse's flight response is controlled by reflexes, it becomes clear why it is completely pointless to punish him for his reactions. In fact, it's crucial that every trainer schooling young horses watch out *not* to trigger the defense system with its consequent flight responses by using her aids incorrectly: Once such a motion pattern has been established in the horse's brain, it is very difficult to change the respective automatic reactions. In some cases, change becomes impossible. A typical example is the "cinchy" horse. The first time a saddle is put on his back and he experiences this action as painful—or frightening—the memory will be engraved into his defense system. One single traumatic experience can influence the horse's behavior for the rest of his life.*

Proprioception provides you with information about the position of your body in space—the position of your individual body parts in relation to each other; the position of joints; and the degree of flexion and tension of your muscles.

You are only able to specifically use your individual body parts when you know how they are positioned. However, your perception tends to play annoying tricks on you. For example, if you deviate from sitting in an upright, balanced body—the correct "middle" riding position—it will feel quite normal to you after you've kept it up for some length of time. Then correcting the "false" position is what feels wrong or unnatural!

A typical example is your head: When you keep your head sideways for a while, the normal "straight" position will feel "crooked." Only when you combine balance reflexes with body awareness can you detect such a wrong "feeling" and correct your position: Say you are not sitting in the middle of the saddle (but think you are), it can be helpful to take both legs away from it so your balance reflexes can "report" to you that you are not at all centered (no matter what you felt). For detailed exercises, see page 76.

In riding instruction, this piece of knowledge is important. Riders who have difficulty feeling their center can regain this proper feeling by doing balance exercises, and asymmetric positions can be corrected more easily this way than by verbal commands from an instructor, such as, "More to the left," "More to the right," "More forward," or "More backward."**

*Advice to stay calm and patient when training a young horse is not offered only for humane or ethical reasons: It comes from knowledge of the horse's sensory system and its connection to the flight response.

**When you specifically use your knowledge of the different areas of the tactile system, you will be able to ride in a way that is gentle to your back, and your horse's, too.

1.3 The Importance of the Senses and Perception

Rider & Horse Back to Back

Sense of balance

The *sense of balance* detects body position and supplies information for orientation. It is based in the balance organ, which is located in the inner ear and cerebellum. Your sense of balance is not only connected to hearing, but also to eyes and other senses—as well as reflexes. A simple exercise to test the state of your sense of balance is trying to stand on one leg as long as you can with your eyes closed.

As flight animals, horses need good balance in order to survive. They never fall unless circumstances significantly change (for example, sudden slippery ground) or they have a health issue. The danger of losing their balance triggers fear and an instinctive counter reaction—just as in humans. Riders, who think they are about to fall off their horse, often tighten their legs and bend their upper body into a fetal position. This loss of rider balance is guaranteed to make the horse run faster, and the rider eventually make (unwanted) contact with the ground! A problem with the rider's balance is one of the reasons for resistance, which is often misinterpreted as disobedience, and the horse is consequently (and unfortunately) punished.*

Natural posture of horses at high speed is to balance themselves by holding their head high, lowering their back and turning their head and neck outward. The objective of dressage training is to teach horses how to balance themselves in a back-friendly way by using their entire body.

Your sense of balance is a combination of the ability to differentiate between up and down; gain a feeling for angle and inclination (spatial orientation), a sense of rhythm, and the linear and rotational acceleration of your head in all directions.

All of the above proves the complexity of balance and shows that all the senses have to be working together in a system that is operating automatically.

You need to focus on the connection between balance and rhythm since the ability to feel the rhythm of a movement is the basis for a balanced seat. Without rhythm and motion, good balance cannot be developed!

The knowledge that balance sensors exist within your pelvis should help you understand why riders who sit in the deepest point of the saddle and in a relaxed manner do indeed have good balance, which allows them to safely and quickly adapt to the horse's movement.

This sense of balance rooted in the pelvis plays a central role in riding. In daily life, however, you usually control balance through your feet, which makes it difficult to allow the pelvis to take on this task. As a consequence, many riders subconsciously use their stirrups for support and are surprised that they ride so much better without them.

Without stirrups, your automatic reaction to use your feet to balance is deactivated so that you focus on your pelvis to feel the motion without even thinking about it. Now your body can automatically put the balance control of your pelvis first, and your seat will become deeper and more secure. Compare it to the feeling you get when you close your eyes: By taking your sight away your sense of "feel" becomes much more pronounced. By taking stirrups away, you inten-

The entire training process of horse and rider can be described as finding and perfecting balance—together.

Sense of balance in movement is supplemented by:
- Sight—For positioning and orientation.
- Skeletal muscles—For turning the body and, to a lesser degree, speed.
- Pelvis—For speed and "speeding up."
- Hearing—For determining speed with the help of the sounds produced by air.
- Touch—Air resistance against your skin indicating speed.
- Feet—For stabilization of upright position when standing and walking.

The Back—The Center of the Body and All Movement

Riding without stirrups improves balance reflexes.

*Your balance can be improved by riding without stirrups in the walk phase at the beginning of each session.

sify use of your pelvis to achieve balance—most important in order to be a good rider (see photo).*

A sixth sense

A sixth sense is often used to describe the ability to perceive things the other senses are presumably unable to notice. These seemingly supernatural abilities usually turn out to have relatively normal origins: An astonishing amount of sensual stimuli are received subconsciously and are unknowingly processed by our brains. Intuition, for example, is based on experience we are often unaware we possess.

In contrast to animals, human beings have the ability to simulate perception in the brain, that is, to imagine feeling something without any actual outside stimuli.

The entire complexity of mental training is based on a sixth sense. It enables you to achieve the necessary visualization skills and depth of thinking by way of imagination and the ability to associate. You are able to imagine changes in systems and processes, to play out alternatives and their consequences while coming up with different scenarios—the perfect jumping course or a successful dressage test, for example. Your imagination allows you to relive the results of a training session and to create variations of it in your head. This is the only way you are able to analyze complex contexts and to find solutions with regard to the training of horse and rider.**

A sixth sense helps you memorize, remember, rethink, and even create a complete picture of something in your head. These kinds of pictures are projected in your mind's eye where they make a lasting impression. Usually, the subtlest keywords are enough to reactivate them. In this way, the riding instructor is able to activate in a student a complicated chain of movements with just one memorized keyword.

**Improving your imaginary perception has additional positive effects on your actual perception as your senses become increasingly sensitized in this way.

1.3 The Importance of the Senses and Perception

Rider & Horse | Back to Back

*A sixth sense, empathy, and imagination are essential to riding!

It is possible to improve a sixth sense by consciously concentrating on the things in our environment. This way, the power of imagination can be combined with reality.

All of this requires time, however—time we often do not have or think we do not have. Nonetheless, the reward is certainly worth the trouble! Only positive pictures in your head will allow you to create positive movement. In this context, you can understand why watching top professional athletes not only motivates, but downright inspires you to get better at riding—with the "perfect picture" in your mind's eye.

A sixth sense helps you improve your riding skills and increases the fun, as well. It's impossible to make good decisions in favor of a back-friendly riding style without imagination.*

Using all your senses while riding can improve the riding experience.

1.4 Awareness and Motion

Be aware of your own back

Playing on a German saying that everyone is responsible for her own good fortune, you could say that everyone is responsible for her own back. If you treat your back well, you increase your chances of never experiencing any problems with it. This means that even people with back conditions can lead pain-free lives—but as said earlier, there are no perfect backs anyway.

As already discussed, it is difficult to be aware of your own back. It is much easier for you to see, feel, and control your hands and feet than the individual vertebrae of your spine.

You often experience back pain as *referred* pain—not local or confined to the back itself. Instead, the pain travels to other body parts such as the stomach, for example. The back contains reflex areas that can influence all organs. Between the shoulder blades, for instance, you can find a spot that can have an effect on the heart. The connection to all your internal organs ascribes to your back an additional function; being aware of it can sometimes be very helpful.*

The biggest challenge in regard to being aware of your own body is to gather as much information as possible with the help of all your available senses. You need to know about the leverage your joints give you, the length and mobility of your body parts, to which side you can turn more easily.

In order to assess all of this as realistically as possible, most people need outside support such as having photos or videos taken of them; being observed by an instructor; or watching themselves in a mirror while riding in the ring. It is most important to know as much about yourself as possible in order to "see" yourself.

Every form of perception is subjective

When you perceive yourself you usually believe that what you *feel* and *experience* is true. But, the way someone else sees you might paint a completely different picture.

Even when you use all of your senses, you are always limited to taking in only a small part—a fraction of the whole of what makes up *reality*. This phenomenon is known as "tunnel vision." You experience your subjective reality as a sort of jigsaw puzzle piece, which is part of a complex structure you are unable to see in its entirety. In order to grasp as much of it as possible, you need to get out of the tunnel! This means that you must take off the "blinkers" you are wearing and start to look at yourself and the way you ride—on a regular basis and from all angles. The more puzzle pieces you collect, the better you will be able to see the whole picture.

In the process, you will reach your limit over and

*Even though you are not always aware of your back as long as it is healthy and works fine, you should develop a feeling for doing what is good for it when needed ("rounding" it and stretching, for example) in order to actually be able to make use of its strengths. Remember, you need to ride with your back, not against it!

Every body is unique and develops its own unmistakable motion pattern.

Rider & Horse Back to Back

over again since it is impossible to see, hear and feel everything at once or to experience all of it consciously. Your brain automatically decides which stimuli are to be processed consciously and which, subconsciously.

You should never underestimate your sixth sense and the amount of information you are able to perceive through your *sub*conscious—it is usually a lot more than you think. *Consciously*, you can only focus on two or three things at the same time—despite what the word "multitasking" implies.

As a logical consequence, you have to walk a fine line taking in as much as possible without letting yourself get confused by an overwhelming amount of different stimuli.

Riding also requires you to understand the "species-specific" perception of the horse. What can seem completely harmless to you is often perceived as very dangerous by the horse.

The instructor as a "medium" for your perception

Every instructor has to be very aware of a student's specific body shape—especially her back since it defines everybody's individual movement. Understanding the rider's conformation tells the instructor what is going to be easy (or difficult) for her and to choose appropriate exercises. Since the back is the body's motion center, it determines the mobility of each student, whether good or limited. Each rider's body works like an individually operated "motion system." To learn how to be empathetic to a student's problems, an instructor needs to put himself in someone else's shoes. It's important to remember that although every student has many faults that need correcting, there is always one most important issue that dominates the others, and it is this one that needs to be recognized and worked on first.

Some advice that might prove helpful in practice is to look at the "leverage-relationship" of the individual body parts. Using the hip as the body's dividing line, are the legs longer or shorter than the upper body? What is the proportion of thigh to lower leg and—even more important with regard to the back—the proportion of upper arm to forearm? (See the photos below.) When the forearms are particularly long, they act like powerful levers, which are difficult for the rider to balance (see pages 9–11 for interesting examples illustrating various body proportions).

Long forearms are heavy and this is "extra" weight to be carried in front of the body. Unfortunately, this weight pulls you forward and down, which means strain on the back. When you do not have enough muscular, dynamic stability in your back to handle it, you will have to counterbalance: In

A rider with especially long forearms.

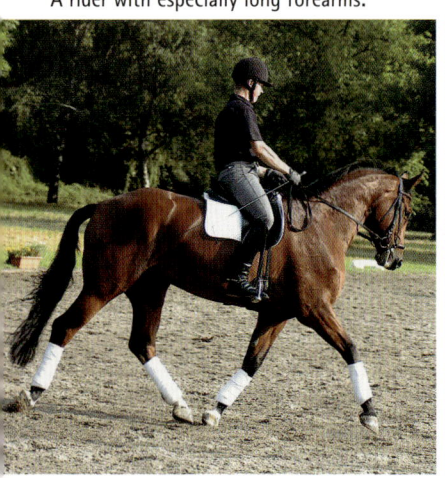

A rider with very long legs (middle and right).

The Back—The Center of the Body and All Movement

the far left photo on page 26, you can see how this rider rounds his back and shoulders to counterbalance the weight of his arms. He will need to work on his stability and strengthen his abdominal muscles as well as those muscles between the shoulder blades to be able to remain upright and supple while carrying his hands free and independently in front of his body.

An old saying among teachers says that they always teach what they themselves need to learn most. It's common knowledge that when teaching students, instructors tend to focus on what they are working on themselves at that time. For example, if they are perfecting their own balance during turns, this is what they will concentrate on in a lesson.

This parallel of learning and teaching is quite normal and can be valuable, too. Since you only master a skill when you are able to teach it, when an instructor continues to improves his knowledge, his instructing will change focus accordingly. In time he will help his students improve their seat from all different angles.

It is a particularly important to make sure that every successful improvement in the rider—no matter whether a shift of weight, better hand and head position, or placement of feet in the stirrups—always leads to an improvement in the horse, too. As a matter of fact, improving parts of the body individually often leads to a "chain reaction" with a positive effect showing up in the rider's seat. Since riding involves complex movements, there are many different areas of the body from which to start dealing with a problem.

A competent and experienced instructor is able to offer an individualized solution to a rider's problem and not just point out as many faults as quickly as possible. Nothing is worse for a student than being given too many corrections at once since she cannot possibly process more than three in her brain at a time.*

Develop a feel for movement

Working with a horse, you should always concentrate on one single aspect at a time. For a while, focus more on rhythm; later, you can work toward achieving correct bend; then transitions; after that, you can aim at improving the activity of the hindquarters. Then you can work on rhythm and balance again. It's like a circle on which you concentrate on your riding from different angles and work your way around—the picture of perfect harmony. Among other things, on any given day, good, experienced riders have the ability to notice which aspect of training they need to focus on.

Just as priorities change during the course of a horse's training, a good rider also has to face the challenge of detecting the issue her body is currently dealing with so she can concentrate on fixing it. Sometimes, you work more on correct balance, sometimes on the position of your hands and other times, you struggle with your stirrups ...**

Consequently, good riders need to not only develop and practice a feeling for the horse's movement, but also for their own. A rider may be able to tell an instructor how she can feel the horse's activity from behind, and how supple or straight he is but, at the same time, have poor awareness of her own balance, straightness and movement. There can be an astonishing discrepancy between a rider's ability to talk about the quality of her horse's movement versus her own.

Riding is all about the harmony of motion between horse and rider, which is why, as a rider you cannot simply limit your perception to yourself or your horse. One of the biggest challenges in learning how to ride is developing complex awareness, the focus of which constantly adapts to what the current situation demands.

There are, however, extraordinarily talented riders who have never learned how to be aware of their body in this way. If you start riding as an athletic adolescent with a well-developed sense of balance you will be able to instinctively adapt

*Too much correction all at once ruins a rider's "feel."

**You need to develop a sense of motion in order to be able to move in a way that is both efficient and gentle to your back. This is a feeling you have to take with you when you mount a horse so you will be able to ride in a back-friendly manner.

1.4 Awareness and Motion

to the horse's movements. If your body works just great, training your body awareness may seem to be unnecessary. Your lack of body awareness becomes obvious only when your body does not automatically do what it is supposed to—either due to injury or a decrease in performance caused by the natural aging process. In situations like these, even good riders have difficulty coping because they have never learned to listen to their body.

What you feel versus what others see

What you perceive about your body is always "real" to you. What you feel is what you feel—there is no other way. But since every form of self-awareness is very personal and subjective, while you are insisting to others that what *you* are feeling is right, always remain "open" to hearing how *they* see you.

What you are feeling about a movement and another person's view of it can be quite different!

Take a rider's impression of how she performed in a dressage test. Quite often, the rider has a good feeling about her performance, but when she sees the score the judges awarded her, it's like a slap in the face. She will only be able to understand the low score and critical assessment that came with it after she improves her self-awareness through more training and experience. It takes time, energy and self-criticism to reconcile her own feelings with the picture she is getting from observers on the ground. It often happens that people deceive themselves—even riders at the highest levels. So, in order to prevent mistakes from creeping into your riding (balance issues, for example, can become so deeply ingrained in your seat that it takes enormous effort to correct them), you need to regularly expose yourself to the critical eye of an instructor who can tell you that even though you feel straight and centered, you are actually not. And no matter how hard you try to "feel" this, you cannot. So you need help to "change" your self-awareness to feel more like what the instructor is seeing.

Here is a simple experiment to prove the unreliability of perception: Take three glasses and fill one with hot, one with cold and one with lukewarm water. Next, dip a finger in the hot water, a finger of the other hand in the cold water, then dip both fingers in the glass with lukewarm water.

Now you will experience a conundrum: Even though both fingers are in the same water, it feels cold to the finger that was in the hot water, and hot to the finger that was in the cold water. The fact that you "know and understand" that your fingers are now in the same lukewarm temperature does not change the way they feel. "Reason" is unable to supersede your feelings—as often happens in life! In order for your fingers to feel the same, they will need to be in the lukewarm water for some time until they adjust. Moving your fingers around in the water can accelerate the process.

Projecting this experiment onto riding teaches you that even though you think you are sitting with an upright, balanced upper body (the middle position), your perception does not always correspond to reality. You could actually be sitting in a "chair" seat (which can feel very comfortable to riders), and when the instructor tells you that your upper body needs to come forward, the correct middle position makes you think you are now leaning much too far to the front of the horse!

Body awareness and seat corrections

Correcting *lateral asymmetries* is even more difficult than finding the middle position by moving your upper body forward and backward. After successfully changing her lopsidedness, many a student has said: "Oh, I get it. When it feels to me as if I am leaning too far to the right, I am actually sitting in the middle." However, this is not the way to learn how to sit in the saddle. Teaching students to experience a posture as "incorrect" eventually will lead to overcompensation and miss the actual goal, which is to instill what the middle position is *supposed* to feel like.

The Back—The Center of the Body and All Movement

Once a rider has been sitting correctly for a period of time, this position is stored in the brain's memory as normal—similar to the water glass experiment, when, after a while, the fingers reported to the brain the actual "reading" of a lukewarm temperature. The experiment teaches two things: It takes time to get used to feeling that a new position is correct, but the process can be accelerated by "stirring the lukewarm water with your fingers." For example, to successfully sit in the middle position you need to improve your feel for it; this is best done by movement, not desperately trying to "hold onto" the way you were positioned when corrected. You need to move your pelvis left and right and through this become more aware of where your seat bones are in the saddle. Afterward, you will feel the correct position more easily and securely. (Just being told to sit more to the left and stay there is not helpful and only leads to *negative* tension.)

The result of this experiment is particularly important for an instructor to understand because it helps explain why it is often so difficult for a student to carry out a "correction." Even when a student trusts her instructor and believes him when he says that sitting in a certain way is sitting "in the middle"—the student's feeling for her own body will try to convince her of the opposite as long as possible, just like the example of the fingers in lukewarm water.

Riding against what you feel is difficult. In most cases, this happens at the expense of relaxation and slows down movement, which in turn gets in the way of your being able to apply precise and subtle aids.

The goal of good riding instruction is for the student's feeling to correspond as much as possible to reality as experienced by the person on the ground. Good instructors are able to empathize with students and their problems, that is, they basically "ride" along on foot. It is very informative to watch an enthusiastic instructor and his body language during a lesson, with his own body also carrying out the correction directed at his student.

Here's another example to illustrate this point: Say you are asked for the middle on a scale of one to ten, you would answer five. Now, imagine someone who does not know the whole scale yet and has only learned to count to six (okay, you need to suspend disbelief for a moment). Asked for the middle, he would, with quite some conviction, answer three. So a student who does not yet know, and has not experienced the entire range of movement and balance, may feel he is in a different middle position from the position he is actually in, which is what the instructor is seeing.

As a consequence, you always have to move your joints and muscles in a way that allows them to actually use the whole scale, like learning to count all the way to ten. This means you learn to make use of your entire scope of motion, for only then can your body awareness tell you where the middle position really is.*

An enthusiastic instructor often "rides" along on foot.

*In order to sit straight, you need to be able to move equally in all directions. This way, you will automatically assume a better middle position as your autonomous and often reflex-controlled movements allow you to ride in a better and more sensitive manner.

1.4 Awareness and Motion

1.5 Pain—A Challenge to Your Perception

Feeling pain

Pain is a special case of body perception and feeling. Researchers specializing in pain even describe it as the most complex form of body awareness. When people talk about pain, they always name the location of its origin: headache, backache, stomachache or even heartache (the latter, of course, in a figurative sense).

Acute pain is usually caused by a sudden problem, which can be often found and treated. Acute pain arises quickly and usually goes away again at some point. *Chronic pain*, however, is constant, sometimes more severe, sometimes less, but basically always there. Therefore, it is more difficult to describe, locate, and treat. Patients with chronic pain get stuck in vicious cycles of pain, which are difficult to influence and almost impossible to break.

The spectrum of pain is enormous and the way it is experienced is diverse, so people often find it difficult to correctly describe what they feel: tugging, stabbing, burning, sharp, dull, flashing, blinding, dark, throbbing, pounding...The difficulty of aptly describing the quality of pain indicates that individuals in similar situations experience and process pain differently.

A *pain threshold* (defining what is actually considered pain) and *pain tolerance* (the degree of pain you can take without it having a negative influence on your well-being) differ from individual to individual. Even the exact source of pain in the body can become difficult. While, for example, pain in the sole of your foot or in a fingertip can be precisely located, back pain is often hard to pinpoint. It can radiate into unaffected areas of the body to such a degree that the actual source of the pain completely vanishes from your awareness. A famous example is the sciatic nerve, which originates in the lumbar spine and can have negative effects on the entire leg: from the hip down the outside of the thigh all the way to the foot. Issues concerning the thoracic spine can spread and interfere with your cardiovascular system and, thus, breathing.

The location of where you experience pain strongly influences how adversely affected you feel. Nail-bed inflammation, for example, is usually very painful, but hardly anyone gets depressed because of it. However, the closer pain is to the central nervous system, head, heart, and back, the more likely you are to be influenced psychologically.

People who suffer from chronic pain are mostly preoccupied with it and consequently much less aware of their surroundings. Pain not only affects your perception but also your breathing and digestion: The entire autonomous nervous system reacts to painful situations. Pain equals stress on the body and every person reacts differently to this kind of stress. It is typical, for example, for pain to cause stomach problems.

Like all forms of chronic pain, back pain has destructive effects. Someone who experiences constant pain often gets depressed, extremely irritable, and less tolerant. These psychological impairments are part of the complex of symptoms—not necessarily a consolation to those affected, but important to know.

The area where pain is most intense is not always the location with the worst problems—especially with regard to back pain. From a medical point of view, there is a huge gap between the intensity of the pain experienced and the actual severity of the medical condition. Bone—including the spine—does not actually contain any nerve endings that would report painful sensations to the brain. It is the tissue adjacent to the bone, however, where nerves are abundant. Problems with back muscles can cause pain more severe than serious injury to the spine.

Riding with back pain

In industrialized countries, back pain is by far the most common medical problem, not only in adults but children, too. It has developed into the number one complaint in the modern world. Statistics predict a significant probability that riders will have to deal with back pain multiple times during their active riding career. Moreover, wear and tear of the spine is a typical occupational hazard for professional trainers and riders.

To decide whether you should go riding or not, even though you are experiencing acute back pain, you might want to consult a doctor (preferably one who has knowledge of riding). It goes without saying that you should not ride if you suffer from extreme pain or acute inflammatory or degenerative illness. When in doubt, you should base your decision on the following questions: "Am I able to sit on my horse without experiencing the acute pain?" and "Does my chronic pain not get any worse—neither directly after riding nor the day after?"

Distinguishing whether pain is *protecting* or *harming* you is not always easy. Successful treatment consists of visits to experienced therapists, keeping up good body awareness, and taking responsibility for yourself.

"Protecting" pain is really telling you: "Watch out or you will get hurt!" This kind of pain is necessary and useful as it stops you from overstraining, prevents overly high expectations of what you can do, and reminds you to check your posture. You should always look at pain as a warning and respect it—trying to ignore or hide it hardly ever works out in the end.

Pain demands consideration! Avoiding pain is one of the strongest reflexes you have. You automatically move away from it: You pull your hand away from a hot plate or jump onto the other leg when you step on something sharp. These reflexive movements are a form of self-protection, which is not controlled by the brain but by the spinal cord. Therefore, these reactions happen very quickly and are highly effective—your will has very little influence over them.

If you have ever had sore knees during riding, you will know how difficult it is to sit with your lower legs relaxed and correctly positioned. If you suffer from back pain connected to a certain position of the pelvis, you will instinctively avoid the position during riding—even at the expense of sitting balanced and at the deepest point of the saddle.*

With regard to chronic pain, however, repression can be a helpful strategy. Nevertheless, even repressed pain can have a lasting influence on motion patterns.

In order to work on pain, to lessen it in general or—in the best-case scenario—get rid of it entirely, you need to make yourself aware of it first.

*It is impossible to ignore acute pain and simply shut off the body's pain-avoidance reflexes.

Rider & Horse Back to Back

Take care of your back

More than anyone else, talented, strong riders in their adolescence and early adulthood tend to exploit their body and ruin their health. Unfortunately, there are no warning signs to protect them from overstraining the stabilization capability of their back. Those who take naturally to riding are particularly able to compensate for hidden weaknesses over a long period of time—though at the expense of making their muscles work evenly and efficiently. Negative effects such as degenerative disorders usually only show after years of misuse. Riders, who are used to a body that functions well without any problem are often downright shocked when they cannot depend on their physical capabilities anymore. Resignation, however, is the worst remedy.*

Constructively dealing with backache always requires you to face the pain and to get to know your body once again. Since sitting on horseback is very much like walking—the horse's back moves your pelvis in the same rhythmical, three-dimensional way—chances are good that it might actually break the vicious cycle of pain.

Riding when your back is hurting obviously requires you to be considerate of it—trying to improve your skills should not be attempted at this time. You need to avoid a situation that results in a sudden movement or one that puts additional strain on your back—even when you are an experienced rider. Riding unpredictable horses and jumping fences is, of course, out of the question. In order to protect their back, trainers also need to avoid any "confrontation" with a horse—even though they might find this hard to accept. It is important to ride in an environment that allows you, first of all to focus on your own body. (If necessary, free school your horse or longe him before you start riding.)

It is not a good idea, however, to have a strong rider get on your horse before you. Even though riding a horse that has been "prepared" by someone else might give you the benefit of learning from the horse, his back will already be relaxed and "swinging" while yours is still stiff—possibly even tensed up—and this is not a good combination. Planning a warm-up phase that both you and your horse can do together is one of the most important requirements for consciously taking care of your back.

*It is never too early and seldom too late to learn how to ride in a back-friendly way.

The walk phase at the beginning of your ride offers you the chance to listen to your body and let the horse's movement mobilize your back.

The Back—The Center of the Body and All Movement

Developing a style of riding that treats your back in a gentle way is a great challenge—it takes imagination, good problem-solving skills and, most of all, an understanding of classical riding. Usually, there are multiple ways to reach this goal, and one of them will be the best for your back.

> **What to do if you want to ride despite preexisting back problems:**
> - Relieve—Find a pain-free position (position of pelvis, type of seat/discipline, stirrup length).
> - Mobilize—See how far you can move your joints (try exercises targeting the suppleness of your pelvis and hip joints).
> - Strengthen—Build up positive body tension especially in your core (alternate between contracting and relaxing muscles according to the rhythm of the horse's movements).

Dynamic stability of the core is necessary for riding. This stability is controlled by the interplay of the deep trunk muscles (stimulated by the horse's movement) and your upright seat secured and actively rebalanced all the time. When these muscles work properly and support the back, they can ensure the back is pain free. When the rider is in acute pain, these short deep muscles often stop working and the longer superficial muscles take over. However, since it is not their function to stabilize the spine, the latter can tire out quickly and become tense—and thus painful.

Riding constantly challenges body awareness. This is actually a good thing: Chronic pain—which frequently dominates all your feeling and sensation—is moved into the background. This phenomenon of *positive distraction* can contribute to improving the quality of life of someone suffering from chronic pain. In this way, the vicious cycle of pain can actually be broken in some cases. The brain, which was bombarded with pain stimuli, can get a rest and concentrate on other things. Ideally, pain can be reduced to a bearable level and sometimes even vanish completely for a while.

Painful experiences can have a lasting, negative effect on how flexible you are on horseback. Strategies to avoid pain are stored in muscle memory and will stay there for a long time. If certain motion patterns have been associated with pain over a long period, you will actually have to relearn them after the pain is gone.

The advice in this book is not a magic formula to deal with back pain. It takes a lot of self-knowledge and self-discipline to understand what is good and what is bad for your back.

Long-term studies of patients suffering from chronic back pain have proven that those who take things easy during a phase of acute pain in order to return to everyday activity showed the best results—regardless of whether they had an operation or received conventional treatment. Their experience is supposed to motivate you not to give up riding even when back problems restrict your movement for short or long periods of time.

Mastering the challenge of developing better body awareness and riding in a back-friendly way can actually lead to more fun—and success—with your riding! ■

1.5 Pain—a Challenge to Your Perception

1.6 Learning How to Move

Different ways to start riding

There are many different ways to learn how to ride. Few other sports have such a wide variety of approaches to take you to your goal.

No matter if you start with lessons on a longe line in an arena, or go out right away on trail rides (or if lucky enough, have parents who ride themselves that statistically give you the best chance to become a successful competitor)—riding careers always progress individually.

Longe lessons are a well-established way to learn how to ride and move with the horse.

No matter if they are competitive or not, there is one thing all good riders have in common: The way they learned to ride is always connected to an instructor who correctly taught them the basics. Even the most talented athletes need to learn the right motion patterns on horseback before they can become really good. They also have their weaknesses and make mistakes so they need instruction on how to move and someone to correct them.

The most important thing about successfully teaching and learning how to ride is to understand that riding is based on mutual movement of horse and rider. Even though this might sound banal, it has powerful influence.

Life is motion

Motion is a natural thing. It is one of life's characteristics. We move constantly and most movement happens subconsciously: You do not have to think about telling your muscles to work in a certain way. Since there are so many reflex-driven movements, it is difficult to learn or correct motion patterns. In many cases, they cannot be controlled deliberately.

In order to understand the basics of how you learn to move, you need to look at the motion development of toddlers. It takes about a year to go through the process necessary to sit upright and to walk—these steps can be taken as an example of how you learn new movements in general. A toddler's development demonstrates all the little steps it takes to learn a movement right up to the point where he has control over a motion pattern. How fast children learn to walk has no bearing on their basic ability to move. A very young child's back, still relatively weak, needs to be considered: sitting up and standing should not be attempted too early.

Some children may learn to walk late but still can become successful runners. In riding, there is no rule about how many longe lessons a young rider needs, or how long she needs to be on a lead rope before starting to ride alone. It depends on the situation—and the quality of horses, too. Therefore, you cannot assume that the rider who needed fewer lessons on the longe at the beginning will be the better rider at the end of the day.

The pace of learning always depends on the individual and is influenced by many different factors. Often, more time spent on the longe line or being led by someone else builds a stronger foundation. The most famous example to prove this point is the Spanish Riding School in Vienna where, for months, horse-trainers-to-be are only allowed to ride while being longed.

Is age an issue?

With regard to the development of the back and the stability of the spine, it is important for toddlers to learn a wide variety of movements before they start putting strain on their back by standing straight. Examples are turning around, belly crawling, rolling, and crawling. Similarly, a variety of movements is the best way for older children to learn how to use their back correctly. However, the changes in lifestyle—now so much more sedentary than in the past—do not help children meet this requirement. Telling a child to sit still before he has developed the muscles to support the position, is about the most unhealthy thing you can do for his back. In this position, he is basically "suspended" in his ligaments and joints without any muscles for support. Sitting too early on in life can lead to back problems in the future.

A child can sit up straight only after he has developed the coordination and strength necessary to do so. This is why children should only be allowed to sit when they are able to do so themselves. Give them incentives to vary their movement as they should not stay in the same position for too long.

Children should be allowed to sit on a horse only after they are able to sit straight without assistance and can stabilize their spine during movement in all directions. A general age limit does not exist in this case—it depends on whether a small child is going to be sitting on an adequate-sized pony without "big" movement (preferable) or on his parents' show horse. Being able to control his head position is a clear indication. When the child lacks stability, his head will wobble uncontrollably during trot. Even without medical training, you can imagine the negative effects these violent, "disorganized" movements will have on a child's back. Unfortunately, you can see cases like this in lead-line classes; officials should consider raising the age limit for these competitions.

Anybody who is able to sit as relaxed and upright as this child and showing control of head movement is ready to ride a pony. Though in the beginning—just walking is enough!

A couple of years later, an upright and relaxed position has almost become a matter of course.

1.6 Learning How to Move

Rider & Horse Back to Back

The following comparisons can be drawn in order to better understand the strain riding puts on your back: Sitting on a horse in the walk is actually similar to your walking on the ground, the trot is equal to running, and cantering to skipping. Naturally, the amount of strain depends on the type, size, and movement of the horse you are riding.

Only after basic back stability has been developed, is it possible to ride sitting trot for a longer period of time. When a rider lacks stability in her core, she will either wobble uncontrollably or tense up and stiffen her back in order to compensate. In both cases, following the horse's movements is impossible.

During this learning phase, sitting trot must only be practiced for short periods of time and alternated with rising trot and walk. By the way, it is much better for a young student to compensate for a lack of stability in the back with the help of a strap attached to the front of the saddle instead of trying to do sitting trot at all costs!

Back stability is paramount

Instructors need to be aware of how important it is not to ask beginners, whether adolescents and adults, to sit in a position their back does not yet have sufficient stability to support. Asking too much can put a student's health at risk.

Your seat (posture) as well as control over the horse are two aspects of riding only *theoretically* dealt with separately; during riding lessons (except when longeing beginners), both need to be taught at the same time. Before any "real" riding begins, a rider needs to have a certain degree of control over the horse.

If your seat and posture are not yet stable, you cannot do anything else but use strength to compensate for lack of riding skill. Even though using strength might cut down on the time you need to convince your horse to do certain exercises, it will not work for your body in the long run: You will be learning incorrect motion patterns and it will take lots of effort to change them later on.

Here's a good example to illustrate this point: If you are asked to push your horse forward before you are able to sit in a balanced way, you will inevitably end up banging your lower legs against the horse's sides. Beginners have not developed the key skill that maintains forward motion, which is to unite precisely their own center of gravity with their horse's at every step and stride. A beginner's lack of balance unintentionally slows down the horse!

Moving forward together—without asking too much of those who are still learning how to ride.

In order to solve this difficult problem, it is best to follow the traditional form of instruction of riding in a group behind a lead horse (see photo).

Asking the horse for any new movement always requires the rider to shift weight. In order to better understand how, it makes sense to divide it into three steps.

> **Creating movement requires both rider and horse to:**
> - Shift weight.
> - Develop stability.
> - Execute the movement.

Shifting weight—rider

Every movement begins with a shift of weight. Strictly speaking, shifting your weight is in itself already a movement!

Standing on both feet, decide which foot you want to shift your weight onto in order to start walking. Normally, thinking about this question is redundant as your body simply decides for you based on preference and habit. There are situations, however, when deciding which foot to use is important. In track and field events (long or high jump, in particular), starting on the wrong foot makes it impossible to takeoff correctly.

The same principle applies to riding toward a fence in a disunited canter: Being able to automatically adapt your horse's canter stride for a perfect takeoff in front of a fence is part of the horse's ability to find a good distance and requires correct rhythm. In addition, another prerequisite is the trained eye of the rider, who needs to have learned how to correctly assess her distance to the fence well before she gets to it.

Ideally, horse and rider do not think about which of the horse's feet moves first in walk. When in doubt, however, dexterous riders are able to apply weight aids to literally organize their horse's legs.

As in dancing, you cannot have harmony if you and your partner do not start on the correct foot. You need to automatically move together, with your first shift of weight matching the horse's shift of weight.

Shifting weight—horse

In order to develop a feeling for the very first weight shift, use the following well-tried method: Walk your horse without stirrups and transition to halt. Ask your horse to walk on again (with as little leg aid as possible) and try to feel which foreleg your horse lifts off the ground first.

Ideally, you should know when your horse steps forward with his hind leg (technically the first step in the horse's walk, but 90 percent of horses start with a front leg first when moving out of halt), but it can be difficult to clearly feel this happening. In walk, the hind foot always touches the ground shortly before the front foot on the same side.

Just like us, when he begins to move, the horse first needs to shift his weight, which in walk he does from one side to the other. Once you can feel the front foot touching down, you will become aware of how the horse's back arches upward when his hind leg swings forward. This will help you feel the hind foot step down shortly before the front one.

The "engine" of the horse's movement is the hind legs. In order to use them, the horse's front feet have to move out of the way to make room for this "power from behind." So, ride a transition into halt and walk on again to get the feel of how the horse moves underneath you. The better you acquire this feel, the better you will be able to influence the horse's movement. An excellent halt—that is, one with even weight on all four legs and a straight and fluid "takeoff"—will be reward for this concentration on the horse's balance and footfalls.

Rider & Horse Back to Back

Halt is a difficult balancing act for horse and rider.

anything else. This is a key function of control of movement. Stand on both legs before shifting your weight to just one, and try to feel how you can stand on it securely. Push into the ground and, without straightening the knee, feel how all the muscles around the joints work together as you actively straighten up the whole side. You will feel you are becoming taller while the other leg is almost hanging freely from your hip. By shifting your weight onto one leg you are freeing the other to move.

When you do this exercise on both legs, you will notice a visible difference: Similar to being left- or right-handed, everybody has one leg that is more stable.

Notice this same difference when sitting down and shifting your weight from one seat bone to the other. Be sure you do not "collapse" at the waist and hip when you shift your weight. If you do, it makes it a "passive" shift of weight—rather than active—and your body bent like this stops your upper body from being stable. It also puts a lot more strain on your back and joints. If you collapse like this when riding, the horse is not receiving a good, clear seat aid, and will not respond without extra strength on your part.

This next exercise consists of predicting or "feeling" in advance which foreleg your horse will use first when you ask him to start walking. To see if you are right, start from a halt and see which leg he uses first. Once you know how it feels when your horse shifts his weight, you can try to influence him to start with the leg you would like him to use. This exercise will challenge your awareness, balance, and the interplay of all your aids. You can use these exercises as valuable little "breaks" in the middle of a ride, a breather from trot and canter work, while still keeping the horse focused.

Developing dynamic stability—rider and horse

After shifting weight to one leg, you need to build up stability in your upper back before you can do

Here, the rider planned the turn, she shifted her weight correctly and built up stability in her upper body.

The Back—The Center of the Body and All Movement

Every turn and many exercises require you to shift your weight to your inside seat bone *without* collapsing or bending in the inside hip. Since horses are naturally crooked (see p. 147) and their spine rotates better to one direction, many horses cause their rider to collapse in one hip. It is not surprising, therefore, that this mistake ranks first in the list of incorrect motion patterns riders often show.

In order for your horse to swing his legs forward in a relaxed manner, he needs to have stability on the other supporting legs. In order to develop this, he needs to use his back. The better the dynamic stability of his topline, the looser, easier, and freer his movement will be.

Executing a movement

This is the third step in the creation of forward movement: first was shifting weight, then came developing dynamic stability. Moving forward can only be achieved when the first two steps have been completed.

Before you are able to set one foot in front of the other, you need all your back's deep muscles to work as a team plus have a stable core. You are only able to precisely and efficiently move one foot when the other leg builds up a stable foundation. When the leg you are standing on is insecure, automatic balance reflexes may well stop you from falling, but they will cause counterbalancing movements from other parts of the body. (As a result, your hands, for example, cannot be kept quiet, a serious riding problem seen all too often.) You can easily find this out for yourself: Stand on one leg and when your foundation is stable, you will be able to move your other leg wherever you want. When your foundation is wobbly, however, any movement forward becomes unstable and you will need your arms and upper body to help you stay in balance.

Knowing about these "pre-steps" to executing a movement is important so you can analyze and correct any problems occurring in motion patterns that relate to riding. In many cases, the root of the problem lies not in actually doing the movement itself, but in the weight shift or instability beforehand. No matter how much effort you put into improving the execution of forward movement, you will not be able to change it unless you first establish a correct weight shift, and develop stability of your upper body.

The connection of the three steps just outlined is the foundation for understanding aids and their application. At this point, you can see once again that the classical riding principles—in their role as training theory—contain important information for the rider: *first* weight aids, *then* leg, and *last* rein aids.

Knowledge of how you create movement will help you understand weight aids. From analyzing the criteria outlined above, you can see that every application of an aid begins with a shift of weight of both horse and rider. Even though your legs and reins support this process, they can only be effective after the application of your seat bone, that is, a correct weight shift in combination with your stable upper body.

The ability to find your balance on a moving horse is in itself already a "weight aid" in that it is an essential part of correctly applied forward-driving aids.

Rider & Horse Back to Back

Riders, who are able to follow the horse's movement, shift their weight the same way as the horse and move harmoniously—in a back-friendly manner.

An inexperienced rider, who has not yet mastered this skill, will continuously disrupt the horse's rhythm and gait. Your weight is always influencing the horse—whether you want it to or not.

You also have to remember that the horse has strong reflexes that drive him to always keep his balance. But even a horse that, for the most part, has already found his balance when being ridden, can let himself be disrupted by his rider—and, of course, an unbalanced horse even more so. Riders who lack balance will always influence their horse's movement—another reason why inexperienced riders should ride experienced horses and vice versa. Only a balanced rider is able to actually *school* a horse.*

In Part 2, you will find many exercises and ways to improve your balance on horseback as well as your ability to influence the horse's movement by voluntarily shifting your weight.

In the beginning, riders inevitably act like passive pieces of baggage in the saddle. They just "piggyback" on the horse's motion and get pulled along. Consequently, every time the horse speeds up, a beginner will be slightly behind the horse's movement—spatially and in time, especially during upward transitions. The first thing a beginner needs to learn is to follow the horse's rhythmic forward motion. Only then will the rider be able to "trigger" and control the horse's movement.

The transition to trot, for example, illustrates this fact very well. When trotting for the very first time, it is advisable to hold onto the saddle or, even better, a strap fastened to the saddle in order to pull yourself deep into the saddle. Otherwise, this unfamiliar movement surprises you and causes you to lose your balance. Your hands on the saddle, or strap, give you the security and stability necessary for balance—and prevent your using your legs reflexively to hold on. (Once you find your balance, you will not need your hands anymore.)

When you know what the trot feels like, prepare yourself for the motion to come by visualizing it in your mind. This way, you will be balanced and able to follow the trot motion from the first step. When more experienced riders ask for trot, their center of gravity easily shifts in front of the horse's. Starting the trot should happen in such a way so that someone watching from the ground cannot tell who began trotting first—the rider or the horse. At this point, harmony in motion has been achieved.

Planning a movement

In order to precisely execute a movement, the human brain always needs a plan. This plan should consist of a picture of the movement you have in mind, an idea of how the movement can be executed. All your senses help you get the feeling for the movement to form a complex mosaic.

If you do not have any idea of what you want to move, your brain will not be able to create a plan. And if you have no experience how the movement is supposed to feel when done correctly, you will not be able to control or adapt it to the situation.

Once you have a picture of a movement in your mind's eye, your brain works like a supercomputer and plans all conscious and subconscious movements necessary. The execution of a movement is constantly monitored and optimized by all your senses and the control mechanisms your body awareness has to offer.

Once you understand this complex process, you can see why "technical" corrections from an instructor such as, "Lift your hand up 8 inches, and turn it out 2 degrees" is hard to put into practice, while an image-based description is more effective.

The Back—The Center of the Body and All Movement

A good imagination is a prerequisite for being able to create as precise an inner picture of the movement as possible.*

Train your sense of body motion

In addition to a plan, a rider needs to experience how to *correctly* execute a movement in order to control and optimize the picture in her mind's eye.

For someone who wants to learn how to ride, it is most important to practice this correct feeling of how to coordinate all movements—some of them very difficult. Unfortunately, incorrect motion patterns can be learned very quickly.

As mentioned, putting young riders on an experienced horse is the best way to learn. The feeling for a movement is obtained by experience, trial and error, as well as constant practice, repetition, and fine-tuning.**

Good riders are able to direct their horses with the subtlest of aids so an observer can hardly see them move: In their upper body, especially, movement becomes almost invisible. A beginner needs to understand that these subtle aids are connected to a complex system of motion patterns.

A beginner is not able to give an aid to her horse in such a precise manner, She must start with an exaggerated aid, though once it is mastered in this "larger" form, it can be constantly refined until it can be given with minimal effort.

Horses learn the same way. A large "aid" can help a young horse in particular learn how to eventually react to it in a much more subtle form. For example, if you start by taking your hand away from the horse sideways in the direction you want him to turn, later on he will react to just the first bit of your hand motion and move as requested. Here's another example of training your body motion: When you ride corners, turns and circles you use the "spiral" seat explained on page 90. That is, your outside shoulder needs to be brought forward so you follow the horse's shoulders. Many riders tense up or stay behind the movement. By patting the horse's inside shoulder with your outside hand—an exaggerated action—your outside shoulder turns as needed while, at the same time, you learn the feeling of your trunk rotating correctly (see photo on this page). Later on, you can refine this movement to a nearly invisible rotation (see photo on p. 151.)

The challenge an instructor faces when teaching a beginner is to be able tell the difference between the rider's *correct* movement however "rough" it looks at this stage versus a "fine-tuned" movement that is actually *incorrect*.***

*A lack of imagination will quickly limit (even halt) any progress in riding.

**If you are not allowed to make mistakes, you will never learn!

***Learning always takes time and never proceeds as quickly as you would like.

Practicing in this way "teaches" your outside shoulder to be in the correct position for a turn.

1.6 Learning How to Move   41

Rider & Horse Back to Back

*It is much more difficult trying to change incorrect established motion patterns and compensations than to learn new, correct ones.

It is necessary to practice some movements slowly at first until you have gained the required degree of coordination. A pianist, for that matter, does not start learning a new piece at the tempo it will eventually played.

But all students are individuals when it comes to the pace at which they learn new things. For some, it is easier to practice with faster, rhythmical movements, while others need to do everything in slow motion in order to memorize a new motion pattern. The instructor needs to be experienced in order to present ways of learning that suit each student.

Compensation

Everything explained so far tells you how important it is to take the first steps correctly. Nobody is perfect, however, and this is certainly true for riding students. If your back is a problematic area to begin with, your muscle memory will make it difficult to naturally take to new complex motion patterns. Fear of pain, less flexible parts of the spine, and muscular weaknesses do not make it easier to learn how to ride.

Each person's body always chooses the path of least resistance. This means that your movement is guided by physical strength and fitness, and your body avoids using the parts where you are weaker. Therefore, your body tends to quickly compensate for certain movements, which leads to actual mistakes in new motion patterns.

You can often observe parallels between a person's motion patterns on horseback and in his everyday life. If you walk with a hollow back, not "stretching" your hips, you will have difficulty when riding because you will not be able to stretch your lumbar spine and swing your hips forward.

People limited in their ability to rotate their thoracic spine or lacking dynamic stability in their core often swing their arms more intensely in order to compensate. These riders have a hard time keeping their hands still and experience difficulty learning how to balance without holding onto the reins.*

Changing an incorrect movement is more difficult than learning a new one. Prevention in the form of a back-friendly riding style is, therefore, the most promising method of keeping both your own and the horse's back in good health.

The occurrence of back pain is usually a sign that incorrect motion patterns have already been established and will lead to a vicious cycle. Fighting this cycle is a highly demanding task, which usually requires the help of professionals (doctors, physical therapists, for example).

Improve incorrect posture

Since learning processes are "paths" with many detours, it is important to learn from your mistakes. But you should not have to carry them around with you like unnecessary baggage putting a strain on your back and your riding.

Steps to successfully change incorrect motion patterns

- Recognize the problem.
- Analyze—Find the cause of the problem
- Go back to the basics.
- Eradicate bad habits and break compensations.
- Train correctly by using easier movements and exercises.
- Train a new movement going both ways, and coordinate it with other movements.
- Visualize a movement first to get a better mental and physical (inner and outer) feel for it.
- Improve awareness to be able to prevent a vicious cycle from getting started.
- Build confidence in your ability.
- Train the correct movement so you can do it automatically.

The Back—The Center of the Body and All Movement

Recognize the problem

In order to correct a bad position or movement, you need to recognize—and admit—your mistake. Awareness of problems and incorrect movement goes together with the willingness to do something about it. Giving up does not solve your issue: When you accept your hollow back, crookedness, or imperfect posture—out of laziness, perhaps, or fear of failure—you will hardly make any progress. Moreover, when you ride demanding movements with more collection, for example—you are putting your health at risk if you don't work on your bad posture.

Of course, you cannot ignore or completely change your body type. If you have the genetic disposition for a hollow back, you will never develop a round one—even the upright position of the pelvis will be difficult for you your entire life. Your challenge is to learn how to prevent excessive strain on the lumbar spine, find movements to improve your posture and avoid those that harm it.

Another typical example is the common "desk" posture characterized by round shoulders and shortened abdominal and chest muscles. If you sit on a horse in this position, you need a lot more strength in order to apply forward-driving aids or collect the horse. Tense muscles in the back of the neck are usually the result.

Analyze—find the cause

When you want to improve your weaknesses, you need to find their causes first. Analyzing your movements can help you understand why certain body parts display more—or less—positive or negative tension. You need to do some ambitious detective work and use common sense to find the correct cause among all the possible ones: conformation, fitness, coordination, balance, rhythm, flawed technique, and subtle incorrect habits. There is usually more than one problem since movements are organized by long chains of muscles. If you find the one problem that started it all, you get the chance of eradicating a whole bunch of flaws at once.

In addition to self-evaluation, you need input from others. Since your subjective perception only provides you with an imperfect image, you need instructors, trainers, mirrors, and/or video recordings on a regular basis. Be prepared to face the fact that an outside critique might not always be pleasant!

Go back to the basics

You will only be able to make a change if you get to the root of the problem. There is an important connection between beginning work (the basics) and the upper levels.

All basic work is really just a simpler version (often performed "bigger," riding a larger circle at the lower levels, for instance) of the movements performed at advanced level. So a regular turn or corner is the basis for a pirouette. And problems that occur riding a pirouette seldom get solved by riding another hundred of them, they get fixed by returning to the basics. Therefore, working on the basics is always part of training horse and rider—no matter what the level.*

*You are only going to be successful if you are prepared to return to the all-important basics and improve them.

A student–instructor relationship based on trust is the best way to detect problems and develop solid solutions.

1.6 Learning How to Move

Rider & Horse Back to Back

In order to improve an incorrect movement, you first have to analyze the origin of the problem: Is it in the picture in your mind; the shift of weight; the stability in your upper body; or the actual movement itself? When your visualization of the movement is not right to start with, the movement can never be correctly ridden.

When beginners doing rising trot for the first time literally take the instruction to "stand up and sit down," they will never be able to do the movement correctly because rising trot is actually more like "kneeling down"—just sometimes higher and sometimes lower.

Misunderstandings like this are relatively common. When an instructor fails to explain his image in enough detail, he can easily mislead the student. Let's say he says, "Head up," but actually means "Grow and sit tall." The student may just lift her chin and lose her balance even more. "Pictures" in the mind need to be shared and explained with both parties visualizing the movement in the same way.

When both have the same plan in mind, the student has to master the challenge of executing the movement. The next thing she needs to focus on is shifting her weight (see p. 37).

The rider's knee and heel can only stretch down when weight is shifted correctly.

When a rider shifts her weight properly, a bystander should hardly be able to tell. You can try this at home by sitting in front of a mirror and practice shifting your weight onto your seat bones from one side to the other. Your shoulders should stay level and move sideways as little as possible. If they bend sideways, forward, or backward, your upper body is not balanced. When you shift weight too far, your arms reflexively move to compensate for loss of balance. When practicing this by sitting on a chair, you can often tell which of your sides has better stability over the weight-bearing seat bone.

When you encounter a problem while riding and want to analyze it, the first thing you need to look at is where you placed your weight. If during transitions to canter your inside knee and heel always slide up, check where most of your weight is positioned at the moment your horse transitions to canter. You will only be able to stretch your inside leg downward when your weight follows the horse's movement diagonally from outside back leg to inside front leg. All your attempts at solving the problem by just concentrating on your inside knee and heel are inevitably going to frustrate you. Every rider would like to have perfectly positioned legs, but no one is able to compensate for their balance reflexes!

Once your weight is positioned correctly on a seat bone, you need to quickly build up dynamic stability on that side of your body. This stability is the basis for your ability to be able to perform a controlled movement that influences the horse's hind leg, for example. But as the horse moves and shifts his weight again, your shift of weight will need to change too, and you must redevelop the dynamic stability every time.

As a prerequisite, you need to have, most of all, good coordination skills, but also strength. Take a flamingo, for example, that can sleep balancing on one leg: Here you can see that dynamic stability does not require a maximum of strength but good automatic coordination skills. You can develop the latter by practicing "large" movements first before proceeding to subtle, more refined motions without changing posture. Now you understand why stability can only be corrected through rhythmic movement and not by being told to keep a static posture.*

Once you've established your mental "picture," correct weight position, and dynamic stability, it's time to concentrate on the body part that will execute the aid (the hand, for example). Do you have a stiff shoulder or elbow that will prevent you from "giving" your hand forward without moving your upper body at the same time? Do you have any tension or weakness in the arm's muscles that could negatively influence your ability to move it? If so, you lose contact and the horse's rhythm will be disturbed. Can you reestablish contact in a soft and sure way? Do you have the necessary coordination skills to perform the movement easily and effectively using the least amount of strength needed?

The greatest difficulty in riding is that the intensity of the aids varies according to the each individual horse. Therefore, you cannot simply teach your brain to apply leg aids at the intensity of "x" in walk, at the intensity of "y" in trot, and "z" in canter. The aids need to be constantly adjusted. If during a riding lesson or training session you realize that you are now able to reduce the intensity of your aids, you have done very well and taken care of your back at the same time.

Eradicate bad habits and compensations

When you know your mistake and have discovered its cause, you understand why your body compensated as it did. Movements compensating for loss of balance usually take a lot of strength and put additional strain on your back.

In addition, these incorrect motion patterns are now unfortunately ingrained in the brain, which is why people tend to slip and always go back to them. Therefore, the first step you need to take is to actively eradicate these bad habits from your mental image so they cannot spontaneously take over again.

Working on eradicating these compensatory movements takes concentration, time, and patience. While you are trying to do this, you cannot afford to get involved in a confrontation with your horse: Your body will just automatically return to the old, incorrect motion pattern as soon as your mind is occupied with controlling your horse and other tasks at hand. Stress makes learning impossible and in such situations, the brain only has access to old, ingrained motion patterns.

Train correctly by using less demanding movements

New, improved mental images are possible only when the "compensating" movements are not occupying brain capacity anymore. Basically, these new movements have to be learned from the ground up and newly programmed into the brain's motion center. The path for new movement needs to be cleared—only possible through repetition and practice. First, you need to do the new movement slowly and in an easy fashion. Later, you can increase speed and become more subtle. All the while, you need to repeat it over and over again until it has been saved to memory.

In order for the rider to be able to concentrate on this demanding task, all other parts of the riding lesson should be kept as simple and familiar as possible. Sometimes, longe lessons can be helpful as they allow riders to focus entirely on themselves (see photo p. 46). During the usual lessons, however, you can also vary the degree of difficulty of the exercises you are planning to do. When you are starting to learn a new movement, you should, of course, begin with easy exercises and only increase them at a pace that does not endanger progress. A pace that is too demanding forces you to concentrate too much on the technical aspects and not enough on the "feeling" of a movement.

One of the great difficulties in riding is that because the horse is continuously in motion, it makes it hard to learn a new movement—the

In order to develop dynamic stability, you need to move rhythmically.

Rider & Horse Back to Back

moments come and go so quickly. You manage to sit in balance for a couple of strides, the horse "swings" his back, you feel great—then it is gone. The horse cannot be asked to trot or canter in slow motion to give you more time to establish your seat! You actually need a nice steady rhythm—not too slow—to help you gain a secure balance. It's similar to riding a bicycle where moving at speed contributes to finding your balance.

This rider is concentrating fully on her own body.

However, when you have a horse that is a big mover, it is more challenging to precisely apply aids. Trot and canter are gaits with a moment of suspension. The more powerfully a horse moves, the more he swings through his back and the harder it is to sit to the gait. Preparing a transition to canter from sitting trot is not easy and often the rider becomes tense when trying to put her outside leg back and apply the aid. This tension then causes the transition to fail. In walk, however, the rider has more time to sort out her seat and her aids, so she disturbs the horse less during a transition. This is why, particularly for riders who have trouble staying supple, transitioning from walk to canter is much easier than trot to canter: They can take their own time preparing the aids without being unbalanced by the impulsion of the horse's trot.

First, visualize the movement

An improved movement is only possible when you visualize a clear positive image how to actively execute it. When your brain confronts (hears or sees) a "No," all action gets blocked.

The following example will help you understand this paradox: You are told *not* to think about a pink elephant! Instantly, you see a huge pink elephant, which you wouldn't have thought about if you had not been told not to!

Telling students *not* to do something conjures up the same fat pink elephant, which stands in the way of correcting riding errors. "Do not pull on the inside rein!" Instantly, this makes your body prepare for a backward movement of the inside hand. "Let your inside hand go forward!" produces a completely different image in your brain and you will be able to improve your actions much more quickly.

You need to think *positively*: Set a task for yourself and not get stuck in mistakes and restrictions. You need "Do's" instead of "Don'ts."

Improve awareness

You need to work on body awareness at the same time as you practice correct movement. Only when aware of it, will you be able to improve yourself—and recognize old habits and mistakes sneaking in. The sooner you feel you might be falling back into an old pattern, the easier it is to prevent it from happening. Once again, it is easier to prevent a cycle from become established than it is to break it.

After you have successfully changed a movement, you need immediate feedback to confirm the feeling you have is correct. In many cases, your horse will give you this feedback: Every improvement of your seat and aids always has instant effects on the horse and causes a reaction.

Riders need to experience a new movement over and over again until they have developed trust in their ability to recreate the correct path all by themselves. Only once you are convinced that you will able to execute the movement again if need be, have you actually mastered it.

You also have to gain positive experience while doing the movement you have learned. This is why you need to go back to simple, promising exercises many times! Positive experience is the basis on which constantly practiced movements can become automatic and eventually (and ideally) part of your subconscious. It is at this stage, that the newly corrected movement will finally be possible in stressful situations and under difficult circumstances.

Reciprocal movement

Weight shifting (as discussed on p. 37 on) is an integral part of all movement. The rider performs it constantly together with her moving horse. The walking pattern of both horse and rider show that the shift of weight is integrated into the flow of motion. The end of the shift of weight to one foot is the beginning of the next shift of weight back to the other foot. For the rider it means that the shift of weight to one seat bone leads to the shift of weight back to the other seat bone. This constant change of direction is the basic key to all reciprocal movement, and typical for all forward movement. It can be observed clearly in the walking pattern.

Insight into reciprocal motion patterns helps you understand why rhythmic exercises and quick changes of direction are particularly important to learning a movement. They equip you with the ability to follow the horse's movement, shift your weight in balance with the horse's movement continuously while becoming independent in your arms or legs in order to apply the aids.

This is why exercises such as juggling, bike riding, and rhythmic variations of rising trot can be of great help.

Giving you some insight into the great complexity of movement is not meant to scare you or make you give up because of the problems you will most likely encounter. Every little success is another piece of the puzzle of becoming a good rider and using your own movements in a better and more conscious manner. Your back will always benefit from it.*

*A movement that turned out well always feel good—for both horse and rider. Having a good feeling about how you move can make you beam with joy and lets both you and your horse shine.

Successfully learning a movement is the key to achieving harmony in motion.

1.7 Sense and Nonsense about Exercises

Practice makes perfect

Riding can only be learned through riding!
(GERMAN SAYING)

Practice is the proverbial requirement to become perfect or skilled. You can only practice something you already know, which means you need to have experienced a certain movement to be able to practice it. Mastering a skill means that at any time, in any situation, you can perform it at will. However, without practice, you will never achieve this. There are specific exercises for practicing motion patterns to teach you how to gain the coordination needed, which must become *automatic* (see p. 56).

Learning rising trot is a good example. You need to know how to do it to practice it, but this is hard to do at the beginning when the horse is changing rhythm or direction. The more you practice, the better you will handle and perform it—and in more difficult situations, too (see specific exercises starting on p. 85).

One such exercise might be the fact that you execute a movement on a daily basis. In this way, you become an endurance walker just by walking; this is called *functional* practice and happens every time you do an exercise: Complex movements become ingrained in muscle memory. Thus, you will become better at a certain motion simply by repeating it often enough.

Practiced movements are memorized and can automatically be repeated if need be. In this way, every person's body develops her own, individual and mostly subconscious motion system. Unfortunately, an incorrect seat and bad posture also fall into this category. They will become deeply ingrained in the rider's motion system as part of regular practice.*

The only thing that can prevent faults is *intentional* exercise, that is, motion patterns that are based on a goal-oriented plan. This form of exercise is the only one that can change and perfect movements. If you think about how much "faulty practice" you get simply by riding "unintentionally"—without thinking—you can easily understand why there are no miracle exercises to eradicate ingrained habits.

Seat-improvement practice works wonders, however, and breaks the vicious cycle caused by an incorrect seat: A rider's tight hips make her uncomfortable and put stress on her back. The horse's back is affected because he cannot swing through the movement, and he moves stiffly. This stiffness makes it hard for the rider to sit, and on it goes. While many riders recognize the necessity of general fitness and cross-train by using other sports to supplement riding, seat-improvement sessions on the longe line have become less popular for many reasons in recent years—especially with advanced riders. This is unfortunate because working on your seat like this is enormously beneficial.

*In every moment of riding, you are practicing something—no matter whether it is correct or incorrect.

A good lesson on the longe line is an excellent way to learn balance, and it's fun, too.

The Back—The Center of the Body and All Movement   1

Patterns of evasion and compensation

There are many common rider problems such as a hollow back, fidgety hands, or a collapsed hip, just to name a few. And there are no specific exercises to offer as a solution to these issues without clearly knowing each *individual's* motion system and recognizing the issues' causes.*

When you pick an exercise targeting a specific weakness, you need to be prepared for your body's "evasive" maneuvers. With regard to the subconscious control of all your muscles, your body follows its own "efficiency protocol," that is, it uses resources (strengths) and avoids confrontation with weaknesses. This can be understood when looking at a rider's body proportions, for example. All riders instinctively use their longer (and mostly stronger) body parts to compensate for weaker areas; or they develop instinctive and automatic habits to rebalance their body proportions—like bending their fists inward to shorten the length of long forearms.

Each person's body develops specific ways to deal with weakness and uses its strongest parts to compensate. A not very well-balanced upper body gets compensated by stronger use of the legs. Weak (i.e. short) legs need an extremely well-balanced upper body as compensation, which riders instinctively use for communication. All riders are different and must use all the tools their body allows them to find a way to produce a willing, obedient horse.*

Trying to use a specific exercise to target a weak spot will most likely not be successful at first. Complex movements, in particular, can be executed in many different ways, which gives your body—clever in its capacity to seemingly fulfill the tasks you want it to do—the chance to instinctively protect the weakest links in the chain of movement. An exercise can only be successful when your body accepts it—punishing your body is pointless.**

When your core does not have sufficient dynamic stability for you to keep your hands still and upright (i.e. your hands cannot work *independently*), you will not be able to enforce this skill through longe line work carrying weights in your hands (one of the many absurd pieces of advice that can be found among the booming number of equestrian books). Classical understanding of riding instruction defines relaxed forearms and elbows as the key to a soft and sensitive contact to the horse's mouth. If you already have difficulty carrying your hands with relaxed forearm muscles because you are lacking stability in the core, you will be all the more unable to carry additional weight. Moreover this form of continuous "static" exercise leads to fatigued and tense muscles in the shoulder girdle and back—negatively affecting your effort to improve the way you hold the reins.

Problems with hands (horse leans on them or rider is not able to carry them independently) may be solved with the rider moving in the same rhythm as the horse's motion (see photo on this page and refer to Part 2, p. 79). If this does not fix the issue, another step in the right direction is to—temporarily and correctly—use special equipment like side reins, for example.

*Simple standard exercises cannot solve complex problems if they have not been customized to meet the needs of the individual rider.

**Working against your body is a dead end: You cannot ride against your body, you need to learn to ride with it, instead.

Moving your hands together with the horse's rhythm prepares you to be able to carry them independently.

1.7 Sense and Nonsense about Exercises   49

Rider & Horse Back to Back

The importance of a schoolmaster

There is a combination, however, in which *functional* and *intentional* practice come together perfectly and can be schooled: by riding a correctly trained and adequately warmed-up schoolmaster.

An inexperienced rider will only be able to experience what seat and other aids are supposed to feel like if the school horse is safely balanced, shows good self-carriage, comes equipped with soft, relaxed movements, and trustfully accepts the rider's aids. In reality, these basic tenets are often violated for many reasons even though choosing the right horse for a rider can make all the difference in her training.

Riding a well-trained horse every now and then can have the same effect. An experienced and sensitive rider is able to optimize the interplay between the rider's aids and the horse's movements, thus increase the horse's willingness to obey even the subtlest aids. Moreover, a good rider is able to improve the horse's balance and quality of his movement.

If you get the chance to ride immediately afterward, you will experience the amazing fact that such a horse can correctly "place" you in the saddle.

One minute of practical experience that you can "feel" is more valuable than one thousand hours of explanation! You can get an "aha" moment from lessons like these. Sitting correctly all of a sudden makes sense and feels easy to your body. Once you have experienced how a horse's back swings and takes you with him in forward motion, you will have gained a clear idea of what you need to feel as a rider.*

*On a correctly trained, well-ridden schoolmaster, you are able to learn more in a single session than in countless lessons where your own incorrect motion patterns are further ingrained into your memory.

Fitness and cross-training

A lack of upper body stability clearly illustrates the problem riders have with certain exercises. In addition to being balanced and able to move rhythmically, riding as a sport requires the body to have coordination—and this is the first skill you lose when you are tired. Basic physical and mental fitness is a prerequisite for being able to ride in a way that is healthy for your back.

There is a huge difference in the fitness of riders who ride once or twice a week as opposed to every day; ride only one or many different horses; ride all kinds of disciplines; train young horses or ride a well-trained one; or ride for pleasure rather than competition.

You need to look at each person individually and, with a good understanding of her body, decide which way might be best: Does she lack general endurance training (for example, an aerobic activity like jogging) or would swimming supplement her riding best? Skiing and dancing go well together with riding as they challenge rhythm and balance. All sports that help keep the spine flexible without putting too much strain on it are good for riders. In addition, stretching the muscles most used during riding, the hip flexors, for example, is advisable in order to prevent sore muscles after lessons.

Every form of gymnastics helps improve body awareness, flexibility, coordination, and balance. Even weight training might increase the stability of the back—though it will most likely require professional guidance.**

Nevertheless, you will not automatically become a better rider by going to physical therapy, the gym, or by doing different sports to work on your physical shortcomings. The real challenge is putting your newly acquired skills into practice while riding your horse. The power of muscle memory must not be underestimated: Learned mistakes

**Every kind of exercise for your body can improve your riding skills when done within the parameters of sports medicine.

The Back—The Center of the Body and All Movement

that originate from muscular weakness do not go away just because you strengthened the respective muscle—your body needs to experience and memorize the newly acquired strength first.*

Adolescents: growing tall and becoming lanky

The muscles of children and adolescents are not at all designed for strength but for coordination, balance, and dexterity. Physically, strength training is possible only after a child has entered puberty. By the way, the horse is very similar in this regard: You can only begin developing carrying power and, eventually, collection, when the horse is older and more mature. All preceding training steps should prepare the horse and especially his back for these subsequent demands.

During growth spurts in particular, an adolescent's back can become very unstable. He needs to regain posture and coordination in a gentle and careful manner. One-sided strength training is harmful to his back.

If you understand the classical principles of schooling horse and rider correctly, you will find they contain all you need to learn about keeping your horse's back—and your own—healthy (see p. 98). These principles offer clear guidelines and large variety of movements that cover basic training in all disciplines. As far as your back is concerned, developing dynamic stability during exercises that school rhythm and balance needs to be the center of all training.

The specific exercises described in the following chapters can always be used during warm up and breaks—for all riders.**

*The German saying "Riding can only be learned through riding" is based on the experience that equestrian "motion patterns" cannot be schooled on the ground.

**A weekend pleasure rider needs different exercises than those practiced by someone who rides every day. Children and adolescents require different exercises.

Every rider needs to find her own individual training and cross-training fitness program.

1.7 Sense and Nonsense about Exercises

Rider & Horse Back to Back

*Observing, analyzing, and understanding movement requires a willingness to be constantly open to new ideas in order to broaden and improve your understanding of motion.

Recognizing, understanding, and influencing motion

Finding an appropriate exercise requires a deep understanding of the respective motion systems of both horse and rider. Usually, an instructor needs to come in at this point because understanding the motion systems of both horse and rider requires trained observation skills and a varied experience. To find the right exercise, the instructor needs to be able to analyze all the factors that influence their movements (see pp. 27 and 45 for information about learning a movement).

Movement analysis as an area of scientific research has revolutionized and influenced the training program of many athletic disciplines. With regard to riding, however, scientists over the last decades have been facing the difficulty of producing verifiable and reproducible data about the interplay of horse and rider in motion in order to give helpful results.

Since movements of horse and rider are unique, individual, and variable, they are almost impossible to statistically evaluate: Knowing how much strain sitting trot puts on the average human body does not help the individual person. There is a huge difference between riding sitting trot on a horse that is relaxed and a horse that tenses his back muscles, making him stiff and uncomfortable to sit on. Even on the same horse, trot can vary greatly between the beginning and the end of a training session and cause the rider's back to feel tense or supple (and happy!)

A good motion analysis is based on being aware of various complex factors at the same time, which are depicted here in the form of a network. Before focusing on details and specific problems, it is important, first of all, to take a look at the big picture of movement in order to understand the connection between individual motion patterns. Only after you are able to understand the connections between the movements of horse and rider as a team, does it makes sense to systematically go through a list of all the little issues. While you are observing horse and rider, your most important task is to look for cause and effect—and the key factor.*

This figure shows the connections between the factors causing the individual motion of horse and rider as a whole.

Tension
Mobility
Conformation
Horse's motion
Balance
Harmony
Rhythm
Horse's training level
Fitness
Suppleness
Stability

The Back—The Center of the Body and All Movement

Your individual motion pattern

Every single new idea produces insight—and raises helpful questions—that bring you closer to understanding the individual motion pattern of horse and rider. If you don't start analyzing and questioning new information, you cannot improve and learn about the difficult subject that is *movement*.

Conformation of horse and rider:

- Looking at the impression the horse and rider give you as a team, how harmonious does it seem? What fits—what does not?
- Which of the rider's body parts are the longest, giving her the most leverage? Where do these "levers" influence her movements?
- What is the conformation of the horse's back: length, muscle tone, and elasticity in motion?
- Do horse and rider fit together: height, length, and width; flexibility and comfort?

If you find a significantly dominating factor while evaluating all the above, you can look at it in relation to the other factors on your list in order to understand what influences the rider's movement.

The following example of a female rider with long trunk and pelvis (upper body) illustrates how to go about your evaluation:

■ Rhythm

Riders with long pelvic bones have difficulty sitting on a horse with short, quick movements and feel more comfortable on a horse with longer, slower strides. Riders with short pelvic bones, on the other hand, often have a hard time following long, slow strides.

■ Balance

An extremely long upper body needs to work harder to keep its balance. A long pelvis acts like a strong "lever," and this can greatly influence the horse, since the pelvis, via the seat bones, is the contact point where all movement from the horse gets passed onto the rider—and vice versa. When a long pelvis doesn't have a counterbalance from strong abdominal muscles the rider's back will not have sufficient strength to prevent the pelvis from tilting (putting the rider out of position) as the horse moves her seat bones forward.

■ Suppleness, tension

A long upper body requires a higher level of muscle tension in order to stay balanced so the slightest loss of balance is usually compensated by increased negative tension in shoulders and arms or clenched knees.

■ Mobility, stability

A long pelvic bone often comes in combination with a lot of mobility in the lumbar spine. Therefore, the rider needs to have sufficiently toned abdominal muscles in order to prevent overstraining

A rider with a long upper body and pelvis.

1.7 Sense and Nonsense about Exercises

in the lumbar area. Together with a long pelvis, the hip joint constitutes a powerful "lever." When the hip cannot stretch well or is restricted in its capacity to stretch, the lumbar spine is often not flexible enough to support a rider with long stirrups.

■ Coordination, dexterity

A rider with a long pelvis is not as quick as one with a shorter pelvis when reacting to the horse's movement felt through her seat bones. (It takes a bit more strength, control and time to coordinate a longer pelvis.) Therefore, she must always prepare for the combination of aids well in advance in order to apply them precisely. And, when you cannot coordinate your upper body enough to ensure it is stable, your arms and legs react accordingly to protect your balance. When moving around to compensate for balance, both arms and legs lose the dexterity needed for riding.

■ Fitness, level of education

An inexperienced rider is not always able to effectively and correctly use her long pelvis as a "lever." At this point, an instructor's critical observation skills are needed more than ever. When the rider succeeds in using her abdominal muscles to stabilize her pelvis in sitting trot, at first, she should not be asked to do it for too long. Practice and correct training will eventually improve the rider's stamina and fitness necessary for sitting trot.

Instability in the lumbar spine is a sign of overburdened muscles in this area. In this case, sitting trot can be harmful to the back! Moreover, the rider's coordination and reactions will slow down as soon as her deep back muscles get tired. Then, subtle aids become impossible.

Be aware that the rider herself will often not feel tired at all as she is not out of breath—nevertheless, her back is really exhausted! This is often the key to understanding the common observation that repetition does not necessarily improve an exercise. On the contrary, it does not. Unfortunately, these shortcomings in the rider's body and the ensuing mistakes are often blamed on the horse.

*A complex chain of movements is only as strong as its weakest link!

■ Movement and level of training of the horse

Can a rider comfortably sit on a certain horse? Does the way the horse moves match her seat? Is he reacting obediently to the aids? When the horse does not let movement pass through his relaxed back from hindquarters to poll, the rider needs to support him a lot more than she would with a horse that moves in a naturally relaxed manner. The not-so-relaxed horse can put additional strain on the rider's back.

Both lazy horses and ones that like to take the bit and run may not be suitable for riders with a long pelvis: These horses need a rider to be stable and strong in their lumbar spine and this is often these riders' weakest link.

This play of ideas can be continued endlessly. You need to think about movements as being connected to each other and understand how motion can be influenced. Good coordination skills can compensate for weaknesses and prevent overstraining.*

The key factor

The key factor of motion analysis is the characteristic trait that defines the interplay of horse and rider, which can be used to significantly influence the partnership.

To help you better understand this concept imagine some children who, together, swing a huge blanket with a ball rolling on top of it. To keep the ball from falling off, the children need to develop a mutual feeling for the rhythm of their swing and coordinate their movements together as a group. The ball will always fall off the blanket at the weakest point, which is where the motion has become too slow and the blanket could not be kept up high enough.

If you were to try and only work on that one child, he would soon become disinterested in the game. An obvious physical weakness cannot be fixed that easily. However, if you could get the other children to move a little slower, the "weak-

The Back—The Center of the Body and All Movement

est" child would be able to learn to be part of the group's motion. Only then, would all the children together be able to increase the pace and level of difficulty of their play.

When analyzing the motion of horse and rider, it is important to find the key factor. In order to improve weaknesses, it is not helpful to point out the obvious and simply add insult to injury—most riders know what their problems are: They just cannot find solutions!

Choosing exercises to fit the individual rider is difficult. You must always try to help the body, not "punish" it!

Instructors need to be aware of the fact that it is always the student herself who can and must improve her seat—the instructor cannot do it for her. It is not helpful to tell her *not* to do something; she needs help to find the key to a solution.*

*An exercise can only be successful when the rider herself finds the solution to her problem! Only then, will she be able to repeat the exercise and make it a habit.

You need to find your own favorite exercises.

1.7 Sense and Nonsense about Exercises

2 Practice Strengthens the Back—Go Easy on It to Protect It

2.1 Plan and Organize Your Own Schedule

Take responsibility for your back

If you want your riding to be as back-friendly as possible, you need to take the decision-making into your own hands and not replace it with well-meaning advice from the most experienced instructor. In order to take responsibility for your back during riding you need to know what you are doing. It is impossible to be gentle with, protect, and strengthen your back while you are on a horse if you have not worked with and looked at your own body.

Seven steps to a back-friendly riding style

- Get to know your own body, especially your back.
- Reconsider how you structure your riding—how it fits into everyday life—taking into account the strain it puts on your back.
- Acquire a theoretical understanding of the challenges riding poses on the back.
- Practice correct, back-friendly motion patterns on horseback.
- Get to know and choose helpful exercises that fit you as an individual.
- Learn about back-friendly alternatives to your usual training methods and everyday riding.
- Organize a generally back-friendly concept for all the demands riding puts on your body.

Plan your riding sessions

Scheduling your riding yourself—as much as your private and business life allows you to—affords you the luxury of riding according to your own preference and biorhythms. For most riders, mornings are the best time to ride. People who ride several horses a day have different strategies about which horse they like to start off with: Some like to ride the most difficult one first, others prefer the easiest.

Unfortunately, many horse enthusiasts are forced to spend their "best hours" at a desk. The most important thing for these people is to give their mind and body some time to switch from "job mode" to "riding mode." It is ideal to have an active shift of gears in between, such as riding your bike to the barn. In any case, you should groom and tack up your horse yourself, using the time productively by mentally and physically preparing for your lesson. Good body awareness and a sense of how you are feeling on a certain day can help prevent you overstraining your back.

Suddenly doing stretching exercises in the barn without having increased your heart rate and the blood flow to your muscles is questionable. Jogging with or without your horse is a better transition between sitting in a chair and sitting on horseback. A good way of relaxing your lumbar spine, which is constantly stressed while sitting, is walking—or even running—backward (see p. 137).

Riding equipment

Choosing the right clothing—besides well-fitting breeches and adequate shoes—can make a huge difference, especially for a rider whose back reacts with pain or stiffness to the slightest strain. With all outdoor sports, it's a good idea to dress according to the multilayer principle in functional clothing that absorbs moisture and sweat, wicking it to the surface in order to keep your body as dry as possible. Irrespective of season and temperature, it is normal for all riders to sweat in the area of the lower back. Changing the layer of clothing closest to your skin directly after riding is, therefore, a smart and back-friendly choice.

Wearing a well-fitting, comfortable, and approved riding helmet should go without saying—your spine reaches all the way up into your skull after

Rider & Horse Back to Back

all! An ill-fitting helmet can lead to headaches and, thus, interfere with your muscle tone in general. It might even affect your back.

The current fashion of wearing back protectors or safety vests not only during jumping but also during a beginner's lessons (especially children) can be looked at in two ways. On the one hand, they afford useful protection when jumping solid fences, but on the other, they interfere with improving body awareness as well as restrict your mobility. If your equipment limits your movement, you will have a hard time finding your balance and sitting in a relaxed manner.*

Technological equipment such as microphones can be a valuable asset when used correctly. Unfortunately, riding is a very traditional sport and slow to embrace modern devices even though hearing what an instructor says should, in the end, have positive effects on your back!

*The best way to protect yourself from injury is by not falling off in the first place. To make sure of this, you need good balance and quick reactions.

The importance of the saddle

It makes sense that a properly fitted saddle is very important in preventing back injury to the horse. Palpate his back regularly in order to discover tender spots or bruises as early as possible (see photo below).

Saddles are available for different purposes, in various designs, widths, and seat sizes. Specialized saddles (dressage or jumping, for example) are limited to their purpose. Jumping saddles do not support your leg when you are riding with long stirrups, and dressage saddles cause your knee to either slip in front of the saddle flap or to have trouble with the panels when trying to ride with a shorter stirrup.

The fit of the saddle is as important to the rider as it is to the horse. Unfortunately, many inexperienced riders in particular let themselves be fooled

You can draw conclusions about the condition of the horse's back by knowing where and how to palpate it.

Practice Strengthens the Back—Go Easy on It to Protect It

by the first impression or feeling they get when sitting and walking the horse in an unfamiliar saddle without understanding its actual usefulness. The smaller (shorter) seat size, which forces you into a specific position, is not always the best! The more advanced you become, the more space you will need in order to apply differentiated aids.

In a saddle that is too small for you, you will not be able to move freely, and you will stop moving your hips. Thus, you immediately put additional strain on your back and that of your horse. Some saddles with high pommels designed for horses with high withers increase the risk of soreness in the area of the pubic bone. A saddle that is too big for you is the lesser of two evils even though its center of gravity might not be correct for you so that you will need more strength to find your balance.

The width of the saddle is another factor that has a great influence on how a saddle feels to you. A saddle that is too narrow makes it difficult for you to develop stability and find your balance, while a saddle that is too wide can irritate the end parts of the muscles of the seat bones where the tendon is attached to the point where you cannot relax your hips anymore. The panels and angle of the saddle flap influence the position of your thighs. Most important in this regard is that your hips must always be able to move. Even though panels afford you a secure feeling and seat, you need to maintain basic mobility in hips and pelvis. The biggest movement your pelvis has to be able to make occurs during rising trot and canter—this is why you need to extensively try out every new saddle while riding in the faster gaits.

By the way, a saddle is heavy—often of significant weight—for young riders, especially, so should only be carried in a back-friendly manner by walking upright and holding it close to your stomach.*

*The basic training of every rider should include information on how to handle equipment correctly.

It is never too soon to start learning back-friendly posture and movement.

Only a saddle that fits well allows a rider's pelvis to follow the horse's motion and adapt to his back movements.

2.1 Plan and Organize Your Own Schedule

Rider & Horse Back to Back

*Correct stirrup length based on the rider, horse, and task at hand is a prerequisite of back-friendly riding.

Correct stirrup length

Choosing the correct length of your stirrups depends on the purpose and type of saddle. The increasing popularity of discipline-specific saddles has led many riders to only use a dressage or jumping saddle. These special-purpose saddles limit the potentially back-friendly use of different seats—to the great disadvantage of all beginners. Many dressage saddles do not allow you to sit well balanced. And, in saddles strictly designed for jumping, the center of gravity is often too far back to use them for dressage. Therefore, one important criterion for choosing the right saddle is being able to vary the stirrup length by at least two to three holes and still have your leg on the flap.

The correct stirrup length should always be based on function. It depends on the rider's conformation and level of training; the horse's conformation and willingness to go forward; the particular exercise; or even the way a rider feels on a given day. In dressage, the purpose of the stirrup is to support the front of the foot: You need to be able to rise in the trot without changing the position of your lower legs or using your upper body as leverage. During a rider's training, her stirrup length should start off at *medium*, advance to *long* for dressage, and finally to *short* for jumping.

Stirrups that are too long or too short are equally harmful to the back: Long stirrups pull you into a "fork-seat" posture, while short stirrups put you in a chair-seat position. When in the forward seat, stirrups serve as a stable basis for knees and heels, allowing you to balance yourself. In a jumping saddle, too long stirrups put your center of gravity *in front* of the horse's center of gravity, while overly short ones cause you to fall *behind* it. The latter often occurs when riders in a jumping saddle do sitting trot during dressage practice.*

Mounting and dismounting

In traditional equestrian circles, people feel that the ability to mount a horse from the ground—and dismount with a swing—is one of the decisive characteristics of an experienced rider. If you want to protect your back from injury and be gentle on your horse's, you should forget about

Functional medium length.

Too long.

Too short.

Practice Strengthens the Back—Go Easy on It to Protect It

these "skills" right away. Significantly less strain is put on the back of both horse and rider (as well as saddle and stirrup leathers) when the horse is mounted from an elevated position: The purchase of a solid, and at the same time movable mounting block can be very useful.

Dismounting in a back-friendly manner requires some practice: Your left foot should remain in the stirrup while you swing your right leg over the horse's back while your weight is on your left foot. Then, place your hands on pommel and cantle respectively, to push yourself up high enough so your left foot can just slide out of the stirrup with your leg stretched. As a last step, slowly let yourself slide down to the ground while you position your right arm over the saddle to act as a counterweight. Prepare the muscles in your knees, feet, and hips by building up some positive tension that will cushion your landing. This way, you will protect your back from strain.

Everyone who works with horses knows about mucking out stalls, sweeping, lifting, carrying feed bags and bedding, and all the usual advice about back-friendly lifting and carrying properly applies: Always work with your knees slightly bent and your lower back straight; lift and carry things close to your body.

Tips for riding instructors

Instructors, who teach several hours a day, should also develop back awareness. Wearing riding clothes and moving as little as possible does not take their back into consideration! Standing still requires an exhausting amount of muscle strength, and instructors need to decide for themselves how much they can and have to take.

Walking around in the ring is less tiring than standing still, and there are several good reasons why instructors should choose to be flexible about where they stand: In order to evaluate a rider's back posture, instructors need to be able to not only see her from the side but also directly from the front and back. When teaching a beginner, instructors who move around in the ring with a purpose can very well have an influence on the horse—sometimes more so than a weak rider.

The more "spring" the arena footing provides, the better—not only for the horse's back but also the rider's. Nevertheless, trudging through horse tracks is always exhausting on the back. Good shoes can make a world of a difference though: They provide good support for the ankle and, ideally, cushioned soles.

There are useful ways for instructors to sit and support their back during lessons, which take off strain and, at the same time, allow them to move enough to give an effective lesson that includes body language. Many instructors ride along in their "mind." Unfortunately, they do not always do so in the most back-friendly posture: Some tilt their head and literally "bend" themselves when the horse is not doing it properly. While instructing, teachers should always try to be aware of their own posture, too.

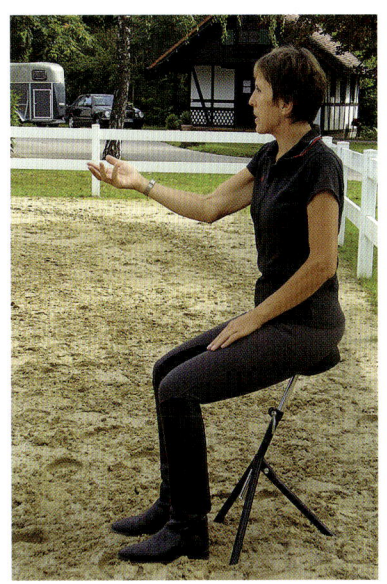

The riding instructor's stool in the top photo should have some back support (like the one below) to help her maintain an upright, dynamic position.

2.2 Versatile Basic Training

Varied movement experiences

The principles of classical riding theory ask for a variety of exercises in the basic training of horse and rider no matter which riding discipline is being performed. The current trends in international riding counteract this idea, however. More and more, riders and horses specialize in one discipline, and very early at that. Endurance racing, for example, which used to be part of the original concept of classical training, has become a special discipline in itself. Even the Olympic disciplines of dressage, show jumping, and eventing keep drifting farther apart with regard to theoretical and practical training.

In this book, the emphasis is on the importance of dressage training as a basis for a solid, ever-expanding communication between horse and rider. However, equestrian sport in general contains many more possibilities to integrate back-friendly elements into your daily training. Students of all ages need experience in riding "movement" that is as diverse as possible since this is the key to becoming a successful rider. Including interesting and versatile "tasks" in your daily training routine is also important, of course.*

Since riding has so many possibilities, it provides you with many alternatives when making back-friendly decisions; you just need to know how. This means, for example, that when horse and rider are used to going out on the trail, it can be a relaxed and gentle alternative to strenuous dressage training. But only in that case! Otherwise, the risk of some unpredictable behavior causing injury to your back would be too high (see p. 117).

Riding in different ways such as switching from dressage schooling to forward seat or jumping exercises can be of much more use than just being less tiring to your back overall. Training in different "seats" increases your ability to stabilize your back on the one hand while improving your motion skills on the other—the best way to prevent injury.

Training in an outdoor ring or on a trail ride offers many ways of creating back-friendly and back-strengthening exercises.

Forward seat—back-friendly?

There is a controversy about whether the forward seat puts additional strain on the rider's back or, just the opposite, relieves it: Leaning your upper body forward turns it into a long lever, which requires the back muscles to work harder to stabilize it than they do when it's in an upright position. Once again, the horse's motion makes all the difference: When the horse is unbalanced, has stiff back muscles, or is not at all straight, he will pass on his irregular movement to the rider's back. If the rider's back muscles are too weak or react too slowly, the ligaments and tendons have to provide the necessary stability—clearly a strain on the back. Sitting in the dressage position may put less strain on the muscles and tendons, but constant pressure on the seat bones means more strain to your joints and intervertebral disks. This means the answer to the question about whether a forward or dressage seat is better for the back lies within the back itself. If you have a problem with the joints or disks, forward seat is more advisable; and if you have sore, stiff, or weak muscles, the dressage seat is probably better.

In summary, riding in the forward seat can indeed be a useful exercise for the deep back muscles, but at the same time, be careful about the possibility of overstrain, especially riders that tend to sit with a hollow back or ones that have a problem with their spine like a slipped disc. Similar to

*Varying training sessions makes work more fun while also decreasing wear and tear caused by monotonous work.

Practice Strengthens the Back—Go Easy on It to Protect It

Practicing forward seat activates and strengthens the back muscles.

bending over and lifting or carrying things, leaning forward with your upper body is not harmful as long as the spine remains straight in itself.*

Dressage riders, who improve their forward-seat posture, gain better mobility and balance. Therefore, it makes sense to include forward seat as a constant part of the warm-up phase, especially for more mature riders. Jumpers, on the other hand, would benefit tremendously from practicing the most demanding of all exercises—the sitting trot: The coordination needed plus the interplay of the deep back muscles that secure the spine make sitting trot ideal training for the forward-seat position and jumping. However, there is one little caveat: Sitting trot in a jumping saddle with short stirrups often leads to a chair seat.

There is a simple way for jumpers, however, to systematically tone their deep back muscles: trotting without stirrups for a few minutes on a regular basis while concentrating on just letting their legs hang down from their hips in a relaxed manner, with no tension in their adductors. They should simply allow for the horse's movement to pass upward through their spine.

How much strain does jumping put on your back?

During jumping, particularly when landing after a fence, the rider's upper body has to stabilize and support enormous forces (see top photos on p. 64). Only if back and abdominal muscles are well-toned and work in a coordinated manner will there be no negative effects on the back. Naturally, jumping is potentially more dangerous to your back since you are dealing with more dynamic motion. Nevertheless, fluidly jumping a small course will be a lot more gentle on your back than long periods of sitting trot on a stiff horse. You can plan and do jumping exercises in a way that makes your horse "round" his back and relax his back muscles, taking you with him in his rhythmic motion.

Jumping is a matter of practice: In order to be able to coordinate and adapt the motion sequences of riding toward a fence, during takeoff, in the suspension phase and landing, your brain and body must execute the sequences almost automatically. In order to jump fences, you need to have a stable forward seat, which you must have schooled beforehand. If you are an inexperienced jumper who only jumps every once in a while, that is, not often enough, you are putting your back at risk. This is often the case with people who take up riding in later life. The same applies to jumping badly trained, inexperienced horses or those that are not ready for jumping; on these horses, even experienced riders might quickly lose their inner and outer balance.

*A systematic training concept adapted to the needs of a rider's back allows dressage and riding in a forward seat to perfectly complement each other.

2.2 Versatile Basic Training

Rider & Horse Back to Back

Landing after a fence puts the most amount of strain on the back of both horse and rider.

Riding on the trail

*It is important to maintain sufficient positive body tension while on a trail ride to be prepared for your horse to make a sudden move, which can happen at any time.

Trail riding challenges horse and rider in numerous, interesting ways: different footing and surroundings, changes in weather as well as people and horses in a group. Based on this, you would think that riding like this would be a back-friendly way of riding, but in reality, the opposite is often the case.

When going out is the only form of riding practice its disadvantage is, in most cases, that it lacks systematic gymnasticizing of horse and rider. Physical problems will inevitably worsen when you do not know about—or don't pay attention to—straightness, stiffness, or incorrect ingrained motion patterns. At the same time, people usually lack a concrete plan to improve these issues. Even many years of riding experience do not help: When you stop trying to improve your seat and your horse's training, your ability and fitness inevitably deteriorate. This deterioration of motion skills (becoming stiffer, more crooked, one-sided, weaker, slower to react) usually progresses so slowly that most riders do not notice. In addition, outdoor surroundings provide plenty of diversion in order to keep you from concentrating on your body—it takes an extra effort to maintain body awareness. If you want to ride in a back-friendly manner when out on a trail ride, you need to start by practicing body awareness (see p. 14) and by showing the willingness to always stick to a systematic plan.*

There is a reason why working in an indoor arena —sheltered from the distractions of the outdoors— is considered the best place for elementary systematic gymnasticizing. When outside and your horse pulls on the reins, canters on two tracks, or shows other schooling deficiencies that can harm your back, you need to go back indoors.

However, despite all the possible disadvantages, the interaction between dressage and training outside can have positive effects. First, good flatwork learned in the arena improves your horse for riding outside. And, systematic practice while on a hack can be used to train both basic and advanced

Practice Strengthens the Back—Go Easy on It to Protect It

dressage exercises in a fun way. Everyone knows that that riding outdoors can be very motivating for the horse, and you can improve his willingness to go forward and work, as well as his endurance. Horse and rider are able to improve their balance by going uphill and down—and, by the way, climbing hills consists of the same motion sequence as jumping, just in slow motion.

Advanced riders can use the gradient of the terrain to gymnasticize their horse: When the ground determines the level of difficulty, the rider doesn't need to summon so much strength and energy to apply aids, and this translates into an immediate relief of the back.

Riding your horse in the countryside or at least in an outdoor arena, asking him go forward on long straight lines is a perfect choice for warm-up and cooling-down phases; active relaxation; and reward for intense periods of collection.

Doing piaffe on a slight slope: A demanding exercise that helps to reach the highest level of collection.

The best way to reward the horse after tiring collected work is by riding him forward in a relaxed manner.

Going uphill and downhill are great ways for a horse to learn to use his neck as a "balancing pole."

2.2 Versatile Basic Training

2.3 Back to Back

The horse's spine

All motion patterns and all forces affecting the rider's back are caused by the horse. This is why you need to have a basic understanding of how horses move in order to be able to ride in a back-friendly manner.

In many aspects, the horse's spine is very similar to yours, especially in regard to its function. The horse's back is both flexible and stable at the same time, while the pelvis plays a central role in transforming movement into forward motion. Movement originates in the pelvis and hips; the hind legs' "long levers" supply the horse's forward motion with sufficient impulsion. This is the basis for the familiar image of the hindquarters being the "engine" of the horse's motion.

The horse's spine compensates for the movement of pelvis and hind legs by "swinging" lightly. The more rhythmic and balanced a horse moves, the more evenly and effortlessly this swinging motion will be: The horse creates a highly effective interaction of all muscles and their balance of tension and release. The term "suppleness" (*Losgelassenheit*) is usually used to describe this state. Only then will you (and your back) be able to feel comfortable on your horse.

It might seem contradictory at first that the horse's spine is supposed to swing and carry weight at the same time: The rider is sitting on the horse's back, after all, acting as an obstacle that makes it difficult for the horse (especially when young) to obtain suppleness.

The horse's spine is securely "fastened" into his body with ligaments and tendons so that he can carry weight without well-developed back muscles, but carrying too much passive weight (the rider) is a big strain on this "support" system with resulting inflammation and damage to the horse's joints; the condition known as "kissing spines" is a good example.

Ligament and tendon injuries in young horses are often caused by training methods that try to tone their muscles—but in an incorrect manner. (The effect is similar to the harmful habit some people have of "overstretching" their knees when they stand or walk. This may seem like the most comfortable way of standing—a less exhausting exercise for your muscles—but in the long run, your knee joints and ligaments will be damaged.)

In contrast to humans, who have to work hard to learn all movement step by step, horses already have full access to their entire repertoire of motion when they are foals. Young horses are able to show spectacular movement and free jump the highest fences. This is why the talents of many young horses are exploited: Unless the trunk's stability is developed through systematic gymnasticizing, the horse's back is unable to cope with extensive collected or jumping work—even though

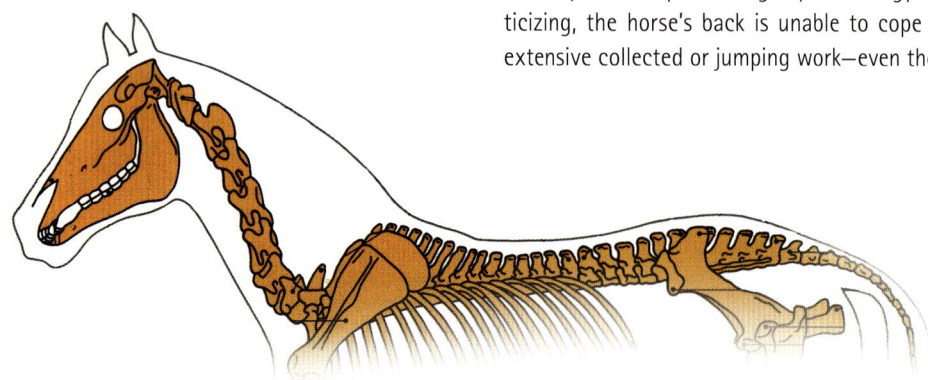

Similar to the human spine, the horse's spine shows the S shape with its characteristic curve in the cervical spine.

the horse may "offer" it. This sort of "large" movement should not be trained too early because the horse will rely on ligaments to carry the rider, which puts more strain on his back thus causing injury to his limbs. Only when the horse has built up enough muscle mass in his topline, will the spine be able to swing freely, that is, allow movement to pass through. It goes without saying that a saddle needs to give the spine sufficient room to swing. Therefore, checking your horse's saddle needs to be on your list for back-friendly riding—ask a professional if necessary (see p. 58).

The horse's abdominal muscles are an important part of stabilizing his back. Its construction can be compared to a bridge; one of the prerequisites for putting up a bridge is to have stability of its underside. It is a fact that soon after a colic operation, a horse can be worked on a longe line; but carrying a rider is only allowed after the abdominal muscles have redeveloped—about three months later.

The horse's internal organs add up to a significant amount of weight. Therefore, it is necessary for the abdominal muscles to be toned and made strong to balance this kind of weight and let the horse lift his chest. The result is the uphill balance riders want to see in a horse. The best exercise for the abdominals—the horse's "sit-up"—is striking off into canter; horses that lack the natural conformation for a good canter, Icelandic horses for example, have a hard time rounding and relaxing their back.

The cervical spine plays a special role in transmitting movement. The horse uses his neck to compensate for a lack of balance in his trunk and the neck acts like a balancing rod or pole. When you see a horse constantly moving his head and neck, it usually means he has issues with his balance.

Forcing his head and neck into a rigid and tight posture (by way of incorrect rein aids or overly short side reins) robs the horse of any chance to establish (or reestablish) his balance. Fear and resistance are usually the result of these methods.

The noblest purpose of rein aids, therefore, is to assist the horse in finding and stabilizing his balance. Once he has found his balance in motion, he can carry his neck freely and quietly while yielding easily in the poll. This is the actual meaning of "putting the horse on the bit." Understanding this close connection to the horse's balance, you understand why you need to push your horse's hindquarters forward toward the bit instead of just using your hands and "riding backward."

The swinging back

Good rein contact can help your horse get his back to swing, that is, to build up positive muscle tension. This effect can be likened to the strings of a musical instrument: It can only produce a sound when it is tightly fastened at both ends. The tension in the strings influences its vibration and results in higher or lower sounds. When you ride your horse, he is "held" between forward-driving and collecting aids. Depending on any changes in this basic tension, which occurs from both ends, the degree of collection changes as well. The image of vibrating strings also underlines the significance of the forward-driving aids as these are the aids that ask the horse's back to swing when in motion.

If your horse's back really swings, it allows you to sit comfortably—regardless of how *much* it swings. Every horse swings differently based on his conformation and level of training—and poses different demands on the rider's back. Horses with less natural movement in their body tend to develop it in their back once truly supple. Horses that throw you about quite a lot, on the other hand, decrease their vibrations once they let movement pass through their back.

Rider & Horse Back to Back

Beginners tend to feel more comfortable, meaning safe, on a horse whose back moves as little as possible in trot. However, you will not be able to learn how to ride on a "tense" horse because you are missing the important interaction between the horse's movement and your back. It is much easier, for example, to learn and practice the rhythm of rising trot on a horse that pushes you upward a little more. The back of a tense horse neither swings nor cushions impact from his feet hitting the ground. As a result, people who are suffering from back problems experience a harder "blow" or impact from this kind of horse than when riding one that swings more but is able to relax his back at the same time.*

Other signs of relaxation or suppleness are the horse's willingness to stretch his topline, a softened facial expression, and a relaxed swinging tail. When the tail is restless—swishing all the time—the horse is most likely tensed up; and when it's held crookedly, the horse's back is not straight and his movement might be hindered in some places.

What happens in the horse's back

The three-dimensional movement of the horse's back can best be seen from behind. The point of origin of this movement is the pelvis. At the widest part of the croup, the bony edges of the pelvis usually protrude quite visibly underneath the skin, which allows you to follow the vertical movement of the pelvis. The horse's hind legs will only be able to swing underneath his center of gravity with the sideways-moving capacity of the pelvis allowing his weight to shift laterally.

This lateral, up-and-down pelvic movement is connected to the spine's forward motion. The fact that the horse also needs to shift his body weight from one side to the other results in a highly complex motion, which is similar to the way you walk. Each time the horse completes a sequence of hoof beats—in any gait (see p. 74)—his back has moved in all directions: forward, upward or downward, and sideways.

The sideways motion of the pelvis is caused by the rotation of the spinal column. When you see a horse displaying little sideways motion, his back muscles are most likely too tense and not allowing it to happen. It is often the case that these kinds of horses have problems in their back, right behind the saddle. When their back muscles are tensed up in this area, the pelvis is not able to move.

The way the horse's individual vertebrae are constructed defines the mobility and possible

The fact that riders need to be able to sit comfortably and drive their horse forward is part of the classical definition of suppleness.

A trot with good impulsion will activate the rider's ability to sit upright with positive tension, that is, from dynamic stability within her core.

Practice Strengthens the Back—Go Easy on It to Protect It

The pelvis as the joint between horse and rider

Your pelvis is what connects or "joins" you to your horse. It absorbs the horse's movements and passes them onto your spine in a way that gives you the appearance of sitting still and upright.

You need to learn to allow the horse's back to move your pelvis—in all three directions—and in a complex manner: Every form of natural movement of a living body always includes all three directions even when it looks as if it is happening in one.

The key to suppleness and impulsion is the mobility of the pelvis of both horse and rider.

The interaction of movement between horse and rider	
The horse's back	**The rider's back**
1. Rounding and lowering/hollowing.	1. Rounding and hollowing in the lumbar spine.
2. Bending (longitudinal bend, lateral flexion in the spine to both sides).	2. Rotation to both sides.
3. Rotation of the spine to both sides.	3. Bending sideways (lateral flexion) to both sides.

1. When the horse moves forward his back moves like a wave: forward up and forward down. Your pelvis following this forward-up movement becomes a little rounder in the lower back as the seat bones from underneath get moved forward and up. During the landing phase the horse's back moves forward and down (hollows) and your pelvis follows this in the same way. In this way, horse and rider perform similar movement.

2. When the horse bends during turns, your inside hip is pushed forward and your spine rotates. Horse and rider perform different movement in this case: *The horse flexes laterally* while *the rider rotates* her spine.

3. When the horse's back rotates (his pelvis drops more on one side), you follow this by performing a lateral movement—flexing your spine. Again, movement is different: the horse is rotating while the rider flexes laterally.

directions they can move—similar to human beings. In both cases, *lateral flexion* (bending to one side) is only possible when the spine rotates in the opposite direction at the same time in order to give the vertebrae enough space. Thus, sideways movement without simultaneous rotation is impossible (rotation without sideways movement is, however). In summary, only those horses that are flexible in their pelvis and allow the rotation of the spine will be able to bend correctly.*

The spinal column of both horse and human are constructed in opposing curvatures—the S shape, which cause the curved segments to rotate in opposite directions. This principle is called *opposing rotation* or *contortion* and contributes to the stability of the spine. It is also the basis for the rider's ability to rotate her upper body when bending and turning (see p. 150).

*A relaxed back is not merely a theoretical prerequisite for bending the horse but also a functional one.

2.2 Back to Back 69

Rider & Horse Back to Back

The neck: mobility and the ability to compensate

For both horse and rider, the cervical spine and the joints in the skull are of specific importance: This whole area controls motion. The cervical spine is the most flexible part of the spinal column; it absorbs and cushions movement coming from lower in the spine before it reaches the joints in the skull. These joints are the highest movable segment of your spine and originate at the ear and eye level.

Structure of the cervical spine

- **The atlas and axis** are the topmost joints in the cervical spine. They look slightly different from other vertebral joints and are specifically designed to turn the head. They form the back of the neck (the poll).
- **The middle segment:** The mobility of the joints between the third and sixth cervical vertebrae "cushions" the upper cervical spine from impact and strain below.
- **The transitional segment:** The seventh and last cervical vertebra (C7) has two functions: Toward the top end (the head) it is as mobile as the other cervical vertebrae, while below, it has the stability of the thoracic vertebrae.

The cervical spine reaches deep into the head.

The neck muscles span from the back of the head (occipital area) all the way to the rib cage. You can clearly see the contraction of one prominent muscle that starts behind the ear and goes to the sternum of the rib cage.

Negative tension in the back of the neck; tipping the head to one side; constantly directing eyes downward; and headaches during riding sessions usually originate not only in the area of head and neck, but also from much further down the spine in the lumbar region (which forms a functional unit with the pelvis and the hips). You are only able to carry your head freely in an upright position when your spine serves as a *dynamic stable* base.

Of all the cervical vertebrae, you can most easily feel the C7 when you touch your spine because its spinous process protrudes the most. In order to make sure you are touching the right vertebra, put a finger on it while putting another finger on the vertebra right above it. Then move your head backward. Now, you can feel how the sixth vertebra slides forward while the seventh vertebra remains in place.

This difference in mobility is purposeful. On its underside, the C7 is attached to the rib cage while on top, it allows for the flexibility of the cervical spine. It might seem paradoxical that the sixth vertebra slides forward to make room for the neck to move backward but it puts a lot of strain on ligaments and muscles. This is one reason why "rolling the head in all directions" as an exercise has been modified in physical therapy to just "moving the head for half a circle" in front of the body.

The most important thing about riding in a correct, upright posture is the ability to carry your head upright in such a way that you secure the position of the sixth vertebra and prevent it from sliding forward. Only then, can a stable cervical spine be maintained. Lifting your head or shoving your chin forward in an exaggerated manner is harmful and improves neither your riding skills nor your health.

Practice Strengthens the Back—Go Easy on It to Protect It   2

Putting strain on the cervical spine: head too far back; neck tension while trying to hold the head still; sticking the chin too far forward.

The common instruction "Head up!" is about much more than just raising your head. It comprises directing your eyes straight forward and stretching the back of your neck. Hollowing the neck is just as harmful for the spine as hollowing the lower back. To correct this you need to actively work at stretching the lower back and lengthening the deep back muscles without ending up in a rounded (collapsed) position. Similarly, you should stretch the back of your neck without bending the neck round and forward, which makes you look down.

In the horse, the neck is much longer than the other spinal segments (see p. 66)—this is why it is so important to see a horse visibly stretch its neck.

The horse's neck is long and the cervical vertebrae are much bigger than the vertebrae in other segments of the spine. Functioning as a balancing tool, the horse's neck needs to be flexible and give stability at the same time. In order to do this, the horse's muscles and tendons along the spine (neck to tail) work similarly to the rider's muscles and tendons from neck to pelvis. Both horse and rider need to activate their back's chain of muscles to support their neck. When the horse hollows his neck, it puts a great deal of stress onto his cervical spine.

When asked where the horse's cervical spine is, many riders point to the topline of the horse's neck; they are assuming that the neck vertebrae are up on top—under his crest. But this is not true! By looking at the drawing on page 66 you can see that the cervical spine of the horse has an almost opposite curve to the one made by the topline of his neck.

For the horse, too, the sixth cervical vertebra is in a very critical place. When the horse lifts his head up, the sixth vertebra (similar to the rider's) can slide out of the way—downward. This leads to a loss of stability and balance. Only when combined with activation of the topline neck muscles can the horse lift his neck in balance and use his back to take weight off his forelegs. Riding the horse in an elevated neck position can actually harm him!*

* To be able to be supple and "swing" through his back—whether ridden low or in a higher collected position—the horse needs to work with a "stretching/lengthening" tendency of his neck muscles in such a way so all the cervical joints stay "open."

The horse becomes more beautiful in collection: When working correctly, his upper neck muscles define his topline.

2.2 Back to Back   71

Rider & Horse Back to Back

Movement control starts from the head

In a human, the first two cervical joints (atlas and axis) are of a "pivot" type, which is of special significance. It allows for more rotation than any other joint so the head can (to a certain degree) move in all directions. These joints are the final destination for impact and vibration from the spine below as well as all strain and stiffness that originate in other segments of the spine and the pelvic bones: It's here, for example, that you see the effects of everything—from wearing uncomfortable shoes (a headache!) to problems in sitting trot that lead to shoulder and neck tension. The close vicinity to blood vessels and nerves that supply the brain increases the sensitivity of this area. Issues involving the joints of the skull can cause many various different symptoms from migraines to nausea, from breathing problems to bad circulation.

Being the body's first movable spinal parts, the sub-occipital joints are closely connected to all other movement. Head control is the first thing babies learn; it is from the head that the rest of the body is controlled. Many reflexes are triggered solely by the position of the head.

The movements of the eyes are also connected to the sub-occipital joints, assigning them an important role in all motion patterns. You can see for yourself that your head automatically turns in the direction your eyes are pointing. Turning your head to the right and your eyes to the left is possible only when you concentrate hard on it, but it always looks unnatural. This phenomenon proves that focusing your eyes in a specific direction defines the course for subsequent body movement; the entire body will always try and follow the eyes. This is the reason for the multitude of comments directed at the rider's line of vision. Focusing in the right direction triggers numerous automatic chain reactions in the muscles, making movements become quicker, easier and natural.*

When you look at your surroundings in a natural and open manner, you often shift your depth of focus in order to observe as much as possible—and as inconspicuously as possible. And your body will prepare to follow your view. Riders, however, can tend to go to extremes: either looking down at their hands or staring with fixed "inflexible" eyes at a specific point, thus limiting their perception.

Looking down limits the rider's "forward intention" from her seat and locks her neck in a position that puts strain onto her lower back. It disturbs the fine balance between the abdominal muscles and back muscles. And controlling hand movement by looking at them prevents a light forward contact with the reins.

Staring fixedly at one point makes your body stiff and does not allow you to take in the feeling you are getting from the horse, so you are not able to adapt to a slight change of situation. Instead, riding with your eyes open and looking ahead with a wide focus—ready to change and take in as much as possible—is what is needed in order to sit in a supple manner to swing with the horse's movement.

Controlling the horse's poll

The horse's uppermost joint (sub-occipital) allows the horse to lift and lower his nose, while the second joint is the center of rotation (where the rider can flex the horse in the poll).

The combined movement of these two joints makes up the horse's lateral flexion in the poll. Similar to the situation of the human, the horse's head position influences the whole muscular system of the horse. When the horse is flexed in the poll to one side, his muscles are automatically prepared to follow: A correctly flexed horse is ready to turn into that direction.**

Use of mechanical force (exploiting the leverage of some bits and auxiliary reins) to gain control over the horse's poll can have dire consequences. During his schooling, the horse is supposed to be taught to voluntarily yield in the poll, and to leave control over his head and neck position up

*The body's movements automatically follow its line of vision.

**Once you have gained influence over the position and flexion of your horse's poll, you have the best possible control over his movement.

Practice Strengthens the Back—Go Easy on It to Protect It

to his rider. The rider needs to allow the horse's neck freedom to work correctly over his topline; too much pulling and force will "lock" the horse's neck joints and have a negative influence on his suppleness.

Horse and rider need mutual trust in order to establish a light and giving contact. The horse needs to be supple—not only in his body but in his mind, too—and any stress or tension will immediately influence the joints in his poll and affect rein contact. As a prerequisite to being trained, the horse needs to have positive experiences right from the first time someone sits on his back and familiarizes him with the aids.

Every horse and human shows a difference in how far he is able to turn his heads sideways, and in which direction he flexes better. This is not necessarily the side that the rest of his neck can bend more easily, quite the opposite.

There is a difference between flexing in the poll and moving the rest of the neck sideways. Sometimes a horse compensates for poor neck mobility with better flexion in the poll. This horse often looks "hollow" on one side, tending to carry his neck to the outside while flexing his poll too far to the inside. (This scenario is true for riders too—some carry their head with their features facing one way and their neck bent to the opposite side!)

Checking your own and your horse's mobility in the poll (first two cervical joints) and in the whole neck can prove helpful to understanding certain situations during training.

You can test the lateral mobility of your horse's neck by using the popular "carrot test": Your horse is supposed to follow the carrot you are offering without moving his trunk. Depending on how high or low you hold the carrot you will see the joints of the neck show different levels of elasticity and mobility.

During the course of the horse's training, lateral mobility of the neck should become more and more equal. If it does not improve at all or only to a very small degree, muscles or vertebrae might be blocked.

If your horse has been correctly trained and is relaxed in the poll, his jaw will relax as well and free the parotid gland, which in turn causes him to foam evenly on both sides of his mouth.

The same connection between the jaw, sub-occipital joints and general relaxation also applies to the rider. "Clench your teeth" would be bad advice because your neck and cervical spine will tense up. "Pretend to chew gum" is better, though a relaxed smile is the most effortless measure.

Clenching your teeth hurts!

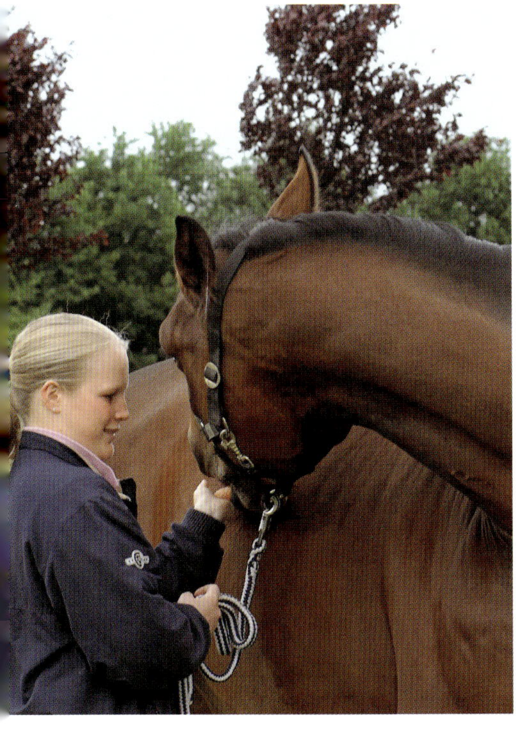

Horses will do almost anything for a carrot!

2.2 Back to Back

Rider & Horse Back to Back

Sequence of footfalls in the basic gaits

In each of the three basic gaits, the horse's legs move in a specific way: The sequence of beats. When the hooves strike the ground, they produce an unmistakable rhythm; this is why you can tell in which gait a horse is coming toward you even when you cannot see him yet. In walk, it takes four, in trot two, and in canter three beats until all feet have moved forward and the sequence starts again. Each one of the beats can be subdivided into two sequences: when the hoof leaves the ground and when it lands on it.

■ Walk

At the walk, the horse shifts his weight from one side over a diagonal support to the other side. Lateral and diagonal support phases follow one another. Like this, even though the horse is walking in a straight line, he always needs to shift his weight diagonally in order to move forward. The rider's pelvis has to follow this lateral movement including the shift of weight.

In order to better understand this process, imagine a direct connection between your seat bones and your horse's front feet: The second a front foot touches the ground, you will simultaneously have shifted more weight to your respective seat bone. Some riders automatically (and correctly) shift their weight in unison with the horse while others instinctively try to "compensate" for the lat-

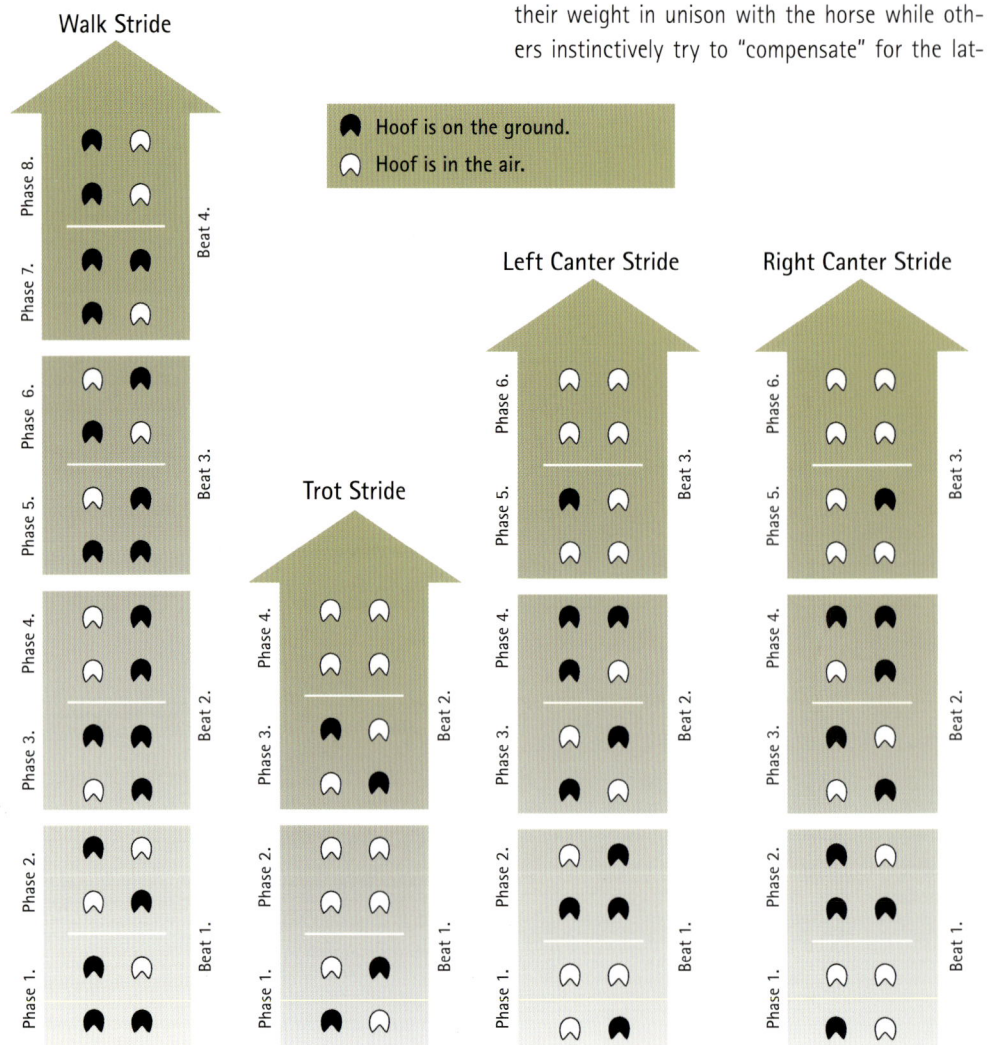

The sequence of footfalls in one stride in the three basic gaits

Practice Strengthens the Back—Go Easy on It to Protect It

eral movement: These people sit to the right as the horse shifts his weight to the left. As a consequence, they demonstrate a high degree of lateral movement without ever becoming part of the horse's motion.

■ Trot

In the trot, diagonal pairs of feet strike the ground together for one beat, the horse is suspended for a moment, then the opposite diagonal pair strikes for the second beat (see photo p. 124). The horse's center of gravity stays in the middle—he does not shift his weight laterally. When you watch a horse trotting from behind you'll see he makes the narrowest track, and it is the gait in which he is balanced most securely. This is why he is able to be calmed down easily in trot.

Trot allows you to clearly analyze and feel the movement of the horse's pelvis. You can feel on the side of the horse where the hind foot strikes off that you are sitting lower. If you have difficulty sensing this movement, start by concentrating on the front legs. Similar to walk, you will lower your left seat bone at the moment the horse's left front foot touches the ground.

The lateral mobility of the horse's pelvis leads to a rotational movement in his spine. This is the key to a truly supple and swinging back. You need to allow the horse's back to lower—alternating on each side—without shifting your weight, which means your pelvis needs to follow his movement. You do this by "lengthening" each of your sides alternately—stretching down in your waist"—while staying in balance (see the photos at the bottom of p. 126). Your pelvis and lower back must allow lateral movement, but your shoulders have to be independent and stay level.

At the same time, the horse is moving forward: What you might feel as a lateral movement is actually a forward-sideways movement. This goes along with the position of your seat bones on the saddle. They are not straight but slope to the front.

When you possess the necessary mobility and co-ordination skills—and rhythm in particular—you will be able to encourage your horse to use his back muscles even more so he can become "loose" and truly relaxed.

■ Canter

In canter, the horse shifts his weight from the outside hind leg to the diagonal inside front leg. This movement requires you to be able to shift your own weight respectively and slide your inside hip forward. Your inside hip should be at its furthermost forward position at the same moment as the horse's inside front foot touches the ground. When you have mastered this motion pattern, do not bend in your hip or change position of your outside "guarding" leg.

A hand on your hip helps you to feel how much your hip joint actually has to move in order to be able to follow canter strides.

2.4 Letting Go, Feeling, and Going with the Flow of the Horse's Movements

Get to know your own back a little bit better

Your back is the center of all movements when on a horse. If you would like to learn how to ride all these and improve your back, you have to get reacquainted with the scope of your mobility and the quality of movement your own body has to offer. The short test on this page (see box) will help guide you on your quest, though remember, it is just a start, not the complete journey.

All the exercises in this chapter will assist you in finding answers to questions in the test. If you adapt them to yourself as an individual, they can even improve the flexibility of your back (the flexion and extension of specific spinal joints) and pelvis. Only after you have gained complete suppleness can you attain better body awareness and feel the horse's movements more intensely as you learn how to follow them better.

You should begin by practicing all the exercises in walk unless they are specifically designed for the other gaits. Getting acquainted with new movements is best done on the longe line—almost all of the exercises, however, can be practiced without being on the longe, though the horse needs to be dependable, of course. In the beginning, it is advisable to repeat each exercise multiple times until you know the movements. Based on this, you can try and modify them to meet the needs of your body.

Useful questions to "ask" your body

- **Your weight on the horse**
  (Can I feel both seat bones equally?)
- **Mobility of the pelvis**
  (Can my horse move my pelvis in all directions?)
- **Stability**
  (Can I align my pelvis, trunk and head so that they form a straight line?)
- **Breathing**
  (In an upright position, am I able to breathe out longer than I breathe in?)
- **Coordination**
  (Can I lift my chest and move my shoulder girdle while my horse keeps moving my pelvis?)
- **Independence**
  (Can I carry and move my arms and hands independently without tension in my shoulders?)
- **Mobility**
  (Can I rotate my upper body equally to both sides?)
- **Mobility of the hips**
  (Can I equally move both thighs sideways away from the horse? And slide both hips forward equally?)
- **Mobility of the ankles**
  (Can I pull up and lower my heels without changing the pressure on my seat bones?)
- **Balance**
  (Do I tend to lean forward or backward?)

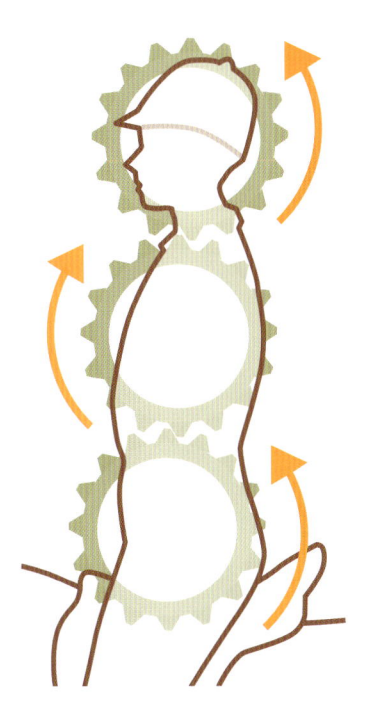

Practice Strengthens the Back—Go Easy on It to Protect It

The pelvis, trunk, and head influence each other.

Feel the position of your pelvis

Every movement of your horse's back passes through your pelvis into your own back. There is a functional interaction between the position of the pelvis and the straightness of your back.

Finding your balance while your back is aligned with an imaginary vertical line is possible only when your pelvis is in the middle position, that is, not too far forward or backward. You can try to see for yourself what the middle position feels like by moving your pelvis and testing its mobility.

Center your upper body

In order for your legs to hang down from your hips without any kind of tension, your upper body needs to be balanced. Imagine your legs are pendulums that can only hang down straight when your upper body is balanced in the middle position.

An easy way to feel the connection between your upper body and your legs is to have your horse go forward in walk while you bend your upper body forward and backward (closing your eyes intensifies the experience). Leaning back causes your

Checking pelvis mobility.

2.4 Letting Go, Feeling, and Going with the Flow of the Horse's Movements

Rider & Horse Back to Back

lower legs to automatically slide forward while your knees come up. Bending over forward makes your seat bones lose contact with the saddle; you will be supporting yourself mostly with your thigh muscles while your lower legs slide backward.

In both cases, your muscles will reflexively react to the state of balance. Even though these automatic movements prevent you from falling off the horse, they interfere with your influence on your horse: Reflexive tension blocks your hips and sends wrong information to your horse. In order to produce a desired reaction, you need to apply more strength and stronger aids: You basically sabotage yourself when you have problems balancing your upper body.

When you move your upper body to the side you will feel the contact of your thighs on the saddle change. One leg will be more "on" the side of the saddle than the other. It is possible to move your upper body in all directions and still stay balanced.

You can test your skills in rising trot or in forward seat: When you transfer your weight to your stirrups your lower legs have to stay in a stable position without your using muscle strength as support. If you are able to rotate your upper body in all directions, you are truly balanced (see bottom right photo).

You will only be able to make full use of the mobility of your hip joints if your upper body is balanced. And you need supple hips in order to allow the horse's back movement to make its way through your seat bones into your pelvis. This is the key to being able to follow the horse's motion.

Being longed allows you to "listen" to your own body.

Good balance allows you to move your upper body in all directions.

Practice Strengthens the Back—Go Easy on It to Protect It   2

Let your horse move you

Letting your horse move you is not as easy as it sounds. Sitting on a horse is quite difficult to co-ordinate: While your hip joints have to follow the horse's movements in all directions, your trunk needs enough positive tension to stay upright. Your upper body must never start working against the horse's motion or avoid following the horse's movement by making counter-movements.

The following exercise can help you straighten your upper body while relaxing your hip joints: Sit on your horse as relaxed and passively as possible. All the while, your back may become a little round. (You can make an exception here!) Let yourself be "rocked" by your horse, so to speak. Now, hold your arms in front of your upper body and turn them outward (see photo on this page). As a result, your shoulders will be pushed backward and your shoulder blades will come closer together. As a next step, hold your arms in front of your body with your palms facing up. Rotating your arms outward helps to lift your chest and develop positive tension. The increase in positive tension should not in any way negatively affect the relaxed feeling you have in your lower back and hips.

Now, when you move your hands back to their normal position holding the reins, you will feel you literally have to "carry" your fists with the help of your abdominal muscles that support the rib cage from below. This movement—improving and renewing the upright position of your trunk will help you do more advanced work like half-halts (see p. 133).

Rotating your arms outward helps to lift up your chest.

Stretch your hip muscles

Since your suppleness as a rider directly depends on the elasticity of your hip muscles, stretching exercises targeting these muscles are always useful—before, during, and even after riding. Rising trot, for example, is traditionally integrated into the horse's warm-up phase. Doing some rhythmic "games" in rising trot (see p. 88) and constantly changing between rising and sitting trot will increase blood flow to your respective muscles.

During all stretching exercises, you should pay special attention to the hip adductors, the muscles on the inside of your thighs, as riding requires them to stretch in a specific way not usually needed in everyday life. There is a reason why these muscles are normally sore after you have taken a long break from riding. If you want to specifically stretch your hip muscles at home, every decent gymnastics routine will help. Just be

2.4 Letting Go, Feeling, and Going with the Flow of the Horse's Movements

Rider & Horse Back to Back

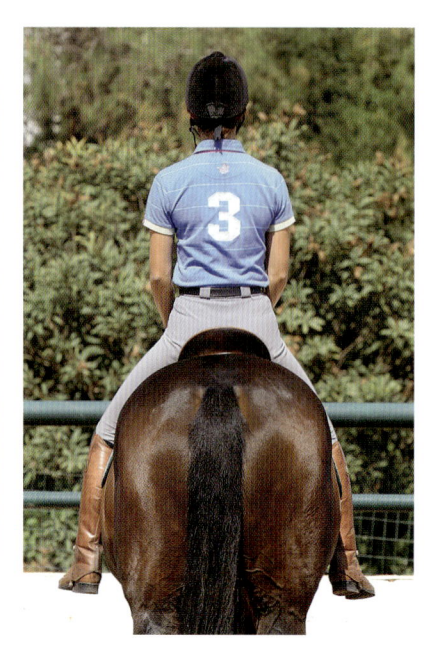

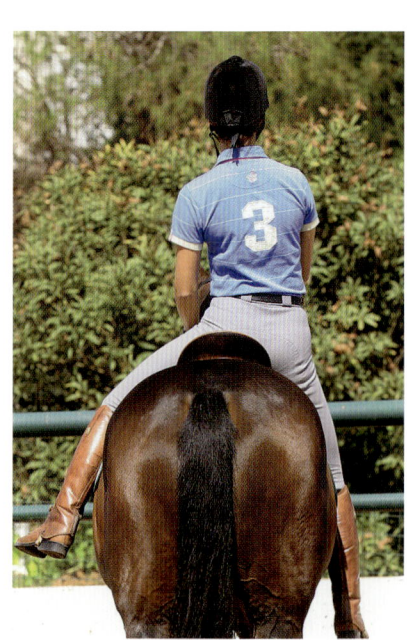

Sliding down the horse's side stretches the hip adductors.

*Stretching exercises are particularly useful when the stretching movement directly relates to your seat or to applying aids.

aware that it is the quality of the stretching that counts—not how far you can stretch. You should be able to stretch both legs to the same degree.

You can also do stretching exercises on the horse in walk. When you slide down the left (or right) side of the horse (without shifting all of your weight to that side), your leg will seem to become longer (see photos on this page). Try not to actively stretch it, but simply let it hang down with your knee relaxed. On the other side, the saddle will be "pressing" into your seat and the ends of tendons and muscles attached there, so, in effect, the horse's movement is providing a "free massage" to those deep areas of tissue.

By turning your upper body and rotating your pelvis you can increase the amount of stretch and change the area of muscles. See if you can detect the differences of elasticity in the hip muscles on both sides so you can target stretching exercises to fit your needs. Even better, do such exercises with a riding issue in mind. For example, if you experience a problem trying to strike off onto a specific canter lead, you can stretch the respective hip forward and downward and remember the feeling during the next canter transition.*

Move your thighs away from the saddle

In order for the hips to let go and relax, your thighs must not be pressed against the saddle too tightly. Holding on with your knees is useful only in an emergency: The supple leg position in dressage and in a forward seat should allow the knees to slide a bit (mainly up and down) along the saddle.

The rider's thighs stabilize the position of the pelvis and, in difficult situations, are important in order to sit deep in the saddle. However, riders who constantly press their thighs into the panels will never get to sit deep in the saddle or learn how to follow the horse's motion in a relaxed manner. Clinging to the saddle like this burdens the back of both horse and rider. An abrupt movement (such as shying or bucking) often catapults such a rider out of the saddle because her muscles are so tense.

Whether you walk, trot, canter, or turn, you should always see to it that both of your thighs have an even contact with the saddle. At first, it might come as a surprise to realize how often one leg has more contact with the horse. Often, this is

Practice Strengthens the Back—Go Easy on It to Protect It

because you are not sitting in the middle of the horse's back.

To achieve better control and relaxation of the hip and thigh muscles, without stirrups try walking your horse and take one thigh off the saddle, then both at the same time, and move them out sideways a few inches (see photo). Remain in this position for a few steps. Be careful: This exercise is very tiring and can quickly lead to cramping in the hip muscles if done too far or without warming up first. On the other hand, this test clearly shows you how mobile your hip joints are.

This exercise is more difficult than it looks—it requires a lot of strength from the muscles around the hips. However, after you "tense" muscles like this, you gain relaxation in the hip area, so it's an excellent exercise for relaxing tight hip muscles.

Riding a bicycle

After the hip-stretching exercise, it's a good idea to do some coordination exercises to take advantage of the new mobility you've found in your hips. Without stirrups, move your legs alternately up and down as if you were riding a bike. Your lower legs should hang down as relaxed as possible so that your thighs and hip joints have to do the most work—not your knees. If your upper body is not stable enough yet, hold onto a strap attached to the pommel. This quite demanding exercise will actually become fairly easy if done in unison with the horse's movement. It also helps

you remain in constant, good (flexible) contact with the saddle. "Bicycle riding" is only possible when your upper body is in the *middle* position; the slightest tendency toward slipping down on one side will be "punished" immediately!

This exercise teaches you that balance is connected to forward motion—in rhythm. And, in the same way as when you learn to ride a bike, you need courage to keep moving forward. Even though the exercise can be schooled in walk, the best results—rewards—will show up in trot. It helps to improve your sitting trot significantly (see p. 142).

Later on, the biking exercise can also be done off the longe line and "minimized." Since hip, knee, and ankle joints are connected by long muscle chains, exercises designed for the hips are useful for the entire leg all the way down to the heel. A scaled-down version of this exercise helps to absorb the movement in hip, knee, and ankle.

When done in unison with the horse's rhythm, this exercise is easier than it looks.

2.4 Letting Go, Feeling, and Going with the Flow of the Horse's Movements

Rider & Horse Back to Back

Stretching exercise: lower back

Negative tension felt in the *lumbar* spine is all too common. A helpful, gentle stretching exercise to improve this area can be done on a horse in walk. The rhythm and movement of the horse's back actually intensifies the stretching of your spine, improving its elasticity.

The following exercise "Giving the Horse a Hug" really does look like hugging the horse around his neck. Slowly, bend forward as far as possible, starting with your head, which you'll need to place on one side of the horse's neck. Repeat the exercise and alternate sides. The horse's back movement will move your back accordingly (see photo bottom right).

To sit up again, first place your hands on the horse's neck to support yourself and straighten up—vertebra by vertebra—beginning in the pelvis; your neck and head are the last links in this motion chain. You can work on the areas of your back where you feel stiff by moving the vertebrae up and down, inch by inch.

Modify this exercise in a way to work on areas where you feel you need the stretch. First, place your hands on the horse's shoulders with your back slightly *rounded*. Using your arms for support, put pressure on your seat bones. This kind of pressure will help to stabilize the contact between your pelvis and the saddle. By bending forward ever so slightly and supporting yourself with your arms, the *upper part* of your back is "fixed" still and stabilized so your lower back can move, and as a result, your pelvis is basically "forced" (in a good way) to truly follow the horse's movement. All you need to do now is maintain this feeling of your pelvis being moved by the horse when you sit back up.

Afterward, you can do the following to counteract the above exercise where you round your lower back: Place both hands on the cantle for support, stand up in the stirrups, move your pelvis forward, and stretch as much as possible (see photo bottom left). If you are riding by yourself—not on the longe line—you should modify this exercise for safety reasons. Take the reins in one hand and place the other on the cantle before stretching diagonally to the hand that is supporting you.

Left: Stretching the front of your body is just as important as stretching the back.

Below: Hugging the horse helps to stretch the whole back and especially the area of the lumbar spine.

When you are able to stretch in both directions, sitting upright will become easier.

Practice Strengthens the Back—Go Easy on It to Protect It

Stretching exercises: upper back

You can take the stretching exercise we just used for the lumbar spine and adapt it to target the *thoracic* spine (upper back). Bend your upper body forward and use your hands to support yourself on the horse's neck (see photos on this page). Put a little bit of pressure on your seat bones with your lower back slightly rounded. Your goal is to feel how all the movement of the horse's shoulders is passed onto your upper body.

To intensify your feeling of the horse's shoulder motion, start by moving your own shoulders in unison with the horse. Depending how far apart from the saddle you place your hands will determine which parts of your spine feel the horse's movements. The closer to the saddle you place your hands, the further up in your back you will feel the motion.

In the course of all these bending and stretching exercises, be certain to focus on the *cervical* spine: Start with your head, then draw your chin as close to your breastbone as possible before rounding the rest of your back. When you sit back up, your head should straighten last and you should concentrate on slowly pushing up your cervical spine to give it a good stretch. Your goal is to carry your head effortlessly and be able to easily move it in all directions.

Once you have gained experience in body and motion awareness, you can use the horse's movement to improve your own mobility spinal segment by segment—from lumbar to cervical spine—during these bending and stretching exercises.*

*Stretching exercises on the horse allow you to improve your own mobility through the horse's motion.

Depending how far you stretch your arms, you target different parts of your spine.

2.4 Letting Go, Feeling, and Going with the Flow of the Horse's Movements

Rider & Horse Back to Back

Here is another similar exercise that focuses on stretching your *thoracic* spine: Place your hands on the cantle once again, slightly pushing off the stirrups and roll your pelvis forward (see photo on left). This time, concentrate on stretching open the chest. Lift up your head, too, but do not overstretch your neck as your cervical spine is very vulnerable to strain.

"Opening" up your chest is the key to sitting upright.

*Increasing body awareness and targeted stretching of deep muscles will have a more lasting effect on improving your balance than the most elaborate strength training.

"Opening" your chest and ribs in this way allows you to take deeper breaths. Every time you breathe in, your rib cage extends from the inside out—which is why this exercise is very useful in combination with breathing exercises. Taking a deep breath expands the whole chest; your goal is to keep this chest position even when breathing out (see photo right).

This simple breathing exercise works on many of the deep layers of the trunk's muscles often difficult to reach and the connective muscles deep in between the ribs as well as the diaphragm. It is much more effective than *passive* stretching (using your body weight or an outside force to stretch) after which muscular fibers sometimes simply snap back into place like rubber and end up shorter than they were before. (This is why in many other sports, intense stretching sessions are not scheduled right before competition.) *Active* stretching done by using the muscles themselves is much more controlled, effective, and intensive, and less prone to injury.

In order to target all the deep muscle tissue around the chest, repeat the exercise with only one hand and stretch diagonally. Improved body awareness will help you detect which body areas you should be working on. The ability to evenly stretch the deep muscles in the rib cage automatically leads to improved upper body balance.*

Taking deep breaths expands your chest and ribs.

Mobility of the hips during rising trot

Rising trot is in itself a perfect warm-up exercise for the hips: The sit-up motion requires rhythmic stretching and flexing of the hip joints. Even though it is only moderately strenuous, your heart rate will increase significantly. As a result, blood flow through your muscles increases as well. Focus on maintaining your balance right from the start: When going on straight lines, distribute your weight equally on both stirrups; in turns, put a little more weight on the inside stirrup.*

The following exercise uses the image of a clock and helps to move your pelvis and relax the short, deep muscles around your hips so you are flexible in all directions. Imagine the face of a clock superimposed on your saddle underneath your seat bones with the pommel at twelve o'clock. Every time you sit down, try to reach a different hour with your seat bones. It is very important that you only move your pelvis and that you do not shift your weight from one stirrup to the other as this disturbs the horse's balance. It *is* possible to move your pelvis in all directions without changing your point of balance.

Try this standing on your feet in a "riding position" and move your pelvis right and left without changing your weight over your feet. Equally important, keep your shoulders quiet and don't start moving your shoulders to the left when the pelvis moves right, or turn with the upper body. This helps you to separate—and coordinate—movements between your pelvis, chest, and shoulders. How far you can move your pelvis is influenced by your ability to keep your weight even and your shoulders level.

The easiest way to begin is to move the seat bones sideways and alternate between three and nine o'clock. Your starting position is always the middle position of the pelvis in the saddle. For some riders, it is easiest if they start with the "big" movement (from side to side) right away, others prefer moving from the middle to three o'clock a couple of times, then from the middle to nine o'clock before finally putting it all together. Regardless of how you begin, comparing the mobility you have to each side paints a clear picture of which hip joint you can move more easily and freely. The "clock exercise" helps you significantly increase hip mobility and heighten your awareness of exactly where the middle of the horse's back is.

In order to step up the level of difficulty, begin to change directions between twelve and six o'clock; later on, you can include diagonally opposite "times of day" or circular motions (such as "every two hours" clockwise or counterclockwise).

*You will only be able to influence your horse with "invisible" weight aids later when you are able to make "small" refined movements with your pelvis.

During this exercise, your pelvis moves sideways without shifting your weight.

2.4 Letting Go, Feeling, and Going with the Flow of the Horse's Movements

Rider & Horse Back to Back

Experienced riders, too, should use their pelvis to its maximum lateral extent in their daily training sessions.

"Five minutes past one" and "five minutes to eleven" are important positions for the inside seat bone when the horse is making a turn.

The clock exercise addresses all the complex motion patterns the pelvis needs to follow to be able to move in all possible directions and follow the movements of the horse so fluently that the rider looks "at one" with the horse. Once they are perfected, these movements are almost invisible to an observer, but even those riders you think are sitting absolutely motionless are actually moving constantly with their pelvis following the movements of the horse's back in perfect harmony.

An interesting side-effect of this exercise is the horse's reaction to it. Since you make contact with the horse's back in different places while keeping your balance and moving in the same rhythm as the horse, most horses feel very comfortable with this exercise. Even horses with tense or short back muscles, a very distinctive one-sidedness (crookedness), or downhill balance, find it easier to reach a state of suppleness and balance—more proof of how closely horse and rider communicate through their backs.

All exercises improving the mobility of your pelvis that require interplay—contraction and relaxation—of the muscles involved are of immense functional value in riding sessions. You can use them during warm-up as well as during breaks from the work phase when you want to regain relaxation after intense muscle flexion.

Upper body balance in rising trot

Even though rising trot is usually one of the first tasks a beginner has to master when sitting on a horse, you seldom see it perfected because its demands on the rider's rhythm and balance are very high (see top two rows of photos on p. 87).

It's important not to be behind or in front of the horse's movement with your upper body. Riders who try hard to keep their upper body straight (as required in dressage) often find their balance is behind the horse's movement.

How far you have to take your upper body forward to follow the movement depends on functional aspects of trotting—not some standardized criteria. Most important is that you keep your balance while the horse is moving forward.

The degree to which someone can lean forward depends on body proportion (especially the length ratio between thigh and lower leg), stirrup length, level of training of the horse, and your goal as a rider. As a general rule, you can say that the shorter the stirrups, the further forward the upper body will lean in rising trot.

Rising trot without stirrups clearly indicates how far forward you have to take your upper body during the trotting motion. Do not try to lift yourself out of the saddle by pressing your knees together—a common mistake.

This exercise is not about getting up as high as possible: The movement should originate in the pelvis while your legs hang down in a relaxed manner. How far you come out of the saddle depends solely on the horse's impulsion (see bottom row of photos on p. 87).

Practice Strengthens the Back—Go Easy on It to Protect It

In rising trot, because of her long thighs, this rider has to move her upper body further up and forward than other riders in order to stay balanced.

This rider has relatively short thighs, which leads him to sit almost straight in order to keep his balance.

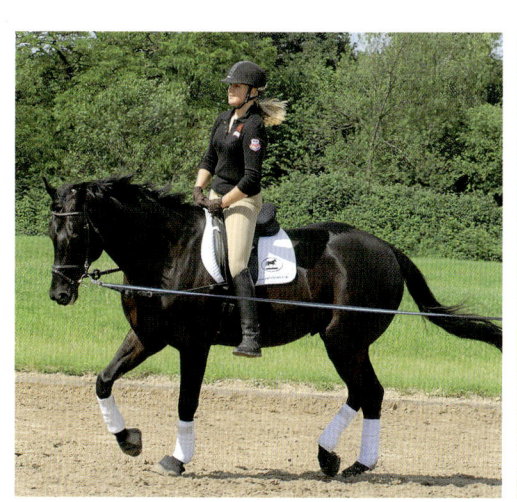

Rising trot without stirrups needs a very secure upper body balance.

2.4 Letting Go, Feeling, and Going with the Flow of the Horse's Movements

Rider & Horse Back to Back

Improve your balance and rhythm during rising trot

Getting good at rising trot requires that the rhythm of trot becomes second nature. Rising trot brings to light the close connection between balance and rhythm in movement: Since you need to constantly move, the slightest loss of balance will cause you to fall behind the horse's movement. As this occurs quite often, some instructors have decided not to school rising trot at all. This decision, however, robs riders of a highly useful tool when training because rising trot improves the equine back and is gentle on the human back, too.

The common practice of sitting down at the same time the inside hind hoof strikes the ground requires you to change diagonal every time you change rein: You sit down one step longer in order to change into the new rhythm. Changing diagonal can also be done by rising for two steps—a very short moment of forward seat. This exercise is more difficult and is excellent for balance training.*

Once you have mastered changing the diagonal by rising for two steps, you can start playing around and varying the rhythm of rising trot with your body: for example, try sitting down for two steps and rising for two steps—"sit-sit-up-up." Another series, "sit-sit-up" or "sit-up-up," is quite difficult. In these cases, since you are moving to a "three-beat" rhythm and your horse to a two-beat rhythm, the slightest lack of balance will upset your rhythm and balance.

Counting out the rhythm in trot "one-two-one-two" can lead to your body putting too much emphasis on the first beat and the same diagonal all the time. This can upset the horse's rhythm and even make some look lame. If you perform a three-beat movement like "sit-sit-up" or "up-up-sit" you will put the emphasis on a different diagonal, and ensure that the horse's rhythm stays regular.

It makes sense to practice these exercises on the longe line first. Holding on to a strap attached to the pommel tells you whether you are able to carry your hands independently from the movement of your pelvis: Try to establish a consistent light contact on the strap and not alter it during the changes in trot rhythm. You can only do this when your hands are "independent."

When you are able to vary the rhythm of rising trot, you can use this skill for other purposes. "Sit-sit-up" is a useful compromise between sitting and rising trot and is particularly helpful for calming nervous horses or familiarizing inexperienced ones with sitting trot. "Sit-up-up" is a good compromise between sitting trot and forward seat and comes in handy when warming up and relaxing horses with a tense and sensitive back.**

There is another exercise that improves the mobility of your pelvis. You can include it in all types of rising trot. Every time you rise (no matter which "sit-up rhythm" you have chosen), slide one of your hips further forward than the other (see bottom photo, p. 89). This movement might look a little exaggerated, but it is the "rough cut" of what will eventually become a *subtle* pelvic movement: Every rider needs to influence the horse's movement through her own.

Follow the horse's movements

All the exercises described in this chapter can help to improve the mobility of your pelvis, hip joints and spine. If you concentrate on your own body and at the same time combine it with the feeling you are getting from the horse's back, you will be better able to follow the horse's movement and influence it. ■

*Your back benefits from every improvement in balance.

**You will only be able to know how to effortlessly change between rising trot, sitting trot, and forward seat without interfering with the rhythm of your horse when you are able to feel the regularity of the beats of the trot.

Practice Strengthens the Back—Go Easy on It to Protect It

Mobility of your pelvis, hip joints, and spine is the key to developing a relaxed, upright dressage seat.

Mobility test: How far forward can you move your hip?

2.4 Letting Go, Feeling, and Going with the Flow of the Horse's Movements

2.5 Improve Flexibility, Stability, and Dexterity

Rotating the spine increases stability

Working your muscles while they are in the "longest" position (known as *eccentric contraction*) is very tiring, which is why it is so difficult to maintain an upright posture. In the section prior, you learned ways to increase your mobility and suppleness in order to be able to follow the horse's movement. This section will offer exercises to build up the necessary stability in order to control the horse with your seat. Rotation of the spine is the key to stabilizing upright posture without become stiff. When riding turns, your upper body needs to perform a specific turn—a "spiral seat." The spiral seat consists of an opposing rotation of the pelvis and the trunk. To do this, your spine needs to freely be able to move in all directions—forward, backward, and sideways.

The greatest challenge on horseback is being able to coordinate the different functions of the pelvis, trunk and shoulder girdle: The pelvis follows the horse, the trunk, provides stability and the shoulder girdle adjusts balance on straight and curved lines.

In walk, start practicing the following exercises that will increase *mobility* of the trunk and shoulder girdle, also improve *coordination* of the pelvis and shoulder girdle. Some of the exercises can later be done in trot and canter.

Try the exercises on the longe line first. You can do them on your horse unassisted if he is calm, dependable and obedient, but it might be necessary to slightly modify them for safety. For instance, should you need to take both hands off the reins, make a knot in them so they cannot slip up the horse's neck and slide over his head. In an unexpected situation you can just grab the knot immediately to gain control.

Diagonal patting

Praising in the form of patting a horse on the neck is a beloved ritual after he has successfully fulfilled a task. According to classical riding principles, you should pat your horse *diagonally*, that is, take both reins in one hand and use your other to pat your horse on the *opposite* side of his neck. This rule is based on the facts about the stability of the spine when it's rotated: You will sit in a much more balanced and safe manner than when patting your horse on the *same* side of his neck (see photos on p. 91).

This diagonal way of patting a horse is the basis for an exercise that turns every act of praise into a functional task that targets your *thoracic* spine. Since your spine needs to move in all three directions, this exercise can also be used to test its mobility and provide you with valuable information. Comparing sides, you will quickly find out to which side you turn to more easily.

During patting, your upper body may lean forward just a little bit, but your seat bones still need good contact with the saddle; your legs must hang down in a relaxed manner. If you are practicing on the longe line without reins, place one hand on the pommel without supporting yourself. Keeping your hand in place this way helps to direct the movement into your thoracic spine.

Practice Strengthens the Back—Go Easy on It to Protect It

thoracic spine. It is not important how far you can turn your body but to feel that you made all the upper spinal vertebrae take part in the motion. In this way, this seemingly simple exercise contributes to improving body awareness and body control, both of them prerequisites for a back-friendly riding style.

During the rotation and while you are bending and stretching, also focus on your *cervical* spine. Start with your head and move it (and your chin) in the direction of your armpit.

If you were not able to tell before, this exercise should definitely show you which side you prefer to pat your horse, that is, the side you can turn better toward and like to turn to most. Shortened muscles in your upper body, which cause one-sidedness when rotating, either end or originate in your head, so you can easily notice the difference.

Patting is a three-dimensional movement.

By stretching the back of your neck you help to remove unwanted tension there so you can carry your head more "freely" afterward.

When riding off the longe line, you need to hold the reins in one hand, maintaining a steady yet light contact with the horse's mouth as your "spiral seat" turns to allow you pat the horse. This movement builds up positive tension in your trunk and shoulder girdle.

By patting your horse further up his neck and by varying the pressure and direction of the patting movement, you can influence the rotation of your

2.5 Improve Flexibility, Stability, and Dexterity

Rider & Horse Back to Back

Turning toward the horse's rear end

If asked to turn around to face your horse's hind end, you would automatically choose the side you prefer to turn toward. It is most likely the side you prefer in everyday life when something unexpectedly draws your attention from behind.

Muscle memory (see p. 48) works highly dependably even if you are not aware of it. If your body has the choice between two opposite directions of movement, it will always choose the side to which it is able to turn most easily, quickly and smoothly. This is one of the reasons why you intuitively use your body's strengths while you avoid "confronting"—and working on—its weaknesses.*

In order to evaluate and improve your ability to turn backward, place one hand on the pommel to support yourself and let the other glide along your horse's croup in the direction of his tail (see photo on this page). Turning should not change the position of your lower legs. Keeping one hand in place secures the back and intensifies the rotation of your upper thoracic spine.

Beware! This movement may surprise your horse, so take your time and make sure he tolerates being touched in this unusual place. If you are sitting on a young, ticklish or nervous horse, keep your hand some inches above his croup.

Stretching and turning combined

The ability to stretch and turn at the same time is required when riding turns, corners, small and large circles, and lateral movements. The following combined exercise will prepare you for this complex motion: Place one hand on the cantle and the other on the pommel or the opposite shoulder of your horse, depending on your arm length (see photo on p. 93).

Your starting position for this exercise is a slightly slumped posture with a rounded back. After some steps in this slouched position, push yourself up with your hands and stretch and turn to one side at the same time. Remain in this stretched and turned position breathing in and out a couple of times before sinking back into the starting position. Your arms support your body in this exercise and are stabilizing your shoulder girdle. This stability allows the trunk underneath to be flexible and mobile. It is able to move more freely.

*Symmetry of movement and balance can only be achieved when you improve your awareness as you work through the systems of learning presented in this book.

Turning round as far as possible.

Practice Strengthens the Back—Go Easy on It to Protect It

Directly after this exercise, it is very useful to ride turns, serpentines, or the Slalom (see p. 161) while keeping your eyes closed, if possible. Every time you change direction, imagine the exercise just explained where you "grow" your upper body as you rotate it. You'll be astonished to see how the horse will react to the slightest of your body movements.*

Rotating the upper body helps establish an upright posture.

The independence of the pelvis and shoulder girdle

Riding requires the highest standard of coordination. Its greatest challenge is to build up *different* degrees of muscle tone in the individual body segments and to be able to move these segments independently and in a controlled manner. All coordination is based on you following the rhythm of the horse's movement—which must become your rhythm, too—as you apply aids.

Your pelvis is supposed to adapt to the horse's back in all three directions and interfere with the horse as little as possible. Only after this foundation has been established will you be able to use the mobility and weight shift of your pelvis and weight to influence your horse and apply aids. To summarize: Your upper body needs to be upright and stable as well as flexible and mobile. These criteria must be fulfilled before you can use your hands "independently"—that is, not need them for balance or stability. All of this is possible only when you can build up positive, dynamic body tension.

It is easy for your whole body to move—whether stretching or bending, tense or relaxed—however, the challenge in riding is that you need your body parts to act differently from one another. You need the trunk to be upright and stable while at the same time you need to be relaxed and allow movement and mobility into your pelvis. You need to activate and control two *opposing* movement patterns. When you can master this you will have obtained an important skill that contributes to being able to apply light but effective aids to the horse. The exercises that follow are to improve "feeling," control and coordination between *mobile* and *stable* areas of your body.

Imagine you are a juggler

To be able to hold your hands "still," which is to say, maintain an *elastic contact* to the horse's mouth, requires specific steps and is part of a learning process. Seemingly still and motionless hands actually must move in the slightest degree in order to maintain even contact. The principle of progressing from "large" to more refined movement applies once again: Moving your hands and arms in rhythm with the horse's movement is good preparation for establishing soft and consistent rein contact later.

At the same time, moving your arms and legs automatically leads you to a better upright posture and helps to stabilize the core. Mini biking produces this effect (see p. 142), while juggling is very useful, too).

*The combination of stretching and turning your spine is a very good way to improve the application of your seat aid.

2.5 Improve Flexibility, Stability, and Dexterity

Rider & Horse *Back to Back*

Imagine you are carrying balls in your hands (palms up) and start to play with them (see photos below). Toss and catch the invisible balls according to the rhythm of your horse's movement. Even though you can do this exercise in all gaits, trot with its two-beat rhythm is especially well-suited. You can vary the pace of your juggling motion by moving your hands at every beat or at every other.

Combine the motion of your hands with upper-body balancing exercises. For example, "juggle the balls" with both hands next to the horse's *inside* shoulder, and then high up while turning a little to the *outside*. It's best to work in diagonal patterns so you cover all directions.

A variation of this exercise is to continue the juggling movement as you ride transitions between rising and sitting trot. You want to be able to do this effortlessly without interfering with the horse's flow of movement. Just as important is juggling between gaits. Establishing the new rhythm together with the horse enables your body to stay balanced during all transitions without using your hands (as many riders do momentarily, especially during the downward transitions). *

* Independent hands—a major stepping stone in riding—cannot be accomplished by trying to keep the hands still at all times. You need to keep moving them in rhythm with the horse's movement.

The game of mobile and stable body parts

To be able to create *mobility*, you need *stability* in other parts of the body. The ability to change one from the other is the basis of coordination (you use it when walking: One leg moves while the other provides stability. The following exercises play with this ability to switch and teach you to gain more control of your body without becoming tense and stiff.

Once you have mastered juggling on the horse, you can begin playing around with the differences between mobile and stable body parts—preferably in sitting trot. By concentrating on the areas of your body that are either mobile or stable, you can specifically influence their function. During juggling, for example, your hands move while your upper body remains still.

You can reverse these movements. Keep your hands still while your upper body moves around: Start by switching between sitting straight or (moderately) slumped. What you are doing is straightening or bending your thoracic spine. This exercise is best done rhythmically and counting the number of trot steps in between bending and straightening.

Afterward, you can try to mobilize specific areas of your body while keeping the neighboring parts

Starting in a middle position, pretend to juggle in all different directions.

stable: Shoulder girdle, pelvis, legs, and head can be moved independently from the rest of the body. All the while, it is very important to always return to the basic dressage posture or middle position with an upright pelvis and upper body. This helps you better feel and control the interplay between mobility and stability.

Mobility of shoulder girdle, neck, and head

When practicing new motion, it is important to always control the movement of your head at the same time. Uncoordinated "compensating" movements of the head put an additional strain on your back. If you are able to move your head effortlessly and freely, it proves you have developed sufficient stability in your spine.

If you tense up the muscles in your neck and stiffen your chin, you are instinctively trying to summon the strength to keep your upper body in an upright position—strength you are lacking and hoping to gain from by building up positive tension somewhere else. Lifting your chin just a little without overstretching it may be helpful. In addition, moving your jaw can loosen up negative tension in sub-occipital joints. Pretending to chew gum can lead to astonishing results as it relaxes a chain of muscles reaching from your neck all the way to your hands. In this way, your chewing can actually encourage your horse to "chew" as well.

Since the shoulder girdle has muscular connections to the rib cage and the neck, specific movements with your shoulder blades will automatically affect the cervical spine. To release shoulder tension, it seldom helps to simply tell yourself to relax so try an "opposite" method: Tense up your shoulders even more, then "actively" relax them. You will find your shoulders become more comfortable this way than if you had tried to relax them without "tensing" them first.

Lift your shoulders all the way to your ears, and let them drop—first together then alternate. This teaches you to become aware of how to relax your shoulder girdle. Remember this feeling every time you encounter difficulty in following your horse's movement: In sitting trot or canter, for example, relaxed shoulders can support and lessen the load on your hands, which get tensed up every time one of the horse's movements asks too much of them. (It's at this point, that the infamous vicious cycle of not being able to follow the horse's motion takes hold: You stiffen up, which prevents your horse from relaxing at the same time.)

In order to find out how flexible your shoulder girdle is, rotate your shoulders forward and backward both at the same time or alternate them. You will quickly notice which direction of movement is best suited for you to improve relaxation and an upright position. Similar to most of the other exercises you have done so far, rotate your shoulder in sync with the horse's rhythm so that you are able to apply the movement later on when you need it to improve the way you apply aids.

Turning your shoulder girdle and pelvis in opposite directions

Being able to freely move your shoulder girdle directly influences the transitional area between the cervical and the thoracic spine and, thus, all the blood vessels around it. Unilaterally tensed-up shoulders decrease blood flow and thus, their efficiency. Other parts of your back have to step in and take over, and this quickly becomes too much for the back to handle. If your horse is supporting himself on one rein and pulls on it, you need to do specific movements to relax your respective shoulder—in addition, of course, to retraining your horse. It is a general fact that horses using your arms as a "fifth leg" by leaning on the reins put a great degree of additional strain on your back.

Exercises that require you to specifically move your shoulder girdle and/or head independently from your pelvis are the most difficult to coordinate. Since all movements start in your head,

Rider & Horse Back to Back

Turning head and shoulder girdle at the same time.

Turning the chest while facing straight ahead.

Turning the head while the chest is facing straight ahead.

the direction the head, neck, and shoulder girdle are pointing to dominates the direction your entire body is going to move in. Once you are able to have your pelvis and legs constantly follow your horse's motion while varying the movement of your head and shoulders, you are fulfilling the prerequisites for applying aids correctly.

Turning your chest but keeping your head facing straight ahead is possible only to a small degree; your head will reflexively try to follow your trunk—a little bit. Nevertheless, attempting to keep your head and eyes pointing straight ahead is a very difficult exercise in itself.

It is not a coincidence that this series of exercises ends by underlining the importance of controlling the movement of your head, and that Part 3 continues with advice on how to make working with your horse friendlier to your back. The position of your head controls all of your movement—an effect that you can make use of in many ways: facing the direction you plan to go when turning your horse in order to prepare for the rotation of your upper body, or looking over your horse's outside ear—a classic solution to collapsing in the hip.

When practicing the preceding exercises, your goal should be to get to know your body a little better and to treat it in a more conscious way. In this manner, the exercises will be helpful and successful. You have to constantly check to be sure the exercises you are doing still work for you and if not, you need to discover new, more effective ones. They serve as tools to specifically improve suppleness, mobility, balance, and coordination and, as a consequence, your riding style—while also meeting all the needs of your back.

Practice Strengthens the Back—Go Easy on It to Protect It too

The most important step toward a back-friendly riding style is to improve body awareness and to self-critically admit that you as a rider are part of all the problems you have when riding your horse. Finding the best solution to your problems is possible only if you start improving the part you play in them. During advanced levels of training and in critical situations especially, you need to learn to always focus part of your perception and awareness on your own body. Your back will be taken care of "automatically" once you sharpen your focus and improve your body awareness.*

*A training concept that focuses only on acquiring new skills (for example, the demands of competitive riding) does not take into account the needs of the rider's back at all.

Being able to ride on a straight line requires mobility and coordination of the rider's body.

2.5 Improve Flexibility, Stability, and Dexterity

3 Putting Riding Theory into Practice—The Back-Friendly Way

3.1 Training without Overstraining

Recognize your own limits

"Stop when things are going well." Oft quoted, this German saying is particularly annoying to young riders (and those who feel young)—even though there is a lot of truth to it!

Back muscles are one of the muscle groups that is least present in people's minds, as described in "Awareness and Motion" (see p. 25). Many of the muscles in this area are very short, sometimes less than half an inch. The conclusion: One muscle by itself does not have a lot of strength because strength is produced by all muscles as a whole. All muscles—working together in a chain—make your back strong and stable. Since riding requires your entire body and all muscles to work as a team, exhaustion does not show as much in your muscles as when, for example, riding a bike where your thighs start burning when you go up a hill.

When riders are getting tired, their coordination will slow down first before they start experiencing slight negative tension in their muscles. Every incident of tension hides a weakness. If you (or your horse) suddenly experience a loss of "suppleness" and relaxation, the deep muscles of your back are probably exhausted. At this point, you really need to take a break or start on a different kind of exercise in order to prevent damage to your back.

If your intention is to take good care of both your and your horse's back, you need to focus your attention on how loose and relaxed you are when sitting and moving. If you know what your basic level of relaxation feels like, you will be able to quickly recognize when your back is getting tired and, thus, prevent overstraining and subsequent injury.

This rider does not have enough power and strength to maintain the stability of her muscles—it's time to take a break!

It may sound contradictory but *relaxation* requires muscles to *work*—in a very refined and coordinated interaction—and you cannot simply try harder to force them as you might when summoning all your strength for a dash to the finish line. When your and your horse's muscles, which have been tense for some time, suddenly relax, you should not continue much longer. Sore muscles will be the result, which, of course, will only cause them to tense up all over again!*

"Below-the-limit" training— and with variety

When training, you should always work *below your limit*, that is, do not cross the line of fatigue but stay right below it. Either practice a simpler exercise for longer, or a more demanding one in shorter intervals.

This becomes particularly apparent during trot work: You can keep up rising trot for a long time while a relaxed sitting trot may only be possible for a few steps.

*Correct suppleness is the key to a back-friendly style of riding.

Rider & Horse Back to Back

Noticing the first signs of exhaustion is very important even though stopping right then and there is not very satisfying. Therefore, you need to learn how to "un-tire" tired muscles, that is, make them able to perform again. In order to do this, you need good body awareness. Often a muscle gets tired simply because it lacks oxygen. By slightly varying the exercise, you give the muscle the opportunity to fill up with oxygen and be able to cope with additional tasks. The level of training defines whether rhythmic movements, subtle turning of your upper body, walk phases, short periods of rising trot, or letting the horse go long-and-low is the right way to give muscles a break.*

The following exercises are included to encourage you to better subdivide your training sessions. These are not meant to be compulsory but are simply offered to give you ideas and possibilities for structuring your training sessions.

The training of horse and rider requires a mixture of simple and difficult exercises plus allowing the horse to stretch downward regularly during collected work and giving him the opportunity to turn collection into forward motion to prevent straining his muscles.

Suppleness is a general indication that you have done the right amount of training in a session—as is the way both horse and rider feel directly after it, the following day. Extremely sore muscles are a clear sign of too much work. In order for a session to be successful, you need to reach the point where you stop just "below" the sore-muscles stage: The next time you go riding, many exercises will feel a lot easier.

The latter applies to your horse, too: It will be much easier for you to adapt his training when you learn how to recognize his reactions during, directly after, and a day after a training session. Effective training may leave both of you very tired at times, but the day after, you and your horse should be looking forward to working again instead of licking your wounds!**

Since every training session should always start at the beginning and proceed up the schooling principles of the Training Scale to the level where the horse is currently working, many trainers are tempted to wait and ask for difficult exercises toward the end of each session. The problem with this method is that frequently horse and rider are not fresh enough to absorb new work. And, even though some trainers do put a lot of thought into the way they increase training challenges, they often lack a basic understanding of *recovery*. Otherwise, you wouldn't witness even world class professionals—right after they have completed a very demanding test or jumping course—handing their horse over to a groom, who then leads him straight into his stall after just a few minutes of walking. Physiologically, this cool-down phase is just as important as the warm up and the ride itself—for muscles of both horse and rider.

Regular periods of stretching prevent your muscles from becoming overstrained, which happens when you work muscles the same way all the time.

Tired muscles do not necessarily mean you have to end a training session—they might just need a different exercise!

**Dividing training sessions into short, varied segments is the most back-friendly way of riding.

Putting Riding Theory into Practice—The Back-Friendly Way

If you want to build up specific muscle groups, the focus of your training needs to be entirely different. Short, intense bouts of training combined with long, active periods of recovery can work wonders for muscles. If you want to do the same for your horse, it makes sense for an experienced rider or trainer to do the initial harder work, and hand the horse over to you for the active period of recovery. You will ride similar exercises as the trainer but at a lower—thus easier—level so the horse's muscles keep working in the same coordination patterns but with less intensity and less chance of strain.

In the same way that a marathon runner does not run an entire marathon during training, you should not push yourself or your horse to the limit of physical fitness every day. A training routine that is diverse and interesting and includes specific short, difficult intervals should be the basis for good, injury-free riding.

When this training system is followed, you can run a marathon without doing harm to your body and when riding, deliver a peak performance without causing injury to yourself or your horse.

In order to make sure that both you and the horse stay in good health, it is very important to develop a feeling for how much, how often, and how high you should jump the horse during training sessions, as well as the degree of collection you can ask for.

Horses trained with their upper level of ability in mind are always willing to work for you and go the extra mile when you really need them to, so work slightly below the limit and focus more on stamina. During competition, you will then be able to mobilize his reserves—and yours—without overstraining yourself or exploiting your horse's trust.*

*Training below the limit will keep you both healthy and the horse willing to perform.

"Thanks, partner!" The horse's willingness to give his very best requires trust.

3.1 Training without Overstraining

Recovery phase for muscles

Physical education guidelines for people suggest that you know the exact method and length of time that your muscles need to recover in an exercise session. In many athletic disciplines, the recovery phase is part of the daily routine and goes without saying: a relaxed jog, and stretching. Many riders, trainers, and instructors do not take into account that the recovery phase should sometimes take even longer than the actual work phase. Therefore, it is not enough to just let your horse trot one lap on a loose rein to stretch out: After doing difficult exercises, you need to move on to easier ones to allow your horse to slowly come down. Give him enough time to really calm down so he goes back into his stall with his muscles properly relaxed and cooled down.

It is no surprise that modern scientific research (at the College of Physical Education in Cologne, Germany, for example) has come to the conclusion that the best thing to do after asking your horse to work hard during phases of collection is to allow him to canter at a swift pace while you assume a forward seat. The same exercise should apply to the day after a strenuous competition: Your horse should not simply spend it in his stall, on the horse walker, or in the pasture.

Many riders also have habits that irritate their own back muscles—often with lasting effect: dismounting immediately after you have just been working really hard so you can go and grab a coffee or beer, or just standing around in a cold arena with your damp shirt sticking to your back.

Scientific research has shown that the way your muscles recover depends on the level of work you have just concluded, among others. After *light* work, muscles best recover *passively*, that is, by simply resting. But when a workout has been more *demanding*, muscles recover quicker and better if they do *active* similar work but at a lower intensity level. This way, they receive enough oxygen in order to "un-tire."

Riding, in particular, offers numerous possibilities to loosen up the muscles in your back after intense workouts. Many of the exercises described in the preceding chapter, the clock exercise in rising trot, for example (p. 85), are a particularly good way to relax your lower back and increase blood flow to this area so you will dismount in a relaxed way.

The way muscles recover depends on the intensity of the workout:

- Light work—passive recovery
- Hard work—active recovery

Moving the pelvis sideways helps to loosen up the lower back.

3.2 The Training Scale: Its Connection to the Rider's Back

The principles of classical riding

The ideal of the rider's seat, that is, her posture, is based on the knowledge and experience of generations of horse professionals. It is amazing to see how every little detail of a correct seat—for example, the way the rider's thumbs build a "roof" on top of her fist and how she is supposed to put more pressure on the inside of the stirrup—are perfectly suited to fit the human anatomy as long as the correctly trained horse contributes his share to make it work.

The best strategy for back-friendly riding is to stick with the principles of classical riding as outlined in the Training Scale. Training mistakes can have very negative effects on the health of horse and rider. But even with the best of intentions, you cannot avoid making mistakes. Perfect moments of harmony are very rare and trying to hold onto them is not possible, so you have to work toward them again and again. You have done it once, so you can do it another time!

Riding in harmony will help you find these "perfect moments"—harmony of movement between rider and horse is the best way to ensure the riding you do is back-friendly. Follow the classical principles in the six levels of the Training Scale—Rhythm, Suppleness and Relaxation, Contact, Impulsion, Straightness, Collection—to make good choices for your own body.*

When training, you are dealing with two living beings and their individual strengths and weaknesses, and these define which path is possible for both to follow. Again and again, you need to take a little detour on the way to your goal—even when strictly adhering to classical principles. There is one principle that must never be questioned or changed: horse and rider as a relaxed, satisfied, harmonious entity, regardless of equestrian discipline or personal goal. The steps that lead to this goal cannot fit every rider and horse, so sometimes, it is best to vary an approach according to your ability.

An experienced rider could, for example, bring a horse back into a collected frame by using a quick, timely half-halt, but an inexperienced rider would not have the strength or coordination skills to deal with this kind of situation. A beginner trying anyway would probably have two negative results: overstraining her own back and causing the horse to resist. Inexperienced riders need different, individual solutions, which probably take longer, but will take them to their goal nonetheless: longer periods of rising trot, different exercises for short periods of time, lots of transitions.**

Training in a back-friendly manner

Every single riding lesson and every situation you find yourself in when you ride requires you to make a great number of decisions, which can be more—or less—gentle on your back. Choosing a back-friendly alternative might take a little more time, but you do not need to lose focus of your goal or switch to a less challenging discipline of riding.

Fear of pain tends to cause a "delicate" back (one that is prone to problems) to "freeze" and block all movement. This kind of fear can only be resolved by gaining trust: A rider who suffers—or has suffered—from back pain needs to gain some back-friendly, positive experience. Lessons on the longe line, and specific exercises for the back will help in this kind of situation (see this book's companion DVD: "Rider & Horse—Back to Back" available from Trafalgar Square Books, www.horseandriderbooks.com). Choosing the right horse also contributes to building trust.

In order to create a back-friendly training program, you need to know which situations put the most strain on the back and which are "toxic," so to speak, to this sensitive area. The entire Training

*The Training Scale is gentle to the back when correctly understood and put into practice.

**Most important for successful training is to correctly evaluate your riding skills and, based on this, choose the way that best suits you to reach your goal.

Rider & Horse Back to Back

Scale can be used as a guideline to build your own individual program. Harmony in movement as required by the Training Scale is created when horse and rider together are able to balance their movement in a way that makes them look efficient and effortless. A good rider never shows how exhausting riding can be! The effects from the horse's loss of balance, however, always show up in the "stressed" back of the rider.

When a horse is unbalanced, you need to look at his body first in order to find the cause of the problem, whether it's from poor conformation or health issues. The typical signs—tensed-up, crooked neck; a tail that is swishing, tucked in, or held more to one side—are just mere attempts at compensating for a lack of balance. Unbalanced horses are responsible for causing repeated "impacts"—both major and minor—on the rider's back.

These horses often use one rein to support themselves, with their outside shoulder falling out. In canter, this lack of balance causes the horse's back to throw the rider back and forth in the saddle, making it nearly impossible to smoothly follow his motion. Rider loss of balance, in turn, can lead to fear—then neither horse nor rider are able to move in a supple or relaxed manner.*

Mistakes that have been made during the horse's schooling will negatively influence your back. The close connection between training your horse correctly and being able to ride in a back-friendly manner needs to always be on your mind.

■ Rhythm

Horses that do not move in a steady rhythm are "poisonous" to your back! Such a horse will always cause you to lose your balance, which puts stress on your back. You will not be able to relax and your muscles will tense up.

Riders, who have a very sensitive back, can sometimes detect the beginning of a lameness based on the slightest irregularity of their horse's rhythm—even before a trainer or veterinarian notices it from the ground. They can feel the hesitation in the horse when he puts weight on that leg, and can sense the change from positive to negative muscle tension.**

■ Suppleness and relaxation

The basic level of muscle tension—whether positive or negative—that the horse is carrying is transmitted to his rider, and vice versa. When the horse does not relax his back muscles, you will not get the chance to sit and follow his movement.

*Good balance in all movements makes you and your horse feel secure, which paves the way for true suppleness.

**Horses that move in a steady rhythm are able to balance themselves and their riders so both can reach an adequate level of suppleness.

A loss of balance leads to a great amount of stress—in both horse and rider.

When in balance, the same turn can be ridden harmoniously.

Putting Riding Theory into Practice—The Back-Friendly Way

Every single body has its own individual basic level of muscle tension. In riding theory, it is often called *positive* body tension. It needs to be adjusted to specific situations: In walk it has to be lower than in collected trot. Horses also have this kind of basic body tension, which must come in combination with suppleness—even when the horse has reached the highest degree of collection and needs a great amount of strength, for example, as he does in passage.

If you look at horse and rider as a unit, you are seeing two bodies with their individual basic body tension, that have been stacked on each other and are supposed to rhythmically move together as one. Physically speaking, their rhythms are adjusting to each other and tension is being exchanged.

This phenomenon explains why riding can, at the same time, relax tense muscles while strengthening or activating the weaker ones. Suppleness equals *ergonomics in motion* and is, therefore, an important building block for the foundation that allows horse and rider to move in a back-friendly manner.*

A riding student is influenced more by the horse, while an experienced trainer will try to have a stronger influence on the horse. Ideally, horse and rider are supposed to equally give and take, in which case, mutual movement will not be tiring at all. If, for every single step your horse takes, you had to produce all necessary positive tension all by yourself, riding would not be back-friendly in the long run.

When the levels of basic body tension of horse and rider do not fit together well, problems inevitably occur. In the same way a stiff rider negatively influences the horse's motion, a horse with stiff back muscles will have extremely negative effects on his rider. And when your level of basic tension is too low, a sudden stiff movement by the horse can hurt your back.**

*Horse and rider are always mutually influencing each other's suppleness.

**One of the most important goals of the warm-up phase is to achieve mutual positive body tension. Only when this happens can you continue with the training session and achieve your goals in a back-friendly way.

Suppleness is the foundation for the perfect balance you need in order to attain collection.

3.2 The Training Scale: Its Connection to the Rider's Back

Rider & Horse Back to Back

Horses that do not look for the contact do not help you improve your upright posture. And, horses that lean on the reins can cause a lot of damage to your back.

■ Contact

Soft and constant rein contact is a hallmark of good and sensitive riding. However, it is impossible to clearly define how strong good contact needs to be. Both extremes—too little or too much weight in your hands—can harm your back.*

Instructors often tell you that you may only exert as much pressure on the horse's mouth as you have just produced by using your forward-driving leg aids. This often leads to riders not understanding that they *cannot* drive forward and hold back at the exact same time. (You get nowhere by stepping on the gas and the brake simultaneously!) There should always be interplay in forward-driving and restricting aids that allows for a very short interval of time between each aid.

Your hands can only resist to the degree your back has the stability to handle it. Otherwise, you will start using your back as a lever, leaning back to ensure a strong enough "pull" with the hands—especially in downward transitions. To make matters worse, the increase in strength needed affects mostly your unstable "weak" spots, which then become stiff, tight, and sore. Areas most often affected are the lower back and the area between your shoulder girdle and neck.

The correct interplay between the aids is not supposed to ask too much of any part of your body. You have to consistently make yourself aware of the connection between rein contact, weight aids, and leg aids. Consistent contact is defined by the horse's willingness to find and maintain his balance in between all the aids.**

Experienced riders who take up riding again after a long hiatus often overestimate their ability. They don't realize they need their deep short muscles to work in a highly coordinated manner. They don't necessarily lose this coordination but they cannot use them strongly or long enough. Since these muscles don't complain about "overuse" but simply lose efficiency, the riders unknowingly compensate by using their superficial stronger muscles in a way that puts all sorts of stress on the back. These riders' feeling for the motion, ingrained in muscle memory, still exists but their back's ability to stabilize itself needs to be built up again slowly. At this stage, less is more: Every attempt to regain former skills by using more strength or

You can only exert as much pressure with your lower legs as your abdominal muscles are able to counterbalance. You can only resist with your hands to the degree that your back can remain stable.

This horse is leaning on the rider's hands, which puts more strain on her back.

Light, correct contact allows her to sit more upright, with less stress on her back.

trying to force their horse to yield in the poll will strain their back. Afterward, it is often the case that these riders suffer from back pain or even slipped discs. Taking up riding after a long period of time always requires patience and a good deal of consideration for the back.

■ Impulsion

A horse without impulsion causes strain on your joints because he is not "inviting" your back to "swing" with his in a supple manner. He is not rounding his back so it cannot "come up" to meet your weight through the pelvis and seat bones when in motion, thus he is not asking you to become part of his movement. If you understand impulsion as the activity of the hindquarters, a horse without impulsion is both lazy and lacking "throughness" by not accepting your forward-driving aids. Constantly having to push your horse forward is very exhausting for your back.*

■ Straightness

A horse that is constantly crooked will pass this lack of straightness onto you. And, he will be uncomfortable to ride. When you always have to compensate for your horse's lack of straightness, you become exhausted and the muscles in your back work unevenly. Vice versa: A crooked rider will also influence the horse and disturb his balance.

If you yourself are tense with poor posture (stiff and crooked) when you get on your horse, take the time to find your balance before you actively ask the horse for a movement, or you will end up with a stiff and crooked horse. Even though the back-friendly alternative requires more time, it is a guarantee for success: You need to use your horse's movement to find your balance and loosen up at the same time he does before you can begin the actual training phase. Only then can you focus on improving your straightness—and the horse's, too.**

*Without forward movement, impulsion is impossible; without impulsion, dynamic movement is impossible; and without dynamic movement, stability within movement is impossible!

**The warm-up phase should concentrate on rhythm and balance, and suppleness as outlined in the classical Training Scale. Without the achievement of these qualities first it is not possible to attain any level of advanced training. Back-friendly riding requires you and your horse to warm up together (and successfully so).

A powerhouse of impulsion!

Rider & Horse Back to Back

Less obvious, but just as wrong, is when the horse slows down as you take up the reins. This leads the horse's hindquarters—his engine—to slow down activity and causes his back muscles to work less. The destructive nature of it all is that you are conditioning yourself and your horse to slow down every time you take up or shorten the reins—right before a transition or any other movement. This is a habit that's really hard to break! It takes a lot more strength to ride a horse with "inactive" hindquarters and puts unnecessary strain on the backs of both of you. In addition, rhythm is often disrupted, which in turn affects your and your horse's balance and the interplay between deep back and abdominal muscles (see photo on p. 121).

There are horses that do not stay straight when you take up the reins but dodge sideways immediately. Some fall out with their shoulders, some with their haunches, others even fall in with their haunches—all signs of a lack of balance. The horse's neck is his balancing pole so when he feels "disturbed" in this area by your taking up the reins, he will evade laterally with his haunches. This is mostly not the fault of the horse but the rider who is establishing contact in a careless and uneven manner, systematically causing the horse to lose balance.

To change such an automatic behavior is just as difficult a challenge for the rider as it is for the horse. When a horse has been upset by a rider badly taking up the reins one thousand times, it will take a minimum of two thousand *good* contact experiences in order to regain his trust!*

To improve your technique, practice on a friend first. The person assisting you needs to take the bit into their hands. Then try and take up the reins while establishing and maintaining an even contact to the bit. The person should not feel more pressure or pull on either side of the bit.

Of course, sitting on a horse adds several additional factors that need to be taken into consideration: forward motion, the nodding movement horses show in walk, and the contact the horse maintains to your hands. It can be practiced while both of you walk, but it needs both of you to move in a coordinated common rhythm.

While taking up the reins, you need to allow your horse to keep walking on the same straight line, at the same rhythm and pace. In the beginning, it might be easier to practice on a curved line, such as a big circle, in order to make use of the diagonal interplay of the aids. Later on, though, you really need to practice on straight lines, first going large on the outside track of the arena, and afterward further away from the wall and its "supporting" function.

Taking up the reins in a correct manner is like familiarizing your horse with your handwriting. If the first impression conveys sensitivity and softness, it will be easier for your horse to trust your hands in other situations.**

Shortening the reins

Shortening the reins is another important technique, which completely influences harmony in movement between horse and rider. Since adjusting the length of the reins has to be done over and over again—especially before transitions from one gait to another—you should be able to do it automatically. Many less experienced riders do not do these kinds of motions often enough, let alone execute them automatically. For this reason, the following slightly mocking comment has become popular among some instructors and judges: "Shortening the reins is always permitted and usually necessary."

Unfortunately, the technique of shortening the reins correctly is not taught and practiced often enough. Many riders upset their horse's rhythm and balance so much that the transition being prepared fails all the more. Others hardly dare shorten the reins because their horse's mouth is so sensitive that every attempt leads to negative tension, head shaking, or irregularities in rhythm.

*The horse's trust in the rider's hands is lost much faster than it can be built up!

**You will spare your back a lot of strain if you concentrate right from the beginning.

In this photo, the flow of motion of both horse and rider has been disturbed by the rider shortening the reins.

Quite often it's the wrong sort of reins that makes shortening them more difficult so reins should be chosen with care: Pick out a width that fits your fingers and decide whether you prefer a smooth rein or one providing more grip that doesn't allow you to slide your hand as easily. When you have a horse that pulls the reins out of your hands, a rubber layer can be helpful, though if your fingers cannot slide softly when shortening, you may upset the more sensitive animal.

Shortening the reins is a complex movement including several steps: preparation, support, taking one hand off, sliding it into its new position and closing it again (see sidebar on p. 112). During the entire process, your constant contact to the horse's mouth must stay light and your feeling for it, remain. Ideally, the movement of your hands rhythmically unites with the horse's motion thus maintaining rhythm and balance. And all the while, your seat should stay as supple and correct as ever.

Learning how to shorten the reins— step by step

An action this complex can only be learned if taken apart and divided into small steps—especially when you are an adult trying to master this task. The number of steps depends on the individual student. You need to be able to make yourself aware of all the building blocks of a movement in order to be successful at it. Only when you understand and feel confident about the little steps that build the whole movement will you be able to perform this complex task without thinking about it.

First of all, you need to decide which rein you actually want to shorten. When you need to shorten both, always start with the *outside* one. Many riders have a habit of beginning with their strong hand every single time. The horse might be irritated by this habit since he secures his balance with the positive contact on the outside rein.

Another incorrect method—but very commonly seen—is shortening the reins with just one hand by walking your fingers down the rein or even "skipping." In this way, it is impossible to maintain contact with the horse's mouth. If you are using this method, you are seriously interfering with the horse's sensitive mouth, and he will lose his trust in your contact. You should not ignore this incorrect practice as it can be the cause of many (seemingly unrelated) problems.

You must never look down on your hands when adjusting the reins. Looking down has serious negative effects on the balance of both horse and rider—but again, it is a very common and "stubborn" habit that is harmful to the back. For your balance, an upright head with forward focus is essential. Looking down at your hands can interefere with upper body stability, and this results in stress and negative tension in your back (see photo on p. 112).

Rider & Horse Back to Back

Looking down causes you and your horse to lose balance.

In the same way that you have to plan ahead and prepare for a transition, you also need to keep in mind that shortening the reins takes time and distance. Beginners might need an entire long side of the arena until they have shortened their reins; an experienced rider should not take more than one horse length.*

*When in forward motion, it is impossible to shorten your reins "step by step in the horse's rhythm" at a specific point in the arena. You always need to start preparing some distance ahead.

Practice shortening your reins correctly. Doing it on the ground or on a horse standing still can be very helpful in order to learn the technique, but it remains purely theoretical. The actual challenge only presents itself when the horse is in motion.

For the act of shortening the reins not to interfere with the flow of motion, you need to do it in sync with the rhythm of the horse's movement. A good way to prepare for it is to juggle (see p. 93). In the same way you learned how to move your hands rhythmically without losing contact with your horse's mouth, you can work on supporting the reins with one hand and sliding your other along the rein you want to shorten in time with the horse's rhythm. Sliding your hand along the reins, in particular, is an important skill you need in order to have sensitive hands.

Taking up and shortening reins— in five steps

(Tracking left, shortening both reins)

- **Counterbalancing support rein**
  Your left hand holds onto the right rein and helps to keep steady contact to your horse's mouth.

- **Ease your grip on the right rein**
  Your right—outside—hand opens up slightly from bottom to top so that thumb and index fingers control the rein. (In these fingers, you have the most sensitivity and control over the movement.) The other fingers remain in their usual position even though they no longer control the rein.

- **Shortening/sliding**
  Let your right hand slide along the rein while applying a little bit of pressure and moving it slightly to the outside. (By applying pressure, you are making sure that you maintain steady feel to the horse's mouth.) You can only shorten the rein as far as your left hand can support it.

- **Closing your hand/second counterbalancing support phase**
  When you have reached the desired length of the right rein, close your right fist once again and support the left rein as described in Step 1. Repeat the previous steps with your left hand.

- **Shortening the reins**
  If it is necessary to shorten the reins a little more, your supporting hand has to take up both reins and does that by holding them in front of the other hand. Your free hand lets go of the rein completely and takes hold of it again when the desired length has been reached.

During some of the steps, your reins will inevitably be of different lengths. Nevertheless, you need to keep offering your horse a steady and even contact.

Putting Riding Theory into Practice—The Back-Friendly Way

Correct technique and a sensitive feel for the horse are both here in perfect combination: taking up the reins of a double bridle in canter.

This exercise shows once again that being able to move rhythmically is one of the basic requirements for riding. If your hands are not following your horse's rhythm while you are shortening the reins, you will inevitably interfere with the regularity of his movement and his balance. Even the slightest irregularity has immediate effects on your balance, which must be compensated with strength—at the expense of your back!*

*A back-friendly riding style requires you to be able to shorten the reins at any time without interfering with your horse.

3.3 Taking Up the Reins—Shortening the Reins

Rider & Horse Back to Back

3.4 Danger to Your Back

Preventing risks

Putting riding into practice requires a vast number of individual decisions, which can be made in a more or less back-friendly way. Keeping classical riding principles in mind, it's best to find back-friendly solutions for specific problems. Taking care of your back does not mean that you have to sacrifice the quality of riding—quite the opposite, in fact.

First of all, however, you need to realistically assess your own ability and skill and the characteristics of your horse, including the way the two of you feel on any given day. If you have a sensitive back, there are certain horses you had better avoid—at least for a while! Many challenges in your and your horse's training, however, can be mastered in ways that are gentle to your back. Some of the known risks can be avoided. Nevertheless, some situations on horseback that are potentially dangerous to sensitive backs cannot be prevented.

High risks for the rider's back

- Horses that lean on the reins.
- Horses with tense back muscles and that lack the natural drive to go forward.
- Horses prone to sudden unpredictable reactions like spooking, bucking, or even rearing.

Leaning on the reins

Every rider experiences moments in which their horse does not carry himself but leans on the reins for support. Even when you are trying to keep your rein contact especially soft, you (and your good intentions) will be facing many tricky situations. If your horse has learned to support himself on the reins, however, and uses them like a "fifth leg," your back will have to deal with serious constant strain.

If a horse leans on the reins, the rider's back will quickly be overstrained.

A few seconds and transitions later, harmony has been restored.

The cause of leaning on the reins is usually the horse's tendency to fall on the forehand and his lack of forward thrust that is not active enough for him to work from behind through his back.

If you increase your efforts of driving him forward, you will simply put more strain on your back while your horse will not necessarily start carrying himself. In this case, a strap attached to the pommel can help you develop the additional upper body stability necessary to deal with this problem.*

*Your entire body needs to be included in driving your horse forward—forward-driving aids are not limited to your lower legs!

Putting Riding Theory into Practice—The Back-Friendly Way

Pulling gently on the strap with a pinkie finger helps straighten your upper body and keeps the horse from pulling you forward. Holding the strap can give you extra support and protect your back should the horse suddenly jerk you forward. Sometimes, in order to increase stability of your upper body, you can build a bridge with the reins by holding the opposite rein as well. Bridging the reins allows you to feel you have support while still carrying your hands independently.

As general advice, you should pay close attention to the *timing* of your aids. When you squeeze your lower legs together and regulate the reins at the same time, you put a lot of strain on your own body while your horse does not understand what you mean. Experience shows that you should not interpret the interplay of the aids as a matter of "everything at once"!

If you want to increase the activity of the haunches and improve self-carriage, you should start by working on your horse's yielding in the poll. For example, you can ride small circles in which you use your legs to ask your horse to bring his legs more forward underneath his body. If your horse's reaction to your leg aids is to lean on the reins even more, you need to try and apply gentle rein aids to flex him in the poll and get him to yield. Every time your horse yields, you need to ask him to reach forward underneath his body with his hind legs. This way, he will learn to react to your leg aids without leaning on the bit.

Only when your aids work together like this, will you be able to drive your horse forward without putting additional strain on your back. At the same time, your horse will improve his self-carriage and balance and allow you to sit more comfortably.*

Another piece of advice that has proven its practical usefulness is the juggling exercise (see p. 93). Especially with horses that lean on one rein more than on the other, this strange-looking technique can work wonders. If you are moving your hands up and down (not back and forth!) while you keep following your horse's rhythm, the reins will glide up and down on the rings of the bit and you can maintain steady and gentle contact with your horse's mouth. Imagine you are moving your hands along an imaginary circle line—the rings of the bit are smaller circles and the reins represent the radius connecting the two.

Inconspicuous but effective—grabbing the strap with the left pinkie.

In this picture, the rider is practicing "juggling" at a halt without upsetting his horse.

This experiment of moving both hands alternately but regularly makes many riders realize that their horse was leaning on the hand they knew was their "stiffer" hand, which demonstrates that it is their stiffness in this hand that is causing the horse to lean on it. While doing this rhythmic juggling movement you can do rising trot, change reins and switch between rising and sitting trot, and at the same time, concentrate on feeling how important it is to have independent arms and hands in order to sit in a relaxed posture.**

*The interplay of the aids does not mean "everything at once" but "everything in the right order," that is, correct timing with the correct intensity.

**If your arms have to use a lot of strength in order to maintain contact, your back will pay the price!

3.4 Danger to Your Back

Rider & Horse Back to Back

Horses with a stiff back

The first and foremost measure when dealing with horses that are stiff in the back and lack the natural urge to go forward is: Do not force yourself to ride sitting trot—at all costs! Sitting trot is possible only when the horse *lets* you sit. In order for this to work out, the backs of both you and your horse need to swing in harmony and as soon as one of the two develops problems, it will inevitably affect the other. Trying to sit on a horse whose back does not move at all often creates a vicious cycle of muscular defense reactions in both horse and rider. Pain and frustration are guaranteed.

This is not to say, however, that you cannot ride such a horse or that sitting trot will forever be impossible. In most horses, trot improves after having cantered. In canter, the horse's pelvis moves differently than in trot: The movement, which in trot is "right/left" becomes diagonal, and this causes the horse's back to flex more in the phase where both his hind legs reach under his body. This motion pattern helps loosen any negative tension so that the back can swing better afterward—even in trot. There is a reason why transitions between trot and canter are among the most important warm-up exercises.

Canter influences the rider in the same way. The rider's pelvis has to follow the horse's "bigger" movement, which means more mobility is required from her hips and lower back. Moving like this warms up her joints for the more refined, coordinated work that is needed in sitting trot, for example. For the most back-friendly way to work on transitions, see discussion beginning on p. 122.

When you look at experienced riders, many of them start sitting trot only after they have cantered—and only when the horse is really relaxed in the back. It is possible to ride almost all exercises in rising trot. Even internationally successful riders do not always sit during collected work: During training, they even ride half-passes and piaffe-passage transitions in rising trot to relieve their horse's back, to improve suppleness and to encourage their horse's back muscles to work better.

When training horses with a stiff back, whether from being ridden too soon or because of an unbalanced rider, it pays not to ride sitting trot at all; for quite a while, even months, you should stick to rising trot. Sometimes you see young, big-moving horses (dressage riders are always looking for such an animal!) producing seemingly spectacular (but "false") front-leg movement in trot. But they have been pushed into it too soon. The result is tension and stiffness—they are too young to be capable of letting their riders sit and follow their

A horse with stiff back muscles does not allow his rider to sit at the trot.

Stretching his topline improves both the horse's movement and the rider's comfort.

movement. It can take a long time for them to develop the necessary strength—and trust—in their rider's weight aids. The reward for these months of rising trot is the moment when these horses actually allow you to sit comfortably. Horses that have been gently trained will thank their rider in their own way: by moving so that you are "sucked into" their motion, at which point even riders with a stiff back can relax!*

Lazy horses

Most "lazy" horses do not lack a good temperament but have stiff back muscles that do not swing. They show no reaction to your forward-driving aids or don't allow consistent rein contact. Correcting a horse that has learned to evade forward-driving aids and contact requires patience, and even a considerable amount of strength. When they are at this stage, lazy horses are extremely hard on your back. You need to find a good training routine and—if necessary—help from a person on the ground or an experienced rider. Only after the horse has begun to go forward and trust you, will you be able to sit more comfortably.

Tense horses use the slightest rider mistake as a reason to stiffen up and slow down again, so it is all the more important that you sit in a balanced manner. If you don't, your attempts to drive the horse forward will slow him instead, and this will put unnecessary strain on both your backs.

The basic rule, which needs to be reiterated here, states: Forward-driving aids do not consist of leg aids alone—weight aids always come first! You can only use your legs to the degree your abdominal muscles can compensate for them by stabilizing your upper body. For example, when you apply too much lateral pressure by pinning a lower leg into the horse's side, your hip joint will shut down and become stiff; your legs will tell the horse "Go!" while your pelvis is saying "Stop!" The effectiveness of your legs as a driving aid is not defined by how much pressure they apply but by their frequency: when you apply them and how well coordinated they are with the rest of your aids. Working rhythmically is once again the key to success: Your horse quickly gets used to constant leg pressure and becomes numb to it.

Unpredictable events

If you suffer from acute back problems, it is important that you do not expose your back to unpredictable situations. As mentioned, the best way to protect your back from injury is to plan ahead by realistically assessing your own ability and the way you and your horse feel on a given day.

Most dangerous are abrupt movements. A young horse that spooks by shying or jumping to the side—or bucks—can injure your back just as seriously as falling off. In extreme cases, the result may be a blockage (where your back gets "stuck" and can't move), muscle injury, or even broken vertebrae. Even though working with animals is always potentially dangerous, the rider with back problems should not get on a horse known for being unpredictable or extremely resistant.

Taking an experienced, safe horse on a trail ride can be a back-friendly alternative to tiring dressage work, but on the other hand, the probability of unpredictable instinctive reactions is a lot higher when you are outside and not "confined" to the arena's border. Forward seat in canter relieves your back—but only at first glance: There may be less pressure on joints and discs, but your muscles have to work even harder. This is true especially when jumping (see p. 63). Moreover, the dynamic motion of the takeoff, suspension, and landing phases make unexpected movement by the horse more likely. Therefore, jumping should not be attempted if you are suffering from acute back problems; it should be reserved for experienced jumpers on experienced horses and limited to moderate levels of difficulty.

If you know your horse well, you are often able to notice the first signs of him being about to spook

*The classical definition of "suppleness" hits the nail on the head: "The rider is able to sit."

Rider & Horse Back to Back

*It is necessary to seek the help of an experienced instructor or good rider when you are trapped in the cycle of fear of pain and negative tension.

or run away. This sort of reactive behavior When you are expecting your horse to buck, your body will automatically build up a protective amount of muscle tension in order to actively deal with the sudden change of movement and avoid getting hurt. Keeping up this kind of preventive tension is very exhausting, however, and almost inevitably leads to negatively tensed and overstrained muscles. When you have to be constantly prepared for your horse to shy hard to the side or whirl around, you will be out of breath much sooner and it is harder for you to keep a relaxed position. A rider with this type of muscle tension passes it onto her horse, and vice versa—the horse back to the rider. This way, the tension keeps rising, which inevitably leads to an "explosion" at some point. "Unwinding" this in time requires a good deal of riding experience.

If you lack the riding skills necessary to solve these problems by making your horse go forward, you should be looking for alternative solutions. Dismounting then longeing or letting the horse run free until most of the tension has disappeared can work wonders. You need to be aware, though, that the whip and longe line act like a long lever: There is nothing back-friendly about a heavy whip and a horse jerking you around at the end of a longe line. If necessary, have someone help you with the longeing. You can hope that after getting on your horse once again, the problems will have gone.

If you are unable to deal with your fear of back pain and, consequently, do not dare to ride forward, you will have a hard time achieving suppleness in your horse and relaxation yourself. Moreover, having to take precautions all the time sends the following signal to your horse: "My rider is not relaxed today so must be afraid!" Quite often this fear of pain not only leads to the rider being tensed up about sudden movement, but also inhibited by ordinary movement, say from a big-moving horse in a trot extension. This concern about back pain can limit your riding in more than one situation.*

A sudden spook is a high risk situation for a rider with a sensitive back.

3.5 Transitions and Half-Halts—Basic Work Presented in a Different Way

Rising trot and transitions

Rising trot is a normal part of every rider's daily training routine. At the same time, it is a rhythmical and dynamic movement that prepares the rider for the more refined dynamic stability of the seat that is needed for sitting trot. Rising trot is often just used in the warm-up phase of a riding session, and consequently not for very long. It should not be this way! On the one hand, correct rising trot is a challenging exercise in itself while, on the other hand, it offers a wide variety of back-friendly riding opportunity for the rider being careful about her back, and fits into even the most advanced training concepts. If you want riding to be gentle on your and your horse's back, it is a good idea to ride transitions to and from the trot in rising trot only.

Transitions require—and improve—coordination between the deep back muscles and the abdominals. To horses, transitions are just as challenging with regard to coordination, balance, and suppleness. This is why they are so extremely important in training. In dressage tests, transitions receive separate scores and are standard exercises in every riding lesson. At the same time, transitions are so diverse and varied that even advanced riders experience new value in them again and again.

Transitions are done *up and forward* (to a faster gait or tempo) as well as *down* (to a slower gait or tempo). Usually, transitioning up is easier. Every transition noticeably changes the movement (and sometimes, balance) of horse and rider, and depending on the situation, either has a positive effect on the rider's back or leads to strain—in some extreme cases, even to injury. When you are able to work on transitions in a back-friendly manner, you will have created the foundation for the entire training of your horse. The back of both you and your horse will be grateful!*

Smooth transitions—in rising trot

The most common transitions are changing from one gait to another. During such a transition, you need to adjust your back to the new gait with its different rhythm and movement. In order to do this, you need to prepare yourself beforehand. Having a picture in your mind, an image of what the new gait will feel like helps you keep your balance during the transition or regain it quickly. Ideally, you will move according to the new rhythm a split second before your horse changes—thus influencing his movement almost invisibly.

In order to transition smoothly, you need to be able to differentiate and change your movement within a gait without disrupting the harmony between you and your horse. In rising trot, it is easier to prepare for this and feel the differences. The constant rhythmic movement requires your hips to be flexible and helps loosen up the muscles of hips and pelvis so rising trot improves your rhythm and balance. When you are equally good at both, you will benefit by being able to ride your horse rhythmically and balanced during rising trot in the warm-up phase.**

One possibility of testing how well you are able to control the movement of your pelvis in rising trot is to vary how high you rise out of the saddle. To practice, exaggerate how high you rise up for some steps before reducing the movement as much as possible. The smallest form of rising trot is "hidden" in sitting trot: Your breeches remain in contact with the saddle while only the pressure of your seat bones varies. You will soon realize that this subtle movement is actually very difficult and requires a lot of coordination and control of all the muscles around the pelvis, abdomen and back.

*Work on smooth transitions: Hesitant, hurried, and unbalanced transitions are harmful to the back of both horse and rider!

**The less you disrupt your horse with your own mistakes, the better and more naturally he will be able to develop the full potential of his movement, which is the foundation of all subsequent work.

Rider & Horse Back to Back

Since the horse is supposed to keep trotting in the same rhythm during all of this, you need to not only control how high you get out of the saddle but also the speed of your pelvic movements. When you rise up higher, your pelvis has to move further, thus, its motion is quicker. When you rise very little, the distance your pelvis moves is less, which requires you to slow it down. Slower motion requires a higher degree of balance.

It is a good idea to practice this exercise rhythmically, for example, for three steps rise up high, for another three, rise normally, and for yet another three, rise very little. The quicker the rhythm, the more difficult it gets—until you change at every trot step. The most important thing is to stick to the rhythm you had in mind without interfering with your horse's regularity and speed. Only when you have mastered this exercise, will you be able to influence your horse's motion in specific ways.

Every time you work on your balance, you also influence your horse's motion—intentionally or unintentionally. If you train your senses to feel this, you are also preparing yourself for making use of weight aids in the best way possible later on. A horse often slows down when, during rising trot, you don't rise as high, so you can initiate and control transitions as well as shorten and lengthen strides by merely using your weight. At the same time, because rising trot requires you to keep moving rhythmically, you prevent a common mistake seen in sitting trot, which is when a rider discontinues "moving forward" with the horse as she attempts to slow down. Your senses will be alerted to how your horse experiences your weight, carries it and reacts to it. With time and experience, you will learn how to control your balance in a way that allows you to use it as a weight aid.*

*Only when you know how to control your own body, will you be able to control your horse!

This exercise is a good way to prepare for sitting trot. It is only a small step from a *minimal* rising trot to riding with constant pressure on your seat bones. You also do not have to completely realign your balance because all your deep muscles are already prepared for the demands that sitting trot and following the horse's movement pose to your back. (For further information with regard to sitting trot, see p. 123.)

The horse's back is usually very "grateful" when you vary the pace by using your balance. Collecting and extending (changing pace within the gait) improve elasticity, suppleness, and back-muscle activity while strengthening the hindquarters at the same time. It is advisable not to ask for the biggest extension or the highest degree of collection right away. Less is more—as is so often the case! It is important that you and your horse develop this kind of balance in a playful manner as it is the foundation for increased work demands: asking for more difficult moves without overstraining your back or the horse's, too.

This is how high you can stand up when learning how to control the full scope of your pelvis' mobility.

Minimizing pelvic movements in rising trot is playing with balance and speed.

Walk-trot transitions

Making a transition up to trot and down to walk challenges your upper body balance. In order not to fall behind the horse's motion when transitioning up, you need your abdominal muscles—and vice versa. When you transition down to walk or when your horse suddenly slows down, your back muscles have to keep your upper body from tipping forward: An inexperienced rider often moves her body a little bit backward during the up transition and tips it forward during the down transition. But, if she is trying to influence the horse with her body, she does the opposite: She leans forward during the up transition, and backward during the down transition. Ideally, she needs to adjust her body so horse and rider move in a common mutual balance.*

There should always be interplay between the aids: To ride a good *forward* up transition, you need to use controlling, restricting aids, too. And a down transition is only good when you are able to *push forward* while slowing down. In this way, well-ridden transitions are ideal training for the coordination between the abdominal and deep back muscles.

Not all transitions turn out smoothly and correctly. If a horse rushes off in the transition to trot, it will upset the rider's balance because her back will not be able to support her. As a reaction, most riders tend to lean backward, which puts additional strain on their lower back. This lack of balance in the upper body forces the rider to use the rein aids too strongly, and this again adds to the stress on her back.

On a horse that starts trotting at a regular pace, balances himself, and waits for you right from the first stride he takes, you will be able to keep your upper body upright. In this position, using the reins puts less strain on your lower back.

If a horse's downward transition is unbalanced and he ends up on the forehand, he will seriously "upset" his own back and his rider's. Suppleness will be lost and, with it, a good-quality walk. This is why it is so important for you as a rider to keep riding forward—to *think forward*—when transitioning down. After all, walk is a forward movement, so it is only logical that you need to apply forward-driving aids. When you apply strong rein aids in order to transition down, you are putting strain on the back of both you and your horse and, in the interplay of aids, the rein aid should not be the strongest, most dominant aid, but used as little as possible. It is better to keep trotting longer until your horse is balanced enough to accept your aids in a way that requires very little rein aid for a down transition.**

For experienced riders without back problems, it makes sense to ride a few strides in sitting trot before and after each transition as the common rule requires. If you are not able to sit flexibly, however, these short bouts of sitting trot might be the source of a lot of problems. Until you are able to smoothly and supply switch between sitting and rising trot (see p. 88) without tensing up or interfering with your horse's rhythm and flow of motion, it is good idea to ride transitions from one gait to another in rising trot.

*Horse and rider play equally important parts in correct transitions.

**If you are riding a well-trained horse, you will even be able to yield the reins during transition to walk!

Horse and rider play equally important parts in correct transitions.

3.5 Transitions and Half-Halts—Basic Work Presented in a Different Way

Rider & Horse Back to Back

*The first canter stride can only be as good as the trot stride sequence that precedes it.

It can be helpful to imagine how children hop or skip when they pretend to be a horse. This is exactly the way the horse's back needs your pelvis to move. It is important to be aware of the fact that the canter actually starts out with the *landing sequence of legs* with just the outside hind leg on the ground. If you hold a picture in your mind of the *suspension phase* (all four legs off the ground) when you are trying to transition to canter, you will not make yourself heavier and sit deeper down in the saddle. Instead, try and get your horse to canter by basically "hopping" up and down on his back. Even though horses can be conditioned to understand this technique as a canter aid, this method is not derived from correct aids nor is it healthy for your back.*

The landing phase of the last trot stride before the canter is particularly important. If you can support the horse in this moment using your pelvis, the weight aids will become a natural part within the interplay of aids. This way, the new motion of the canter will not surprise you and put strain on your back.

**In each canter stride, you must repeat the interplay of aids as if you are asking for the canter transition again.

The horse's outside hind leg strikes the ground first and, thus, determines where you will have to position yourself. It is a relief for the back of both you and your horse if your weight comes down in the saddle at the same time as your horse's hind leg touches down. If you are behind the movement, the horse will feel your weight later together with his front foot landing, so he gets more "pushed" onto his forehand by the rider. As a general rule for the weight aid in the canter, you need to sit down and "land" early enough to be able to support your horse's next stride.**

Following the horse's movement in trot needs the rider's pelvis to swing *forward up* and *forward down* at the same time as it allows lateral mobility when the horse's back changes its rotation from step to step. This combination of a *forward* and *lateral* movement is a small, *diagonal* motion of the pelvis.

In canter, your horse shifts his weight diagonally from the outside hind leg to inside front leg. As a consequence, you also need to shift your weight along this diagonal line.

In trot, the rider's pelvis moves in a quicker basic rhythm in small diagonal directions without shifting weight. In canter, the pelvic movement is slower with a bigger scope and a shift of weight along one diagonal. To use your weight aid in the

The constant change of diagonals in trot requires the rider's pelvis to have quick mobility.

Putting Riding Theory into Practice—The Back-Friendly Way   3

Place your hand on your inside hip to feel where the movement required for a transition to canter is supposed to originate.

transition to canter, slide your inside hip more forward and begin to shift your weight along the diagonal to encourage the horse to strike off into the canter.

In order to learn what it feels like to change the movement of your pelvis in canter, it might be helpful to first concentrate on the lateral motion of your horse's back in trot. Once you can clearly feel this motion and are able to follow it, you can begin to use a change of rhythm (similar to changing diagonals in rising trot) in order to ask your horse to canter. Instead of shifting your weight alternately from side to side, place your weight on the *inside seatbone* for two strides—with its pressure directed at the horse's inside front leg. Your inside hip comes forward carrying more weight, the rhythm changes, and your horse will react by adjusting his sequence of footfalls as he departs into canter. Sliding your inside hip forward in this way (not collapsing it) helps you follow the horse forward without gripping with your inside knee, causing your leg to come up.

Horses that have been ridden by really good, experienced riders need almost no leg aid to transition to canter. When strongly applied, leg aids always have a bad effect on your suppleness, the mobility of the pelvis, and your lower back.

The commonly seen habit of sliding the *outside* lower leg way behind the girth is another misunderstanding of the leg aid for the canter depart.

On a bent line (circle or corner) your outside leg will already be in the "guarding" position about one hand width behind the girth so does not need to be taken farther back for the transition into canter! When riding in a correct seat during turns you are shifting your weight forward to the inside seat bone and keeping your inside hip a little bit forward, so this pelvic position automatically positions the outside leg further back. Checking the outside leg position before the canter transition should be merely a check of your correct balance and pelvic position.

When you apply too much pressure with your *outside lower leg*, you throw your balance off, putting more weight onto your *outside seat bone*, and your hip tightens (see right photo). This throws you and the horse out of balance and puts extra stress on your lower back during the transition.*

Many riders are fixated (because they have been told so often!) on giving half-halts to prepare for a transition so they automatically pull on their inside rein during the canter depart. But there is a great deal of misunderstanding: A half-halt is the correct use of the interplay of aids, never just a rein aid. Pulling on the inside rein causes a rider to incorrectly shift her weight to the outside seat bone, which interferes with the balance of both horse and rider. The flow of motion during the transition is disrupted.**

*Again, correct timing and interplay of the aids is what counts most: shift your weight correctly before applying pressure with your lower legs.

**The inside rein needs to give the horse enough freedom to be able to balance himself during the suspension phase of the canter.

Too much leg aid—here during flying changes—robs horse and rider of their balance.

[3.5 Transitions and Half-Halts—Basic Work Presented in a Different Way   125

Rider & Horse Back to Back

Canter-trot transitions

Making a down transition from canter to trot is significantly more demanding on your seat and back than the up transition to canter. A smooth transition from canter to sitting trot is one of the most difficult tasks for a rider's balance and co-ordination skills. You need to decrease a "larger" scale movement to a "smaller" one and change from a slow, rocking motion to a rhythm that is quicker and full of impulsion.*

During the transition from canter to trot, you need to accelerate the frequency of your pelvic movement. The easiest way to learn how to switch to a faster rhythm is by going from canter directly into rising trot. The key to transitioning from canter to sitting trot is for you to be prepared for the fact that the succeeding motion will be quicker.

In order to ride a fluent down transition, you need to center your weight as the trot requires less weight shifting than canter. At the same time, you have to allow your back to follow the lateral movement of the horse's pelvis. (For exercises to practice working on the flexibility of your pelvis see Part 2.) It is often the case that riders trying to keep their balance and center their weight, automatically tighten their grip around the saddle, which makes them stiffen. This mistake is fatal in the down transition from canter to trot because the horse's first trot stride will "hit" your tense and stiff back, upsetting his and your balance.

In order to center your weight while maintaining the flexibility of your pelvis, the deep muscles in your abdomen and back have to work as a team, and you need good dynamic stability and straightness in your thoracic spine. You can prevent becoming stiff in your hips and lumbar spine by imagining, right before the down transition, that you are stretching your upper back and, thus, giving the joints in your lower back more space to move.**

*The rhythm in trot is faster than the one in canter.

**Being able to sit smoothly and relaxed through a canter-sitting trot transition is a touchstone of coordination skills, stability, and control over your back.

A smooth sitting trot is possible only when your pelvis becomes part of the movement of the horse's back.

Rising trot during transitions between walk and trot

It is not only possible to combine transitions between trot and canter with rising trot but also those between walk and trot. Being asked to do rising trot right from the first trot step requires you to be able to feel the exact moment of the transition and to instantly adjust to the new rhythm. This method is particularly helpful to riders who have a habit of falling behind the horse's motion during the transition. When preparing for rising trot, your weight needs to have a forward tendency in order to be able to rise up in time. This relieves the back of both horse and rider and furthers a smooth transition.

It takes only a little bit of practice before you are able to tell by the sequence of steps in walk which diagonal the horse is going to move forward first when he starts trotting. This way, you can rise on the correct diagonal right from the beginning. You need to feel during walk the moment the horse puts each front leg on the ground. You prepare by sitting on the outside leg and rising on the inside leg. You then need to feel the exact moment the horse is changing so you can start the rising trot from step one on the correct diagonal.

Making a transition from rising trot to walk may be a little unusual but is nonetheless very effective. This exercise will question a habit deeply ingrained in most riders who have learned to *sit down* in the saddle before every transition. By keeping up the rising trot, riders are forced to continue moving rhythmically during the transition itself. Instead of riding *forward* in the transition from trot into walk, many riders stop moving and "block" their seat right before and during it, and only start following the horse's movement again when he is walking. It should be obvious that this behavior will interfere with the horse's balance and flow of motion. By continuing to rise right up to the transition you will prevent this tendency. You get yet another chance to learn to feel the exact moment of transition. Improving your feeling for motion will be tremendously helpful when you are trying to refine your aids and attain an automatic feel for correct timing.

If you have a horse that is particularly sensitive and likes to tense up his back muscles and resist the bit during transitions to walk, you might be able to see how astonishingly easy it can be to transition from rising trot to walk. You will learn to establish a degree of balance that is secure enough to facilitate smooth transitions free of negative tension. Moreover, this method also improves the quality of walk after the transition.

You should not ride all transitions in rising trot. Once you and your horse have relaxed your back muscles and are well balanced, you will be able to support your horse even better in sitting trot to walk transitions. In sitting trot, it is possible for you to continuously align *your* center of gravity with *your horse's* center of gravity in the most exact manner. But if you are tensing up during transitions, you are disturbing your horse more than supporting him. In order to break this vicious cycle, rising trot during transitions might just be the most helpful solution.

Even in rising trot, you can collect your horse and prepare him for a balanced transition.

Rider & Horse Back to Back

Sitting trot during transitions between walk and trot

In preparation for a transition to trot, it's important that you straighten your upper body and increase the positive tension in your body. If, instead of facing up to this challenge, you bang your lower legs against your horse's sides and move your seat around in the saddle, your horse will not only not understand you and most likely not obey you anymore, but you will also cause a negative reaction in your back. Strong leg aids tense your muscles around the hips and pelvis, which work against a supple and upright upper body.

You need to constantly make yourself aware of the order in which aids are supposed to be applied according to classical theory: first, weight; second, legs; and third and last, rein aids. Many riders twitch their lower legs or even their spurs when the instructor merely mentions "Walk on" or "Trot on." This incorrect interplay of aids and their application makes it almost impossible for them to sit in a relaxed way and be able to freely follow the horse's motion. If you catch yourself using mostly lower legs and spurs first in order to influence your horse, you will need a lot of discipline to get rid of this persistent habit.*

*The rule for the application of leg aids is: They may only be applied to such a degree that they do not interfere with the flexibility and suppleness of your seat.

Sitting relaxed and supple does not mean being completely without tension—you do need a certain, well-adjusted level of basic, positive body tension. The necessary prerequisites for this are good coordination skills and sufficient stamina in your deep back and abdominal muscles. Riders tend to compensate for weakness in their lower abdominals by using the flexors on the inside of their thighs. Too much tension in these thigh muscles, however, causes riders to sit more on their tensed-up thighs than deep in the saddle.

The rule should be: Use your lower legs only to such a degree as you are able to build up positive tension in your upper body. The effectiveness of your leg aids is determined not by strength but by correct interplay with other aids, correct timing, and the quickness with which you can relax your legs (taking pressure off the horse's side after the aid has been applied).

The better—and more exactly—you are able to feel and understand the horse's movement, the more you can follow a transition in a way that is good for your back.

Legs need to increase contact ...

... and relax again.

In the walk, it is helpful to get a sense of the sequence of footfalls and learn how to feel where the horse's legs are (see p. 74). The easiest way to do this is to just close your eyes for a moment and concentrate on when the hooves strike the ground. Many riders find it difficult to feel the hind legs so in the beginning, focus on the moment the front legs touch down. Becoming aware of the front legs—combined with knowledge of the walk's footfall teaches how to feel the hind legs as well.

If you can tell when the left or right front leg, respectively, touches the ground, you can keep counting along rhythmically: "And left, and right...." The word "and" signifies the exact moment of a hind leg striking the ground.

You must not let the horse move your body *sideways* too much. Frequently, even though you might feel as if you are following the motion in a relaxed manner, your lower back is actually moving in the area between your lumbar spine and rib cage. When you "rock" sideways like this too much, you are not following the horse's walk in a good way—quite the opposite. This instability makes it difficult for you to drive your horse forward as your weight aids become ineffective. Too much sideways motion from your pelvis usually means you are neglecting forward motion. As in any real lateral movement, you should always emphasize the *forward* rather than the *sideways*.

Increasing your positive upper body tension before a transition to trot can increase the danger of tensing up and inhibit the mobility of your pelvis at the same time. Being able to control individual segments of your body independently of each other is one of riding's greatest challenges. Closing your eyes and trying to feel how your horse is moving is a good way to relax your pelvis. The only way to feel the horse's movement is to become part of it.

Making yourself aware of the sequence of footfalls can also be helpful in the transition to walk. Being able to immediately feel every single step your horse takes will improve your entire sense of motion. Many riders don't understand how they are supposed to drive their horse *forward* during a *down* transition. They tend to apply too much pressure with their legs and tense up their seat muscles so cannot sit deep in the saddle. They slide their lower legs backward and press them against the horse's sides and when, in addition, they turn their legs slightly outward in order to use their spurs, it becomes impossible for them to sit with relaxed gluteal muscles. Their hip joints become "blocked," no longer able to follow the horse's movement. It is impossible to ride smooth transitions this way, and the back of both horse and rider is stressed.

You can find out for yourself what the effect of this poor technique feels like: When you turn both your *lower legs* and *toes* outward, you will feel your gluteal muscles tense up and discover you are suddenly unable to sit deep in the saddle—you are a little higher so your seat bones lose contact with the saddle. Instead, just "imagine" turning your *heels* slightly outward. This will help you relax your gluteal muscles allowing you to sit relaxed and deep.

So, in a down transition, visualize trying to turn your heels a little bit away from your horse's sides to keep the inside of your calf muscles in better contact with his body. This very slight pressure alone will encourage him to bring his hind legs further underneath his body.

"Heels away" from the horse helps you become more supple and sit deeper in the saddle.

3.5 Transitions and Half-Halts—Basic Work Presented in a Different Way

Rider & Horse: Back to Back

You need to learn to keep moving in unison with your horse during all transitions. Try out different ways to achieve this most important aspect of riding. There are no golden rules that lay out exact ways of doing it because everybody has their own unique way of moving: You need to find your own method. For example, you can use rhythmic exercises like juggling or mini biking (see pp. 93 and 142) that *exaggerate* the necessary body movements: As you improve they can gradually be reduced and become much smaller, though you will always need them. Every good rider uses them all the time: When watching an advanced rider, her body's movements can seem almost invisible.

You could fill an entire book with breathing techniques for riders. Generally speaking, *breathing out* usually helps with any tension or cramped-up muscles. It also plays an important role in the quality of a transition: You need to breathe out for as long as you can. However, you must remember to keep your upper body straight.

Breathing in helps build up positive body tension and stability in your back. Do not keep holding your breath!

The first phase of taking a breath can be especially helpful during a transition from walk to trot in order to improve the straightness of your upper body and build up positive tension. Holding your breath can be used when you need a short boost of tension and strength in your upper body; nevertheless, it always interferes with your flow of motion. In extreme situations, you can use this method to protect your back—but it must not develop into a habit, however, and you must always continue to breathe as soon as possible.

Walk-canter transitions

Walk to canter transitions can be especially back-friendly for riders who are still experiencing difficulty with the change of rhythm between trot and canter. They give you more time to prepare yourself: In walk, you can take your time adjusting your position and prepare for the canter movement.

Even though the canter has a different beat than the walk, the length of time the gaits take is nearly identical: One canter stride takes about the same amount of time as the pair of hind and front legs needs to move forward in walk.

It's most important to prepare your horse well enough so that during the actual walk to canter transition you can simply "wait" (by listening and feeling the horse's movement) for him to go forward. Your upper body remains still and straight and you'll have the feeling of cantering uphill right from the first stride.

Some riders have a habit of being overactive in the transition to canter. They are trying to strike off into canter together with their horse and, as a result, they either simulate the canter motion with their shoulders or overeagerly push their pelvis forward. This habit

When all aids are perfectly coordinated, it is even possible to briefly release contact (known as "*über-streichen*" in German), wherein in one clear motion you extend the inside hand and lightly maintain contact with the outside rein during the transition to canter from the walk. As you can see this horse is maintaining self-carriage and uphill balance.

Putting Riding Theory into Practice—The Back-Friendly Way

has negative effects on the balance and stability of their upper body and is harmful to the back of both rider and horse. To the horse, these rider body movements are not weight aids, but simply an annoying burden that disrupts their movement.

Transition from canter to walk

A well-executed transition from canter to walk gives your back the opportunity to build up stability while you can check your balance. However, this transition, in particular, also shows up any weakness or hidden problems. Only those horses willing to begin to collect in canter are able to directly transition to walk. Similarly, only riders who have developed a sufficient degree of dynamic stability in their overall posture should ride these transitions.

Every loss of balance has to be compensated by strength. Horses that are heavy on the forehand during the transition support themselves on the reins and pull their rider forward—especially stressful on the back. To check if you are ready for a canter-to-walk transition, see if you ride a balanced transition from canter to trot solely using your seat aids, that is, not using the reins at all. Working on tight turns like spiraling in and out and small circles can be very helpful for this.

Shortening intervals between transitions

The speed at which you need to coordinate your aids in a transition is particularly difficult for many riders: By the time you have sorted out all your thoughts, readjusted everything and are ready, the actual moment has gone by! It's a challenge to get the timing perfectly right: to "feel" it first and then do it. This is why, during training, it is so important to work on sharpening your reaction and coordination skills.

Same as you, your horse also finds making transitions a challenge to his coordination skills, balance and suppleness. Transitions between trot and canter change the way his pelvis moves. This is why—in combination with frequent changes of rein—transitions can help do away with negative tension or "blockages" in his back.

To help you become more accurate and quick at applying the aids, it is useful to count strides during transitions. Start with 10 canter strides, for example, and follow them with 10 trot strides. In rising trot, only the moment of sitting down counts, that is, every second step. Later, you can begin to shorten the interval between the transitions. This exercise helps you learn how much time you need in order to prepare for the transition. The more "through" ("*Durchlaessigkeit*" in German) and obedient your horse becomes, the more the interval is going to shorten.

The shorter the interval, the faster you have to get ready for the next transition. This is an important lesson for riders in developing "feel" for the horse. All too often, riders stop "riding" after having completed a move successfully. After having jumped a fence, novice riders often need a significant amount of time to prepare for the next: You can tell if a jumper is experienced when you see her keep on "riding" after a fence. Likewise, in dres-

Any down transition from canter can be only as good and balanced as the preceding canter stride.

3.5 Transitions and Half-Halts—Basic Work Presented in a Different Way

Rider & Horse Back to Back

*You need to make every successful moment the basis for the next movement.

sage, you should realize that the transition is always the *preparation* for the next movement.*

Overeager horses tend to become nervous doing this "intervals" exercise, no longer trotting in a relaxed manner and anticipating the strike-off into canter. When this happens, extend the length of the interval between transitions once again and maybe even ask for some turns, small circles, and serpentines until your horse is willing to "wait" for your aids. On the other hand, your horse's anticipation (in moderation) for the up transition can be useful: If he "counts" along too, he will learn to react to the subtlest of aids, which minimizes the amount of energy you need for the actual canter aid.

There are other horses, however, that see this exercise as a chance to take a break and lose the energy from their hindquarters: Consequently, they lose the quality of their canter. Anticipating the trot to come, they fall into a four-beat canter

Trot-canter transitions on an inside track in the ring (i.e. away from the fence) improve the mobility of the lower back of both horse and rider.

rhythm. Ask your horse to canter forward energetically and throw in some rhythmic intervals of lengthening and shortening his stride in addition to the transitions to trot.

The following exercise helps improve the flexibility of the lower backs of both horse and rider: Going large around the arena on the second or third track in from the wall or fence, ride some "interval" trot-canter transitions. Then, ask for counter-canter on the long side and transition to trot before the short side. Once you can do this well, count the canter and trot strides and steps again, and shorten the interval between trot and canter—or counter-canter.

Doing continuous transitions like these require your horse to change his pelvic motion all the time. The regular *lateral rotation* in trot turns into a *diagonal motion* in canter, and by switching between canter and counter-canter, both diagonals are being exercised. This exercise is especially helpful for horses whose muscles are tense right behind the saddle: In a fun manner, they start relaxing and swinging their back. Likewise, you are training your own pelvis' ability to be mobile.

Another advantage of this exercise is the fact that you will learn to feel the *symmetry* of the motion. Since you are supposed to keep your horse on a straight line at some distance from the outside wall of the arena on an inside track, you need to be balanced during the transitions (see photo). Sliding one hip forward is often enough to get the horse to come forward onto the correct canter lead. If your horse wants to move toward the wall during the transition to canter, you need to check in which direction your inside seat bone is "pushing" on the saddle. Quite often, the horse's "evasive" motion is simply caused by the rider pressing it toward the *outside* rather than the *inside*.

The transition between walk and trot is special because it includes a change from a gait *without impulsion* (walk) to a gait with *impulsion* (trot). Whenever the horse transitions from walk to trot,

Putting Riding Theory into Practice—The Back-Friendly Way

he has to push off energetically with his hind legs in order to *produce* impulsion for the trot's suspension phase. Transitioning back down, his hind legs have to *absorb* the trot's impulsion and turn it into a forward, walking motion. Both transitions require strength and elasticity in the hindquarters and back muscles.

For both forms—producing impulsion and absorbing it—you as a rider need a balanced and coordinated upper body. In trot, you have to maintain a greater degree of positive body tension while at the same time, allowing for a "larger" movement of your lower back. Working on transitions between walk and trot is a good exercise for strengthening and stabilizing your back. Many riders find it easier to ride sitting trot afterward because they can better adjust to their horse's movement.

Asking for transitions in more rapid succession (intervals) will increase the effect just described. In order to do this, you have to pick a specific number of trot strides to work with. If you are expecting to successfully transition to walk after just three trot strides, for example, you will have to be prepared for this transition while you are transitioning to trot. Since the aids for both transitions are virtually identical—except for their direction—you must learn to use your weight and your deep back muscles in the right direction. You will develop a feeling of how to control the short trot intervals with your pelvis. The goal of this exercise is to be able to ride these transitions with a light pressure on the reins and without changing the contact.

When making the down transition, you can also ask for trot immediately after a successful transition to walk. In the most "advanced" version, all of this happens in one single step: Your horse brings his hind legs further underneath his body to absorb the trot's impulsion—and pushes off energetically into walk right away.

All of these transitions are actually describing a half-halt: "enclosing" your horse between forward-driving and "guarding" aids. The main goal is to achieve elasticity and "throughness," which shows in the horse's willingness to be slowed down and sent forward with or without changing gaits. What you ask from your horse, you need to be able to do yourself: You have to have good stamina and excellent coordination skills to control the deep muscles in your trunk.*

If, during transitions, you tend to lose positive tension in your upper body—slouching and not pushing your horse forward enough—you had better ride exercises that require more forward motion immediately after each down transition. On the other hand, if you are someone who drives her horse forward a lot and makes him rush, you should not overdo it but rather keep checking your (and your horse's) balance during and after the transition. Knowing *when to wait* and *when to push forward* is an important milestone in the schooling of every rider. If you can feel when the timing and intensity of your aids are right, you are doing your back and your horse a great favor.

*Transitions and half-halts are important exercises, not only in regard to the horse's schooling but also for the rider.

"Enclosing" your horse between all the aids: a half-halt!

3.5 Transitions and Half-Halts—Basic Work Presented in a Different Way

Rider & Horse **Back to Back**

Halt

The halt is made up by the number of half-halts you need to make your horse stop. In order for a halt to be back-friendly, all the criteria mentioned in this section apply.

What is most important here is to be aware of the fact that every halt is based on motion and that there is a significant difference between a horse "doing" a halt and a horse merely standing still. For a correct halt, you and your horse need to maintain your posture, which requires dynamic stability in the spine. When you both are able to develop a common dynamic stability, a full halt can be achieved without any strain at all on your backs.

A successful halt should retain all the energy from the preceding motion: You need to be able to ride forward into every gait, whether an up or down transition, or back.

A halt in forward balance: Let the dressage test begin!

3.6 Sitting Trot—The Standard Criterion of Correct Posture and Influence

Quality over quantity

The sitting trot is a very complex subject to discuss. You can feel comfortable on one horse, while another one upsets your back. Even on one and the same horse, sitting trot might change significantly over the duration of a riding session: from uncomfortably harmful to your back to comfortably stabilizing.

Every rider and every horse has their own individual motion patterns, in which their back serves as the dynamic stabilizer. The rhythmic interplay of the deep muscles around the spine creates dynamic stability. Its intensity and frequency depend on the person and many other factors. Every back has its own individual frequency at which it "swings" best. The better the horse and rider's frequencies of vibration fit together, the more comfortable the rider will feel on the horse. To be able to tell if a rider and horse combination will mesh, it helps to understand their conformation. Riders with a long pelvis, for example, often have a hard time riding horses with a short back, as opposed to those with a long back—and vice versa.

There is a reason why sitting trot is considered a touchstone of riding skills: It has ended many a horse-rider relationship. Not being able to perform sitting trot is considered a typical reason why many riders turn to different riding disciplines. A motion as complicated and difficult to coordinate as sitting trot is not easy to learn and needs to be constantly practiced. Unfortunately, a rider who is cautious about her back because of pain (or fear of it) is presented with a serious obstacle to the learning process.

It is important that you place quality over quantity in order to master sitting trot. When sitting to the trot of a horse for hours, all you learn is that it is at best uncomfortable, and at worst, painful or completely impossible. Riding it for short intervals is much more sensible. When you are able to sit the first two or three steps after transitioning to trot, try to follow your horse's movement—in a relaxed manner—for three, maybe even four steps next time.*

If, out of 10 minutes of trot work, you are only able to sit supply for the first couple of laps, while for the remaining time, you become tense and "fight" your own body, you are developing exactly those muscles that will lead to negative tension and cramping later on. If, however, you keep asking for trot over and over again and either transition to walk or change to rising trot *before* you reach the point (controlled by reflexes) where you cannot sit supply anymore, you will end up with a larger amount of time spent on *correct* sitting trot. Practicing the right "feel" is the only way to successfully school the complex interplay of muscles necessary for sitting trot.

Sitting trot is considered the touchstone of correct posture and influence.

*During training sessions, it is most important to practice the good "feel" during sitting trot.

Rider & Horse Back to Back

When facing the difficult challenges involved in gaining a good seat, the general guideline for all riders should be to work in short intervals adjusted for their individual performance level.

> **Sitting trot contradictory demands**
> - Sit straight—but not stiffly.
> - Sit still—but keep on moving.
> - Build up tension—but stay supple and relaxed.

In order to sit in trot, you need stability, mobility, and adjusted positive tension. Your pelvis will be able to follow the three-dimension movements of the horse's back in trot only if your trunk is stabilized enough.*

Without stability, following the horse's motion in a relaxed manner is impossible!

Sitting trot requires positive tension in your muscles. You will not be able to meet coordination demands without being fit and strong enough—aspects often underestimated in equestrian sport. Adolescents who are still growing often lack the necessary ability to build up stability in their back—a reason why they should not be forced to sit in trot for too long. Short intervals, however, can be extremely conducive to further training.

The challenges you have to overcome in order to follow your horse's motion in trot also apply to walk and canter, of course. Since trot has the shortest "movement frequency," that is, length of time it takes for a stride to occur, it is usually considered to be most demanding of the three gaits.**

**The shorter the "movement frequency," of a gait, the more positive tension you need to build up in your upper body.*

Walking on the spot

Walking on the spot can help you feel how closely linked rhythm and movement frequency are to the degree of positive tension in your upper body. In the beginning, it will be easy and relaxed. The faster you walk on the spot, however, the more tension automatically gets built up in your upper body.

Here's a variation of this exercise: Slide over the floor with your legs straightened, inch by inch, one leg at a time, and as quickly as possible in all directions (forward, backward, laterally, and diagonally). The quick but short movements will literally shake awake your deep muscles so that they can better react to sudden action. You can test your ability to stabilize your upper body. There will be a significant parallel between the directions you prefer to move in on the floor and your mobility in the saddle. Moreover, moving your legs quickly like this increases your blood circulation and prepares your spine for the degree of stability it will need when riding. This is the perfect exercise for moving from office chair to horseback in an active back-friendly manner! Or you can include it in your morning exercise routine.

Walking on the spot helps you build up the degree of positive upper body tension you need in the saddle.

Putting Riding Theory into Practice—The Back-Friendly Way

Being aware of walking

Riding and walking are very much alike. If your way of walking—and posture—is good, your coordination skills in the saddle will most likely also be good. Based on this reasoning, next time you lead your horse, you can prepare your muscles for the task to come by walking in a conscious and controlled manner, though only when your horse is willing to let himself be lead without him pulling you or you pulling him.

The horse's back can also benefit from a few laps of active medium walk to give him a chance to relax before carrying your weight. Especially on cold days, it is much more sensible to walk next to your horse when warming him than to let your muscles get all cold by just sitting on him.

Leading your horse can be a useful addition to your warm-up program.

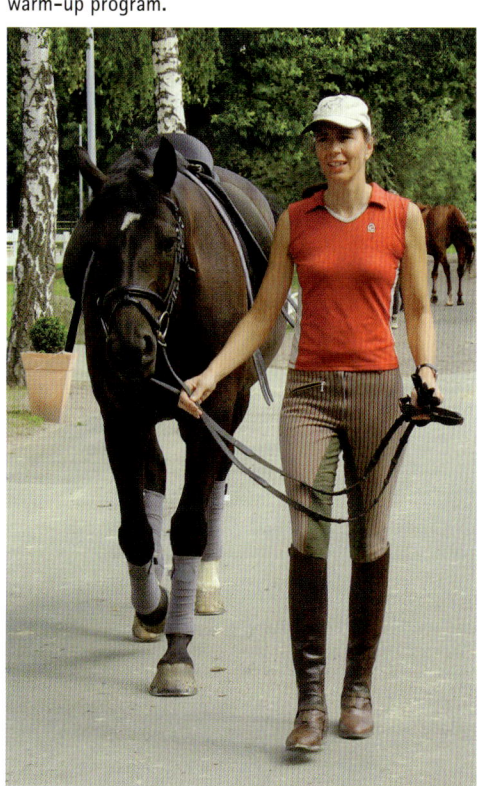

Walking backward

In order to loosen up and relax your lower back, it has proved tremendously helpful to walk, or even jog backward. In this way, your muscles are being used in the opposite order from usual. Targeting the muscle chains this way is one method to "readjust" automatic coordination of the deep muscles in your back. Riders with a tendency to a hollow back or "blockage" in the lower back find that walking backward helps them better stretch their lumbar spine—and simultaneously straighten their trunk.*

*Walking in a "conscious" manner—especially backward—is a good way to prepare for a riding session.

When walking forward and backward, individual motion patterns emerge.

3.6 Sitting Trot—The Standard Criterion of Correct Posture and Influence

Rider & Horse Back to Back

Taking small steps backward can stretch out your lower back: Lifting up your arms intensifies the effect.

Lifting and lowering your hips

In the trot's diagonal leg phases, when the horse keeps his gravity centered, he moves his back up and down and—what many riders fail to notice—from side to side, too. You can see this when watching his pelvis move while standing behind him. You need to be able to follow this lateral movement without significantly shifting your weight left or right.

The following exercise, the hip drop, helps to prepare your pelvis for this complex movement. Practice the hip drop by standing up straight. The exercise trains your pelvis to coordinate with such a movement, and also helps you avoid "collapsing in the hip" when riding. Distribute your weight evenly on both feet and place your hands on the widest part of your pelvis, at hip height. Move one knee slightly forward and down, and feel how the hip on the same side follows the knee. This "dropping" of the hip is part of the lateral movement of your pelvis. Watch out that your other hip does not move out sideways, and be sure your shoulder maintains the same position, not turning or twisting as it "tries" to help. Your weight should remain evenly distributed on both feet.

The hip drop correctly executed. Lifting and lowering the right hip is being practiced in a standing position.

In this picture, the rider's body is "compensating" for the hip drop, effectively negating its effect: Her pelvis has moved sideways and her shoulder has turned forward.

The hip drop teaches you to coordinate mobility in your pelvis while stabilizing your trunk and shoulder girdle. It requires elasticity in your hips and lower back.

Practicing sitting trot in multiple ways

There are many different ways to practice improving the sitting trot on the horse, too. In all of them, your back should be your first priority. Trying to sit despite back pain or even ignoring it can do serious harm to your back.

In trot, what you should focus on most is feeling the horse move underneath your seat bones. You will only be able to sense your horse's back if you relax your pelvis. When your buttocks (gluteal muscles) are tensed and tight—as often required in fitness routines—any "feeling" is impossible.

It has often been noted that the first and last trot steps in the trot-walk-trot transitions are the most comfortable. These moments are also the best time to actually "feel" the lateral movement of the horse's back. Practice this sensation! The more transitions you ride, the more you can practice this feel for your seat during transitions. You'll also gain more strides of comfortable sitting trot.

Initially, sitting at a very slow-paced trot is usually easier than a quicker pace. Sometimes, it is helpful to allow your horse to move in a very slow trot (similar to a jog in Western riding). At a slow pace with less impulsion, beginners have more time to control their seat, find their balance and relax. For the horse to be able to trot slowly, he needs to be in good balance (remember that like a bike, the slower you go the harder it is to stay on). With a tentative rider on top too, slow trot is strenuous for the horse and often makes him go more on his forehand. So ride your horse forward in rising trot before and after intervals of sitting slow trot.

From rising trot, you can prepare for the sitting trot. Make a series of changes of diagonal (see p. 88)—sit for three, four, or even five strides and then rise once. This exercise has multiple advantages: By counting rhythmically, you keep up with the horse's motion and you also keep "riding." Since the duration of the "sitting" time is limited to a few strides, it is more manageable so you can relax more. Rising for the one stride in between the sitting steps requires you to shift your weight forward. Being ready to do this prevents you from falling behind the movement in sitting trot, which often happens with inexperienced riders. This exercise has another bonus: Balance-type mistakes such as "pulling up" your knees are prevented.

The horse is often the best indicator of whether a transition between rising and sitting trot was successful or not. If it goes well, his rhythm is not disrupted and he will keep on moving regularly no matter whether you are sitting or rising. This approach to learning sitting trot is particularly useful when working with young horses.*

The interplay of your aids should not change during these transitions. It is of utmost importance that you keep a steady and light contact with the horse's mouth. It is often easier to establish this contact when in rising trot rather than sitting trot where a vicious cycle of imbalance can get started: The rider who cannot relax in her pelvis is not able to follow the horse's movement, and her upper body will lack dynamic stability and positive tension. As a result, her arms will inevitably compensate for this with reflexive movements. Independent hands become impossible. The cycle continues: The rider cannot provide steady contact so that interferes with the horse's flow of motion. This makes the horse tense up his back muscles, which makes him more uncomfortable to sit. The rider is now more tense, so on it goes…

In order to break this cycle, all riders should use appropriate auxiliary reins until they have found their balance in sitting trot and can follow the motion.

The horse is the best riding instructor!

Rider & Horse Back to Back

When your hands are stiff and uncoordinated during transitions to sitting trot, you might want to try juggling (see p. 93). Even though this might sound a little unconventional, it has proven very helpful when put into practice: Rhythmic movement is the only way to "free" your hands and stop their negative effect on your horse's mouth.

It is a good idea to first practice the juggling movements on the longe line. It is possible, however, to juggle when riding alone, as long as you can keep an even, steady contact on the horse's mouth.

For "independent" hands, practice moving them rhythmically as shown.

Later, just having a mental image of moving your hands rhythmically will be enough to remind you to carry them independently. This will automatically improve your suppleness during sitting trot.

Stretching and toning your muscles at the same time

An important prerequisite for sitting trot is that abdominal and back muscles work together. In Part 1, the special function of these muscles—designed for support rather than forward motion—was described in detail. They operate autonomously—out of your control—which is why it is particularly difficult to activate and "train" or tone them. When done properly, riding—and sitting trot in particular—is a perfect way to train them. But, first of all, you need to get good enough at riding to enjoy these benefits!

One comment you often get to hear during lessons is, "Push your stomach out!" Unfortunately, this advice is usually misunderstood and put into practice incorrectly: The rider hollows her back thus losing all the stability she had in her trunk. A rider trying to tense her abdominal muscles often pulls in her stomach because shortening the muscles is the only muscle function she knows. In order to develop flexible and dynamic stability in your trunk, your abdominal and back muscles need to work as a support; they must not be shortened. They have to stretch *eccentrically*, that is, become longer (when muscles remain the same length, it is known as isometric).

You can check out this function of your abdominal muscles yourself: lying down, sitting, standing, walking, and even riding. Press your fingertips into your stomach about one inch deep. Then tense up your muscles in such a way so you can push your fingers out. You can feel how your abdominal muscles "arch" outward as you tighten them. This pressure not only builds up toward the front of your body, but in all directions and helps to stabilize the lower back. It might help to think of it as a "barrel" of pressure. You can do this experiment in different places on your stomach: up, down, on the sides, and in the middle. In this way, you can find out where your stomach muscles react more quickly, better, and tighten more strongly, and where they react slower and are weaker.

Your buttocks should remain as relaxed as possible during this experiment. It is also important not to hold your breath but to keep on breathing as regularly as possible. When you can talk, sing, move, walk, run, ride a bike, and eventually ride a horse while keeping your abdominal muscles tensed, you have *stabilized your core*. This feeling of improved stability is the actual meaning behind the phrase, "Push your stomach out!"

If you have a hard time tensing the highest abdominal muscles right underneath your rib cage so they will "arch" outward, you are probably unstable in this area and tend to slouch forward. It will be difficult for you to collect your horse and keep

Putting Riding Theory into Practice—The Back-Friendly Way | 3

more...Before you transition to trot, you need to concentrate on how much—or better said, how little—contact there is between your thighs and the saddle so that you change it as little as possible during the transition. In order to do this, it can be helpful to hold onto a strap in front of the saddle for a while. This way, you will more likely relax your legs.

Your thighs also serve as stabilizers that facilitate balance and influence the position of your pelvis. It may seem contradictory that on the one hand, the thighs should be relaxed and not against the saddle, and on the other, their contact on the saddle helps to stabilize and influence the position of the pelvis. Important for the rider to consider is whether she can release her thigh contact again. Often, a rider gets "stuck" and, without realizing it, keeps on pressing her thighs more than necessary. She must become aware of this and consciously relax them.

You "activate" your abdominal muscles by touching them in specific places.

him from becoming heavy on the forehand during transitions. It has been proven helpful to make yourself aware of this area by placing a hand on the upper part of your stomach when you are riding a transition. Especially on a seemingly lazy horse, you will be surprised how little you actually need to use your legs during transitions to trot.

When you are losing your balance, your first instinctive reaction is to hold on with your legs. Once your thighs are pinned to your horse's sides, you have started another bad cycle that you will have a hard time breaking: Legs are squeezed around the horse; hips are "blocked"; horse is upset and becomes tense; your posture becomes unstable; hands start moving uncontrollably; horse becomes irritated and becomes even more uncomfortable to sit; your legs squeeze even

Relaxed thighs allow motion to pass through the entire leg.

Thighs tightly squeezed against the saddle have a negative effect on the entire seat.

3.6 Sitting Trot—The Standard Criterion of Correct Posture and Influence | 141

Rider & Horse Back to Back

Riding without stirrups

In order to better relax your legs and improve the contact between your pelvis and the saddle, ride without stirrups. You should not look at this as some method of punishment and torture but see it as a way to help you improve your seat and balance! If, however, you think of riding without stirrups as simply a test to see how long you can stay on the horse, you will be putting immense strain on your back—without improving your seat at all.

Rising trot without stirrups can greatly help you adjust your pelvis to the horse's motion. This exercise is not about how "high" you can rise up but about letting yourself be *moved* by the horse. Your horse's impulsion or upward thrust, respectively, is what determines how high you will come out of the saddle. Transitions between rising and sitting trot without stirrups can point you in the right direction as to how best to relax your hips during sitting trot and follow the horse's motion.

*Doing movements in the opposite order once again makes you aware of certain chains of motion, which means it is easier later on to execute the movements automatically in their correct order.

Rising trot without stirrups teaches you to sit deeper in the saddle.

Mini biking

Exercises from Part 2 are very important in order to improve the contact between pelvis and saddle. After the biking exercise, especially, you'll find sitting trot often significantly improves (see p. 81).

Many of the exercises can be done without a longe line. While describing the criteria for learning movement in Part 1, it was explained that movement needs to practiced first on a "larger" scale before it can be "fine-tuned" (see p. 34). When you fine-tune biking to mini biking, you will notice how closely related it is to applying aids. In walk, try to maintain an even contact between your foot and the stirrup while, at the same time, you are moving your ankle. Lift your heel as if you were standing on tiptoe, then lower it as much as you can without allowing your lower leg to slide forward. The stirrup should stay in the same position, not be pushed forward when the heel comes down (see top photo on p. 143).

At the same time, there is movement in your knee and hip joints. When your heel is lifted, your knee will slide up as well and your hip will flex a little more. When your heel is lowered, your knee will follow suit and your hip joints are stretched (see bottom photo on p. 143). This movement is similar to the flexibility needed during riding—even though in the opposite order from normal: Usually, the direction of movement is downward from hips, knees, to ankles. Your horse moves all these joints, and the motion of his back is reflected in the "springy" movement of your ankles.*

It is important to do the exercises tuned into the rhythm of your horse's motion. If you concentrate on doing mini biking during transitions from and to trot without stopping, you will not get a chance to tense up and become stiff. Following the horse's movement will almost happen by itself.

Many "lazy" horses show a particularly positive reaction to small movements like these because your leg aids become rhythmic. Horses better understand the meaning of your calf gently sliding up and down rather than bumping against their side.

Unconventional yet proven useful is a method of developing sitting trot on the basis of forward seat. In order to understand the logic behind this idea, you need to think about how and where horses carry their rider. There is no single perfect spot in which you always sit. Even the old masters of classical riding only spoke about the rider's seat in relation to the movements and training level of the horse. As a general rule, it can be said: On young horses, the rider tries to sit less "deep" and take weight off their back mainly by using a forward seat; on more experienced horses, the rider can sit straighter and deeper. In German, the term "forward seat" is known as the "light seat." But that is a misnomer, because the amount of weight the horse is carrying is still the same. However, in forward seat, the weight is placed differently—more at the horse's sides—so it feels lighter and is easier to carry.

Transition between forward and dressage seat

The functional connections between the dressage seat and the forward seat have already been explained (see p. 62). When aiming to improve sitting trot, you need to focus on the fact that, in forward seat, the horse's movement really does pass through your hip, knee, and ankle joints and is cushioned in those places.

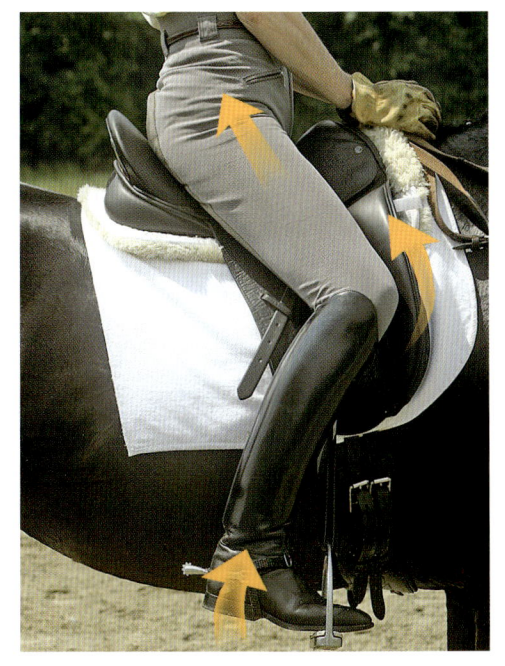

Motion in your ankle joints causes your knee and hip joints to move as well.

A mental picture of how and where the horse carries and feels your weight will give you new insight and understanding about how and where to balance your own weight in the forward seat position.

When you are shifting your weight to your thighs and, thus, to the horse's sides, your horse will no longer feel your weight pressing on his back but onto his sides along his ribs. You need to have good contact on your horse's sides while still allowing him to breathe. Never use all your strength to press your thighs and knees into your horse's sides.*

In this forward position, your center of gravity is lower and closer to your horse's center of gravity. Thus, your horse will find it easier to maintain his

*Using too much strength lowers a rider's awareness and inhibits her feel

3.6 Sitting Trot—The Standard Criterion of Correct Posture and Influence

Rider & Horse Back to Back

balance. During the transition to dressage seat, your weight travels upward along the horse's sides and through your thighs until it is finally resting on your seat bones. In this position, your horse feels and carries you in the middle and on top of his back.

The following exercise will teach you to feel exactly where your weight is meeting the horse and how to control it. While trotting, try to shift your weight rhythmically with every stride. Counting along can be helpful: Starting in the forward position, and within five trot steps, for example, change from forward seat to dressage seat, then ride sitting trot for another five steps before slowly bringing your center of gravity down the horse's sides until you have reached the forward-seat position again (also after five trot steps). The most important aspect of this exercise is not to change position from one second to the other, but to slowly shift your weight in sync with your horse's rhythm and in a controlled manner.

If you are able to maintain balance in forward seat, your legs will automatically be correctly positioned. The deep position of the knee and heel builds the foundation of the forward seat. Changes between forward and dressage seat are most helpful for correcting the lower leg position during sitting trot. During transitions, concentrate on your leg and be aware of the springy movement of your hip, knee, and ankle. This is easier to feel in the forward position but still exists in the dressage seat. Do not let your lower leg move forward when you change to the dressage upright position. This exercise helps you feel and control your seat without building up negative tension in the lower legs.

Once you are able to do this, you can also relax your pelvis and use your legs independently of the rest of your body—an important requirement not only in riding theory but also for your back. The ability to use your legs independently allows your upper body and back to stay supple but stable. Otherwise every use of your legs has a negative influence on the balance and support system of the upper body, and means extra strain on your back.

Changing from forward seat to dressage seat teaches you to feel where and how your horse can best carry you. Even in the dressage seat, this position is not a fixed point but is always connected to the horse's balance and ability to step under the rider's weight. Even on the same horse, this can change during a single training session!*

*Being aware of where your horse can best carry your weight is one of the key skills of a good rider.

A slow change from forward seat to dressage seat...

3 Putting Riding Theory into Practice—The Back-Friendly Way

Being flexible with your weight

When you have achieved basic suppleness and balance you can be flexible about where you place your weight, not necessarily going all the way to forward seat. It is possible to shift more weight to the sides or on top of the horse's back even when your upper body is nearly upright. Depending on the situation and exercise, it is very important that your posture is flexible enough to give you all these options. Shifting a little more weight down along your thighs can be a relief for the horse's back. When he feels more weight there, he can balance more and it's easier for him to round his back and step well under his body.

The foundation that supports your seat in the dressage position (seat bones and pubic bone) is shaped like a triangle because your seat bones run toward each other diagonally to the front. The farther you sit on your seat bones, the broader your foundation; the farther *forward* you sit, the narrower it will be. When starting to learn sitting trot, riders usually feel more secure sitting farther back. If you get stuck in this position, however, you might risk ending up in a "chair-seat" position, lagging behind your horse's movement.

Observing some of the most advanced riders, you might sometimes get the impression that they are trying to sit as far forward as possible, almost showing a tendency to a "fork" seat—without actually tipping forward, though. The more forward they sit, the narrower and, at the same time, more flexible their seat is going to be. The more flexible your seat, the quicker you are able to follow and influence the horse. The higher the degree of collection, the quicker you need to apply aids—and weight aids are the most important, after all.

Sitting as far forward on your seat bones as possible frees your horse's back and allows you to react more quickly.

... teaches you to feel when you have placed your weight correctly in sitting trot.

3.6 Sitting Trot—The Standard Criterion of Correct Posture and Influence

Rider & Horse Back to Back

Subtle weight shifts

During sitting trot, it can be worthwhile to concentrate on where it is in the saddle that you feel your seat bones when the horse's legs land on the ground because it is uncomfortable for the horse when you land in the same spot every time. Following the horse's lateral movements during trot changes the feeling under your seat bones with each step. This helps to relieve the horse's back and improve his suppleness. When you are beginning collected work, it may be quite difficult for the horse to step under his body when all your weight is centered on top of his back. Keeping some weight on the horse's side improves balance and invites the horse's back to round up—thereby making him more able to carry weight. Only when his muscles have become strong enough and he is familiar with collection, can you place more and more of your weight onto his back.

You can vary the subtle shifts of your weight from front to back: Imagine that the entire length of your seat bones are tracks you can move your weight along when you are riding sitting trot. Shift your weight slightly forward and then backward for the duration of a couple of trot steps and try to feel what your horse feels most comfortable with when carrying your weight. Ideally, your horse will let you know where to sit. The position will most likely be the one in which the two of you can find mutual suppleness and where sitting trot does not put any strain on your back.

On seat bones shaped like a sleigh, you can shift your weight forward, to the middle, or backward.

3.7 Naturally Crooked

"Crooked" is normal

In the language of horse training, the term "naturally crooked" is often used—just as if it was unusual for any being to be born with a slightly asymmetric conformation and motion pattern. Actually, the opposite is true: It's quite normal. Not only horses but riders are also characterized by their individual crookedness. Only from a great distance do humans look symmetrical. Taking a closer look, you will notice left- or right-handedness and a preferred leg to stand or walk on. Inside your body, there is no symmetry at all for that matter. Many organs only come as "singles" and their weight is unevenly distributed. This fact is one of the reasons why good balance—and with it almost symmetrical movement and posture—is possible only when *dynamically established through motion.*

Your position on your horse equips you with basic symmetry. In practice and at a close distance, however, many subtle differences between left and right sides of your body will become apparent.*

The spinal column consists of countless small parts and joints, which are nearly impossible to align exactly on top of each other. Moreover, it does not actually concern your horse much if you are sitting straight or crooked—to him, it is much more important that you distribute your weight evenly so he can understand your aids.

The more upright you sit, the easier it will be for you to control your center of gravity and keep it balanced over your horse's center of gravity.

An asymmetric posture requires more strength and energy and puts a significantly higher amount of strain on your back. You constantly disturb your horse's balance when you sit crookedly, thus putting more weight on one side of his back. If your riding is always forcing you back into a crooked position, problems and back pain are inevitable.

On the other hand, a crooked horse will not let you sit straight, either. If you are suffering from back problems, it is very bad for you to sit and work against your horse's crookedness all the time. You are not able to relax, you'll use your muscles unevenly, and most likely end up in a cycle of overstrain and tension.

It is a matter of chance whether the crookedness of horse and rider will balance or reinforce each other's asymmetry. In the worst case scenario, you will be able to ride your horse on one rein without any problems at all, while on the other rein, the two of you will constantly fight. In order to improve symmetry, both horse and rider need to be seen as a whole. Only when both of them can find

*It is really an art to be able to correctly sit straight and ride on a straight line!

"Straightness" has to be reestablished over and over again.

Rider & Horse Back to Back

*All dressage movements influence and improve the horse's straightness; they simultaneously help your straightness as well!

mutual balance and straightness, will riding and being ridden be gentle to their back.*

Only when you have learned to deal with your own crookedness and can sit straight, will you be able to work on improving your horse's straightness. Knowing this, you can reinterpret familiar exercises and use them productively to help your own riding—and your back.

In riding, crookedness cannot be corrected with compensating movement from other parts of your body. This just leads to negative tension and crookedness in other places. Any correction needs to involve your whole body and improve balance, straightness, and stability. The more you are able to stretch and straighten up while maintaining your position, the less significant your crookedness will be.

Similar principles apply to the horse. "Ride your horse forward and make him go straight!" is a well-known and often quoted statement from Gustav Steinbrecht's *The Gymnasium of the Horse*, a famous book written in the middle of the nineteenth century that contains many ideas you can put into practice over and over again during the years you spend on horseback. Some horses straighten better if you ride them forward because only after you have them in front of your aids, can you keep them straight during collection work, too. Without a forward tendency, riding straight is impossible.

To understand this connection, try the following simple exercise: If you yourself were trying to balance on a narrow beam, it would be easier to move quickly. The slower you walk, the shakier your movements are going to be. Horses are no different; in order to maintain balance, they need forward motion—especially during collection exercises.

Once you have understood that neither horse nor rider will ever be absolutely straight and that, to a certain degree, asymmetries are completely natural, it becomes clear that riding on a straight line is not as simple as it might have appeared at first glance.

The difficulty of riding straight

It is a well known fact that people lost in a wood, keep moving in circles—sometimes bigger, sometimes smaller ones. Your sense of what it means to go straight is dominated by the asymmetries of your body. In order to really walk on a straight line, you need optical orientation such as signs on the landscape or a compass.

Moving perfectly straight is just as difficult and unnatural for horses, and the degree of balance required is much higher. The weight of the rider is an additional factor interfering with their balance.

The main reaction the horse shows when losing his balance is a change in his movement. Many horses start to rush as they try to regain balance sometimes even transitioning into a higher gait. You often see the rider of a young unbal-

Riding on a straight line is a demanding challenge.

Putting Riding Theory into Practice—The Back-Friendly Way

anced horse succeed at cantering in large circles. The minute she changes from a curved line to a straight line by heading down the long side, however, the horse usually transitions to trot, starts to rush, or even changes leads.

It is not correct to assume that riding on straight lines in the dressage arena will initially be easier. The long sides are inevitably followed by corners, and the constant change between straight and curved lines requires a higher degree of balance. It is easier for horse and rider to adjust to the even curve that is provided by a large circle.

Oftentimes, a circle is the best place to practice control over your horse's direction, speed, and tempo—basic criteria for the application of aids. Even with a horse trying to ignore your aids by rushing uncontrollably forward, you can usually get him back under control by turning onto a circle.

Balance and obedience to all aids are the prerequisites of correctly riding on straight lines. In the same way your straight posture is defined by dynamic stability, straight lines are dynamic challenges that can only be mastered in forward motion.

When you walk straight, it only *seems* as if your path is straight as an arrow. In reality, your center of gravity keeps being shifted from one foot to the other so you'll always be making a sideways movement to maintain your balance, and consequently move diagonally forward.

The horse' sequence of footfalls also shows signs of diagonal shifts. In trot the horse has the diagonal footfall but no diagonal or lateral shift of weight. Walk and canter include a diagonal shift of weight. This is why it is easiest to establish balance in trot, and why it is the gait where a rider can most easily control direction, speed, and tempo.

Bending and collecting

Bend and collection require excellent coordination skills but as with other more advanced work they require a considerable amount of strength, too from both the horse and rider's back. It's important to find the right balance when training so muscles are not overstrained. When deep back muscles lack stability, too much bending and collection work over a long period of time can be harmful. Correctly adjusted and used with care, this type of work is a perfect way to develop and improve your symmetry and upright posture. It also strengthens the deep muscles in your upper body.*

*In order to keep your upper body in a correct upright position, you need to be able to rotate your back.

The better you shift your weight, the better you and your horse will master curved lines, and the more upright you sit, the more your horse's self-carriage will improve.

3.7 Naturally Crooked

Rider & Horse Back to Back

For a horse to bend laterally, his spine needs to rotate simultaneously (see p. 68). This connection between lateral bend and rotation explains the close relation between bending, straightness, elevation and collection.

The horse in a turn

Observing a horse trotting through a corner offers you some interesting insights into his balance: In trot, the horse always strikes the ground with a diagonal pair of legs. This means that in every turn, the inside hind leg has a significantly shorter distance to travel than the outside front leg. To be able to make the turn balanced and steady on the correct line, the horse automatically needs to perform a shorter, slower stride with the inside hind, while speeding up his outside front for a slightly longer stride. Every turn requires the inside hind leg to be willing and able to carry weight, and collect. The rider need to help the horse bring his outside shoulder forward into the turn to prevent it from "drifting" off the correct line or track, with the resulting loss of balance in the turn.*

For the horse, every turn challenges his coordination because he needs to be able to differentiate between the movement of pelvis and shoulders where leg movement originates. To the same degree that the hind leg needs to carry more weight in a turn, the outside shoulder needs more mobility and freedom to move. This "lightness" of the horse's forehand is one of the goals of true collection, so every turn becomes perfect "preparation" for it.

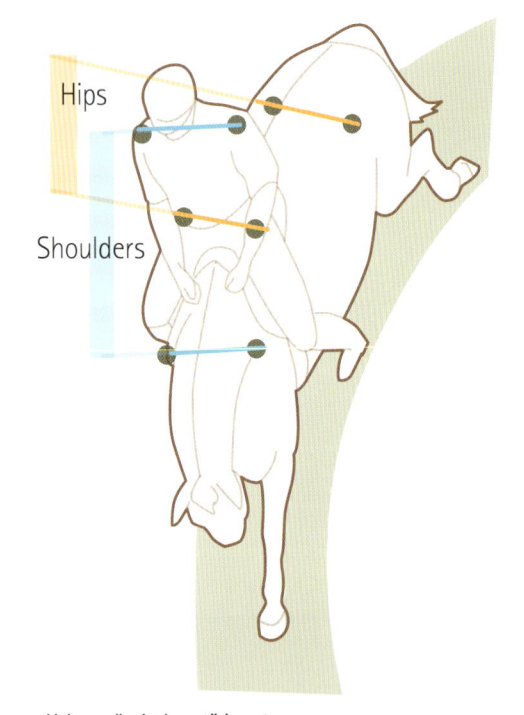

*Along with the horse's outside shoulder, the rider also needs to bring her own outside shoulder forward during the turn.

Using a "spiral seat" in a turn.

Shifting your weight to the inside and bringing your outside shoulder forward—this is how both you and your horse master any turn.

Putting Riding Theory into Practice—The Back-Friendly Way

Riding through turns challenges the rider's coordination skills, too. Your seat in a turn is called a "spiral seat" (see p. 90). Your hips are supposed to be parallel to the hips of your horse and your shoulders parallel to your horse's. In order to do this, just like the horse, you need to differentiate between the movement of your pelvis and your shoulders. All this may appear rather complicated but all you need to do is follow your horse's movements as naturally and as relaxed as possible. Analyzing movement also shows how complex even the most "normal" motion is—the human walking pattern, for example, is highly scientific, and yet, we can all do it!

Good riders only minimally rotate their upper body in a turn. In this case, as in many others related to applying aids, the best aids are the *invisible* ones—the horse still feels these aids as clearly. By invisible, it means riders are just initiating a movement and following it through to a certain degree. Thus, the rotation in their body is less of a change in position as it is a change in *the dynamic tension* of their upper body. This can be explained by the diagonal muscle chains (lines between hip and opposite shoulders) of your body being used to a different degree: the rotation of the upper body influences them differently. The rotation in your upper body alternately works the diagonals by making them stretch and flex (the distance between hip and diagonally opposite shoulder decreases and increases).

Through "large" movements to "small refined" ones, this basic rule also applies in sitting and balancing in turns: To start, visibly rotate your upper body to help you feel which chains are being worked. Later, just *imagining* how your upper body rotates is enough for the required muscle chains to activate.

Every rider has a favorite direction she can turn to more easily. She can better keep her shoulders level that way. If turning to one side is difficult, a rider often compensates by lowering her inside shoulder, which can lead to her collapsing in her waist and hips as well as her weight shifting to the wrong side. Since her horse is now lacking essential support of her weight in the turn, he will lean on her inside rein—another example of how loss of balance leads to the need for more unnecessary strength to be used.*

In order to be able to turn your upper body evenly in both directions, start rotating it from left to right during warm-up and in all three gaits. This way you are preparing for the more subtle movement of the deep muscles and a smooth interplay of the diagonal muscle chains mentioned earlier. Simultaneously, you are improving your awareness of your balance in turns and your ability to move your shoulders and pelvis independently of each other.

Trying it yourself, you will find out that rotating your upper body is possible only if you do not look down. Your cervical spine needs to be straight if you want to work on the rotation of your upper body.

*Looking down during a turn is a bad mistake putting unnecessary strain on your back.

The hips and shoulders of horse and rider move parallel to each other.

3.7 Naturally Crooked

3.8 Tools for Back-Friendly Collection

Basic training: gymnastics for rider and horse

Advanced exercises can only be mastered effortlessly and in a back-friendly way when both rider and horse have developed mutual suppleness and balance.

Based on this prerequisite, the following gymnastic exercises will help you work on the building blocks of classical riding, straightness and collection, in a systematic way.

Even though riding on a large circle is easier than riding on a straight line, working toward a correct and even circle line is an art in itself. You only need to longe your horse in order to realize that on one rein he will pull more to the outside than on the other, or that at certain points on the circle line he will move inward, pull outward, and start to rush or slow down.

In order to be able to make your horse correctly follow the circle line on both reins and at a constant pace, the interplay of your aids needs to be (nearly) perfect and your horse must react obediently. If you succeed, you can be sure that you have worked your horse evenly on both leads. If your horse changes rhythm or pace or leaves the circle line by moving inward or outward, he is resisting the training. The following exercise routines will help to detect and prevent these kinds of evasive actions.

Circle: set cones as marker points

Cones can be used as a visual aid to help you plan and ride a correctly round circle. You can set markers on a circle to indicate the four points where you need to reestablish the horse's balance with half-halts. They are also especially helpful and revealing when riding in a 20 by 60 meter arena where the 20-meter circle doesn't have any barrier on one side (no wall or fence for support). You will clearly notice immediately when your horse tries to decrease or increase the circle.

Since your horse keeps moving forward at a steady pace, every cone is passed in the flow of motion. Applying a half-halt at every circle point—as required in classical schooling—should not interfere with this smooth flow of motion. A half-halt can be ridden without slowing the horse down!

The aids passing the circle point are as they are in every half-halt: not applied all at once but an interplay of all aids. To keep the turn and bend of the circle *even*, the half-halt requires a quick and refined interplay of *outside* and *inside* aids. Imagine bending a stick around your knee, which acts as the circle cone: Your hands "symbolize" where you need to use the outside aids before and after the turn, with the inside aids used in the middle of the turn.

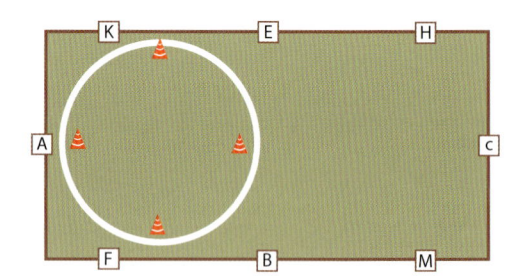

Riding correctly around the circle's points teaches you how to apply outside and inside aids in a rhythmic "automatic" manner, a skill that later on, will be most helpful with more difficult movements like smaller circles and pirouettes.

Circle: counting

Once you are able to apply all aids successfully and in combination, you can start concentrating on counting your horse's strides. This is most easily done in rising trot. Count every time you sit down, that is, every other trot stride. From one cone to the next, a quarter-circle when the diameter is 20 meters, you will count to about six. Depending on the length of your horse's legs and the ground he covers in one stride, this number may vary.

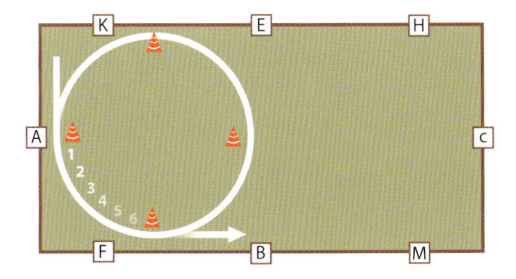

Your first task is to find out the number of strides your horse needs to complete one even circle. This way, you will learn how to correctly assess your horse's speed and assess the exact amount of ground that is covered at a specific pace. This ability is very important in regard to future work on extensions and collection. It's not only jumpers that need to be able to figure out distances—dressage also requires a rider's sensitivity or feel for how much ground her horse covers in one stride.

Counting along teaches you to react quickly and to correct your horse before it's too late. For example if your average number of strides between two cones is six, you should be about halfway between the cones at three. Here you can develop the feel of riding the correct circle and tempo. If you are at three strides and not yet in the middle, you had better speed up, or if you have passed the middle, then you need to shorten the strides.

Circle: using counting to influence the horse's movement

Once you are able to control each circle with the same number of strides, you can begin to influence the amount of ground your horse covers by increasing or decreasing the number of strides on purpose. Walk is the exception: It is challenging enough to master the circle in a controlled, active medium walk while the stride count remains the same. In trot and canter you will realize that *decreasing* the number of strides does not mean riding more *slowly* but, on the contrary, actually requires the horse to *extend* the gait and *increase* ground coverage of each stride. The opposite is true: When you want to *increase* the number of strides in the circle and reduce each one's ground coverage, you ride the horse in *collection*. This is where the markers are particularly helpful, since you can measure from cone to cone. Maintaining the correct circle while lengthening and shortening the stride will make sure the horse stays "framed" between the aids and uphold his balance and self-carriage.

This exercise tells you a lot about your ability as a rider. It also helps you understand your horse better: Some horses can be collected more easily in trot, others in canter, some drift on the circle to the outside or to the inside, and others become slower or start hurrying. Feeling this you will learn to find the right aids using the *full meaning* of the word "aid," that is, to help your horse in this work. You will be able to feel if it is easier for him to collect in trot or in canter, if he dodges to one side or the other when you try to collect him or if he slows down or rushes. The better you know yourself and your horse, the earlier and more targeted you can apply your aids.*

Riding through a corner: triangle

Riding through a corner correctly is a common, yet always challenging task. Your horse needs to be straight before you reach it, then bend his body in the corner in order to stay balanced and "straight." If you pass through the corner successfully, your horse will be in front of your aids afterward. Many riders use corners to make their horses come on the bit again when they have lost contact on the long side of the arena. Correctly riding through corners is one of the key aspects to achieving good scores in dressage tests. Therefore, even experienced riders on well-trained, advanced horses keep working on riding through corners.

*Working in lengthening and shortening strides on a large circle is excellent preparation for performing them later on straight lines.

Rider & Horse Back to Back

In this picture, the horse's haunches are falling in before he reaches the corner.

After successfully correcting the fault, the horse is now straight as an arrow before reaching the corner.

The biggest problem with riding corners is that they come up so often that you get used to them and after a while, do not ride them *consciously* anymore. Most horses are smart enough to start turning the corner by themselves early enough. Unfortunately, this means they are anticipating their rider's forward-driving aids and are not *in front of them* anymore, thus cleverly avoiding work in the corner.

Some horses turn too soon or move their haunches inward before the corner. Often, they hurry down the long side and slow down before the corner. Many horses change their rhythm or pace, especially *after* the corner. In order to reestablish *riding* through a corner, it is useful to turn this task into an unfamiliar situation and exaggerate a little bit, that is, use the big-to-small learning process:

Instead of going large around the arena using all four corners, make a three-cornered triangle.

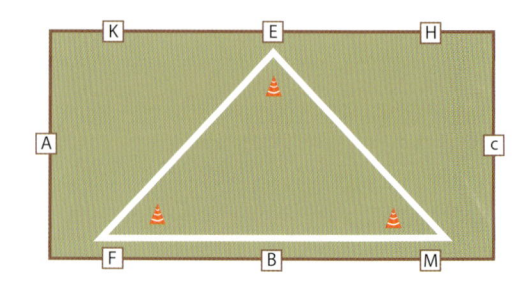

Triangle "map"

The size of the triangle depends on the horse's level of training. Start with one that is as big as possible: When you are working in a 20- by 60-meter arena, watch out that the angles do not become too acute, thus too sharp for your horse to turn. At the advanced level, use the second track along the long side. It's more difficult without the wall as a support.

Since the triangle's corners are "sharper" than usual and unfamiliar to your horse, you need to consciously *ride* him into it. This exercise demonstrates the importance of good balance between the inside and outside aids. You might want to practice in rising trot first, which is usually an easier way to follow your horse's movement. The moment you are rising is the moment when he diagonally lifts his inside hind leg and outside foreleg.

As described earlier, during turns your horse's inside hind leg does the collected work while his outside foreleg has the longest distance to travel. When you are rising, concentrate on making your horse shift more weight to his inside hind leg. During rising trot, the actual moment that you rise—not the one when you are sitting (despite a commonly held belief to the contrary)—is the only time you have the chance to influence your horse's inside hind leg at all, and this is when you initiate the turning aids. You need to help the horse speed up the motion of his *outside* shoulder into the turn. Consistently pulling on the inside rein does not help the horse get balanced around a corner—the aids within the turn must be linked into the rhythmic movement of each gait to help him stay balanced.

If you turn too sharply or too wide, you will not make it to the next corner of the triangle in a straight line. Only starting to turn when you reach the corner is clearly turning too late. The cone should always mark the peak or middle of the turn; therefore, you have to start turning in time. While you are giving your outside aids, the sharp angle of the corner simultaneously slows the horse down, forcing you to use your inside aids to push him forward to maintain the rhythm. Moreover, you will notice how difficult it is to emerge from a corner in a straight line: When you lose momentum in the corner, there goes the straight line you had planned, and when jumping a course, you immediately lose the correct distance to the next fence! The importance of the outside aids becomes more apparent during the triangle exercise. Only a horse that maintains his balance with the help of your outside aids will be able to emerge from the corners of the triangle in the same rhythm and on a straight line.

You can ride around the triangle in all gaits. The exercise can help in prepare for transitions in a playful way. Once you have straightened your horse after the corner, transitions to trot or canter are more successful with a much better uphill balance. You can mix riding transitions before or after the sharp corners of the triangle. This way, the horse will learn to *wait* for your aids and stop hurrying after the corner—or slowing down before it. In walk, this exercise is a good way to prepare for a turn on the haunches, while in canter, the acute corners help you work on pirouettes. Moreover, it is useful in the training of young horses in order to improve their balance in canter and their straightness. Of course, you need to adjust the angles of the triangle or turns to the ability and training level of your horse.

Riding the triangle can help you prepare for turning onto the center line straight and balanced.*

Counting corners

Corners also require rhythmic forward motion. This becomes more apparent when you start counting the steps and strides necessary to ride through a corner—similar to the circle exercise described earlier. The number varies depending on the path, degree of collection and level of training.

Knowing that the average trot stride is about 1.2 meters (3.9 feet) in length, it will be fairly easy to calculate the distance traveled when going through a corner. If, for example, in rising trot you are counting four (counting every time you sit equals two strides), your horse has taken eight strides, which gives you a turn of about 9.6 meters (31.5 feet) in length. A corner should not

*Successfully mastering the more difficult corners of the triangle allows you to ride through the four usual arena corners more easily.

Rider & Horse Back to Back

Riding through a corner requires horse and rider to concentrate hard on their work.

be thought of as "pointed" but more rounded like a quarter of a small circle with a varying diameter.

In canter, it usually takes three to four strides to cover a corner completely. Counting along helps to maintain the horse's rhythm during the turn and to apply your aids well coordinated to this rhythm. The amount and timing of the aids will vary and need to be adjusted to every single corner. The number of strides is a criterion you can measure and give you a clear, verifiable goal to concentrate on. Counting makes you aware not only where to start the corner but also where it is finished, which is when the straight line out of the corner starts.

When you do not straighten the horse on the short side between the corners, however, the positive effect of riding corners disappears immediately. And, if you are faced with footing that does not allow you to ride right into the corners correctly, rather than ride "sloppy" ones, you are better off making the arena smaller with new corners.

Corner: a quarter of a circle

Using the corner as if it were a small circle (10 meters or less) is a good way to work on balance and straightness at the same time. It prepares you and your horse for the correct bend you need during the complete circle.

This "image" has proven useful: Similar to a large circle, a small one consists of four quarters. When you are riding a small circle by starting in a corner, let the corner become the first quarter, and end the circle where it began. The corner then constitutes both the first and an imaginary "fifth" quarter of the small circle.

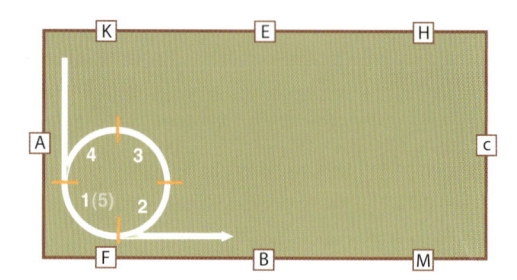

Since your horse can use the wall as support during two of the "five" ridden quarters, it is easier to make small circles evenly round by asking for them in corners. Moreover, you have more time to concentrate on an even bend from poll to tail than you do during small circles starting from a point on the long or short sides of the arena. Consciously riding small circles in corners can sig-

Putting Riding Theory into Practice—The Back-Friendly Way

Prepare, turn, and emerge from the corner on a straight line.

nificantly improve your feeling for an even bend and for straightening your horse afterward. In this way, small circles (and a half circle and return to track) will be easier to manage in other places within the arena.

The same as on a regular circle, counting strides helps to make small circles evenly sized and round while preventing the common mistake of enlarging or reducing the size of the second half of the circle.

Circle: diamond or square

You can think of the line of a circle as "abstract," one that requires the horse to move at a steady rhythm—with or without support from the outside wall or fence of an arena. It is much easier said than done, and performing one correctly is an art in itself. Many horses, but especially young ones tend to pull toward the corners or fall in or out on the open side of the circle.

In this case, the image of a diamond (or square) instead of a circle can be helpful. The cone markers become the corners so that you change between turning and riding a straight line instead of going round evenly.

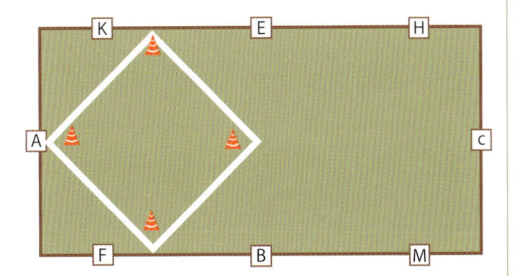

This exercise helps you to turn horses that tend to fall out with their outside shoulder. Knowing how the horse turns, you can understand how difficult it can be for him to "speed up" his outside shoulder during the turn. By falling out, he evades taking more weight on his inside hind leg. This knowledge combined with the diamond exercise will teach you the feel of how you can use your aids to help the horse be in better balance around corners, rather than just pulling on the reins. This is because the only way for your horse to master turns successfully is to allow him to move his outside foreleg quicker without being slowed down by you.

Similar to the triangle exercise, a diamond (square) exercise also improves your ability to co-ordinate your outside and inside aids. Even though the corners are not as sharp as in the triangle, the challenge in the square exercise is to make the

3.8 Tools for Back-Friendly Collection

Rider & Horse Back to Back

changes between turning and straightening more quickly because the sides of the diamond are shorter than the triangle.

The diamond shape also teaches you to concentrate on where you are going. Being able to plan ahead and decide where your horse's next stride is supposed to land on the ground is an important part in the preparation of all exercises. Knowing exactly where your horse's front and hind legs are touching down gives you the opportunity to control and influence an even bend from poll to tail.

Circle: control of the forehand

An important aspect of the principles of riding and classical theory is to align the horse's forehand exactly in front of the hindquarters. When straightening him you should not try to do so by moving the hindquarters in or out by moving the forehand in alignment. The hindquarters are defined as the horse's engine, and even though keeping it "running" is essential, controlling the forelegs and, thus, the shoulders becomes more and more vital during advanced training.

In walk and with your eyes closed, it is relatively easy to feel the front feet touch the ground and to learn how to follow their direction with your respective seat bone. This skill is necessary in order to control the forelegs with your seat.

During a turn, both forelegs are supposed to move in the new direction. However, in order to avoid bending, many horses turn with their outside foreleg only while the inside foreleg keeps moving straight. This "compensating" movement inevitably leads to "irregularities" in all lateral movements, in addition to the fact that your horse will lose his balance in every corner.

In walk, you can begin to find out through feel which direction is easier for your horse to turn toward. Finding this feeling over and over again creates the basis for correct bending, which leads to correct straightening.

Once the horse uses his hindquarters correctly as the engine for all the power of movement, and is stepping well under his and the rider's center of gravity carrying the weight, his forehand will become free and light and the rider can move it to any direction she wants.

Putting Riding Theory into Practice—The Back-Friendly Way

Your conscious attempt to influence the direction of the inside foreleg in the turn will teach you that it can only be done if you don't pull backward on the inside rein. This way, the importance or, better, the *preeminence* of the outside aids in turns becomes self-explanatory. If your horse keeps falling out when cantering on a circle, pulling on the inside rein does not improve the situation at all. On the contrary: Pulling on the inside rein actually helps push the outside shoulder to fall out even more.*

Especially in canter, trying to improve things when your horse's leading leg is about to hit the ground is pointless because every landing sequence of steps is prepared during the preceding stride. So instead of working on the landing sequence, try to influence the next stride by controlling the front leading leg's strike-off.

Loss of balance during a turn caused this horse to compensate for it with some undesirable movement in the front legs...

...however, once he is balanced, he is able to master the same turn.

On the line of a circle, you need to plan ahead where you want your horse to place his front feet for the next canter stride. Having a clear image of the movement in your mind's eye defines how you plan to coordinate your aids, and this "preparation" can be felt and understood by the horse.

The canter stride you are riding right now was "pre-programmed" in the preceding stride, so you can only work on improving the *next stride*.**

When your horse's balance is disrupted, he will not only instinctively compensate for this lack of balance by using his body but also by using his legs. Experienced jumpers know all too well that even horses with a natural talent for tucking up their forelegs over a fence will often just let one front leg "hang down" when their rider interferes with their balance.

Even minor imbalance has to be compensated for by your horse. If a horse that normally shows straight motion patterns starts, all of a sudden, to wing out (exaggerated paddling), he might be trying to regain his balance.

Even though subtle losses of balance will not necessarily be visible in your body, they put additional strain on your back nonetheless. This is why it is important to constantly check if you are still balanced when riding turns and make sure that you are not compensating by using muscle strength in order to be able to follow the turn.

Even if you should need to apply aids more intensely for a moment, you must return to subtle influence right away so as not to get stuck with the horse making compensatory movements. Your horse might exploit these and use your energy to support himself and maintain his balance. Neither of you will experience any positive effects on your back from situations like this.

*If you want to be able to influence your horse's movement, you need to think and act ahead.

**Thinking and acting ahead determines whether you are successful or not—in both dressage and jumping.

3.8 Tools for Back-Friendly Collection 159

Rider & Horse *Back to Back*

*One of the central requirements for developing a good seat is to be able to independently control and coordinate the movements between your pelvis and shoulders.

**Having a good awareness of your balance in turns activates an automatic reaction of the deep muscles in your back, and this improves the dynamic stability of your spine.

Influencing bend with your seat

The first step to influencing bend is to develop a feeling for how your horse differentiates between moving his shoulders and pelvis when he turns. Then you have to learn how to influence his forelegs without slowing down his hindquarters (his engine). In order for you to do this, you have to be able to control and coordinate the movements of your own shoulder girdle and pelvis.*

When you are sitting balanced through a turn, both of your thighs will have *even contact* with the saddle. Being aware of this feeling helps you to control your balance precisely. Once you feel that your inside thigh and knee put more pressure on the saddle, your weight has already shifted to the outside—even though this might not yet be visible to others. If you are among those riders who tend to collapse their inside hip and slide to the outside during corners or circles, you should concentrate on your ability to keep very little or no pressure with the inside thigh and knee on the saddle—especially when turning.

The common mistake of sliding to the outside during turns is intensified by two factors: first, by the naturally occurring centrifugal force of curves, which pushes your weight to the outside, and second, by the natural crookedness of your horse. You will only be able to sit comfortably in turns if your horse's inside hind leg reaches forward underneath his center of gravity to carry more weight. Caused by the rotation of his spinal column, your horse's back lifts a little on the inside, and this gives you the feeling of your seat being pushed to the outside. It is important for the rider to allow the horse's back to move and rotate during turns. Dynamic stability in your trunk and supple mobility in your pelvis is necessary in order to avoid collapsing at the waist or hip.

If your horse tries to avoid bending correctly by not carrying weight on his inside hind leg and back, he will place you noticeably more to one side and will not let you sit in the middle of his back.

Your lateral bend and rotation are also connected. When your horse is correctly bent and the inside of his back lifts up, this movement causes a lateral flexion in the rider's spine starting from the bottom—it is the rotation needed for the rider to be able to sit correctly in the turn. The way your horse's back influences yours and vice versa will automatically lead you to correctly rotate your shoulder girdle and your pelvis if you are balanced and relaxed. The ideal is when you and your horse help each other balance in harmony.

Talented children during their first peak of motor-skills development (approximately the age of nine or ten) sometimes show perfect posture riding turns: Their outside leg goes back by itself, without anyone ever explaining the principles to them in detail.

Unfortunately, the ideal is mostly theoretical. Many riders are pushed by their horse to sit more to the outside without their noticing, or they do not allow for the subtle rotation of their upper body. Both cases lead to negative tension in the long run, sometimes even causing "blockages" between the vertebrae.**

The following exercises offer ways to work on differentiating between the movements of your pelvis and your shoulders in as effortless and back-friendly a manner as possible. In order to prevent overstraining of joints and muscles during practice, remember the principles defined earlier on how to learn new movements (see p. 34): Create a rhythmic basic structure for all motion patterns and systematically return to simpler, "bigger" movements.

Putting Riding Theory into Practice—The Back-Friendly Way

Slalom on a straight line

Set up a slalom course using cones on a straight line. The distance between the cones should be about 16 to 20 feet (5 to 6 meters) and can be decreased to 13 feet (4 meters) for practice purposes. In order to be able to evenly ride through the course and begin from both ends, an uneven number of cones is a good idea.

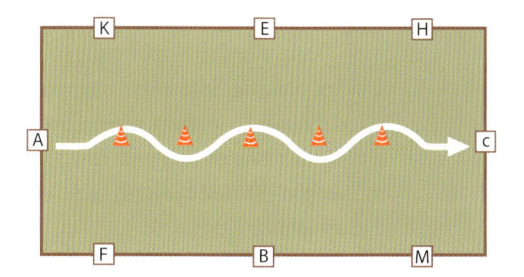

Mastering a slalom course in walk and trot is a fun exercise. How difficult—and educational—it can be for both you and your horse, you will probably only realize later. You will both automatically learn the interplay of inside and outside aids. Because the cones act as a visual aid, your horse can clearly understand what you want him to do and work independently. Using the slalom during the warm up with tense or stiff horses helps them become more supple and elastic.

This exercise gives you the opportunity to concentrate on your seat. You can feel how you and your horse shift weight for every change of direction. When you can do a slalom course well, you will be better able to ride straight afterward because you have been working on fine-tuning your inside and outside aids.

If you use your reins too much, you will over-steer and either miss the next cone or lose the flow of motion. Slaloming without applying outside aids is impossible and the motto "less is more" proves true once again when applying any kind of aids: The lesser the effort you put into getting through the slalom, the more smoothly and easily you will master the task. Other useful variations of this exercise are riding with the reins in one hand or even closing your eyes.

Combining the slalom course with transitions is a good way to learn the technique of preparing for an exercise. Right after you finish the slalom in trot is a good moment to strike off into canter. Trotting through the slalom prepares your horse to listen to the alternating aids; he will be better between your inside and outside aids, which is ideal for a fluent transition into canter. Usually, transitions at this point in time turn out smoothly because your horse is better balanced and able to obey your aids more easily.

In a riding lesson—as is happening with this adult beginner—the slalom is a good and enjoyable way to learn complex motion patterns.

3.8 Tools for Back-Friendly Collection

Rider & Horse Back to Back

The value of flexion and counterflexion on a straight line

For the next exercise, ride on the second or third track or on the centerline: Increase the flexion in your horse's poll and neck to one side and concentrate on keeping all four legs following the straight line. It will quickly become apparent how easily some horses avoid a correct flexion by stepping out with their outside hind leg every time your inside rein asks for more flexion. Keeping all four legs straight while changing the flexion takes coordination and balance. Maintaining a straight line while flexing your horse from left to right and vice versa is a very challenging exercise.

You will be able to feel that you keep your horse's body straight by using your seat and your legs, while your hands are busy asking for a specific flexion and position of neck and head. The importance of your outside aids will immediately become apparent. At the same time, you will feel when your horse obeys your forward-driving aids, that is, when he is "in front of" your inside leg.

During this exercise, you will quickly realize in which direction your horse's shoulder or hind leg falls in or out so you can help him improve his balance.

Since the neck is the horse's "balancing pole," he can only give you control over the position of his neck and head if he is truly balanced in his body. Every loss of balance shows you the quality of contact you need to your horse's mouth. Riding straight with increased flexion helps you feel and analyze the origin of your horse's balance problems. A better understanding of these problems is the key to correct—and simultaneously gentle—training.

How far sideways you can flex head and neck depends on your horse's ability to maintain his balance in motion. If you overdo this exercise and ask too much of your horse, the only thing you will achieve is his supple neck: You lose thrust and impulsion from back to front, as well as proper contact. In the beginning, it is advisable to start with less sideways flexion—moving his head laterally no further than his respective front foot's position.

Flexion to the right, flexion to the left, and going straight ahead: Even though it looks so simple in the pictures, this exercise is the epitome of balance.

Putting Riding Theory into Practice—The Back-Friendly Way

The basis of all lateral movements: shoulder-in

Once you are able to ride your horse straight while flexing his poll and neck sideways, you have created the foundation for shoulder-in. From this point, it is not long before you will reach the goal of riding the first significant classical lateral movement: All you need to do, in addition to head and neck, is move your horse's forehand slightly inward.

Do not worry about your horse drifting inward a little as this is the lesser mistake: The horse's forehand (shoulder) is still moving in the correct direction. There is a far more common and serious mistake, which happens when you end up with a "neck-in and hindquarters-out" instead of shoulder-in. By falling out with his hindquarters, your horse avoids the correct bend of his body and the actual point of the exercise is voided.

Only when you succeed in correctly leading your horse's forehand inward, can you loosen your grip on the inside rein. This gives your horse the opportunity to actively and regularly move forward and sideways and use your outside aids to maintain his balance. You as his rider need to be able to straighten up within your upper body and, at the same time, coordinate and control a slight rotation of your spine to match the horse's angle of bend. Your shoulders are parallel to the horse's shoulders in a shoulder-in position while your hips are parallel to the horse's hips—continuing on the straight line. If you do not concentrate on sitting upright (improved straightness) during the entire exercise, you will immediately collapse in your side and put strain on your back.

If you have to apply a lot of pressure with your legs in order to push your horse into a lateral movement, then he is lacking "throughness," obedience to the aids and needs systematic gymnasticizing. Every once in a while, it might be necessary to encourage your horse by nudging him with your leg, but your goal should always be to get him to step underneath your weight instead of your having to "push" him away sideways.

Shoulder-in: The hind legs are moving forward on a straight line.

In shoulder-in, the forehand needs to be moved inward to a degree where the outside front foot and inside hind foot track on one straight line.**

When riding shoulder-in, the horse's hind legs should not change their track or direction. The horse should only move the shoulders in, so needs to bend between his pelvis and shoulders—the correct bend for the body. Developing a feel for the position and direction of the horse's hind legs (this began in the flexing exercise on p. 164) will enable you to feel and ride the correct bend of the horse. Holding an image of a straight line on which the inside hind leg works toward the outside front foot, helps you to keep riding forward in shoulder-in (see photo).*

In canter, there is a moment in the stride when a diagonal pair of legs (inside hind and outside front) strikes the ground simultaneously. This diagonal supporting sequence is essential to the quality of the canter. If the two hooves do not touch down at the same time, you are facing a four-beat canter, which results in loss of impulsion and additional negative strain on both of your backs.

Loss of rhythm and forward motion are the two most common mistakes in lateral movements.

**When observed from the front, only three legs should be visible—the outside front leg is "hiding" the inside hind leg.*

3.8 Tools for Back-Friendly Collection 165

Rider & Horse Back to Back

Shoulder-in at canter: When, from the front, you see three tracks, the horse is bending correctly.

The key to a successful shoulder-in, therefore, is bend of the horse's body—not the flexion of his head and neck. Experienced riders are even able to ride shoulder-in in counterflexion. Regarding the coordination of your aids, it is always helpful to ask for all kinds of lateral movements, not only along the wall or fence of the arena, but also on imaginary lines such as the second track or centerline.

Diagonally and straight

Lateral movements require the rider to have enough skill to be able to control the horse's forehand and hindquarters individually. The following exercise helps you to manage this complex task by splitting it up into parts, which give you more time to feel and control each step. Start practicing in walk, later in trot and canter. This exercise is particularly helpful as a preparation for half-pass or when working with horses that have been showing problems with half-pass.

Turn onto a diagonal line across the arena and, after a short distance, turn once again and ride parallel to the outside track. As soon as you feel your horse is straight, turn onto the diagonal again and continue alternating like this until you have slowly worked your way forward to the centerline (see figure). It is important that you initiate the turns onto a diagonal with the forehand, the inside foreleg in particular. This way, when you want to go straight again, you can control the

Lateral movements without the support of a wall or fence challenge the coordination of your aids. Here: travers on both leads.

166

Putting Riding Theory into Practice—The Back-Friendly Way 3

forehand while moving the hindquarters sideways. Controlling and stabilizing the forehand, while at the same time asking the hind legs to step underneath your horse's center of gravity in order to go straight again afterward, is the point of this exercise: It is a principle many other classical exercises are based upon!

The quality of lateral movements is to a great degree defined by how you prepare, begin, and end them. Every irregularity of rhythm, every hesitation and acceleration are signs of a loss of balance, and all require energy. Therefore, it is more important to maintain rhythm (flow of motion) of the half-pass than to ride it at a "sharp" angle. Another thing you should not neglect is the ending and riding out of a half-pass. Finishing, straightening your horse, and flexing him to the new direction must not interfere with the rhythm.

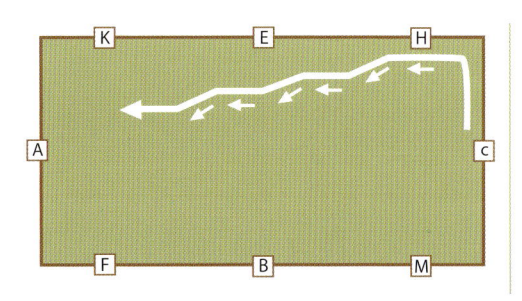

This is how smoothly a half-pass can be ended—by making sure the horse straightens and by flexing him to the new direction.

3.8 Tools for Back-Friendly Collection 167

Rider & Horse Back to Back

A half-pass—here in trot—shows how well the rider and horse are able to keep their back stabilized.

Constant, soft contact is part of the basic requirement for correct lateral movement. Ideally, the contact never changes—no matter if you are riding straight, asking for shoulder-in, travers, renvers, or half-passes. The more you need to support your horse with rein and leg aids, the more you are straining your back. In order to ride back-friendly, you need to constantly assess how

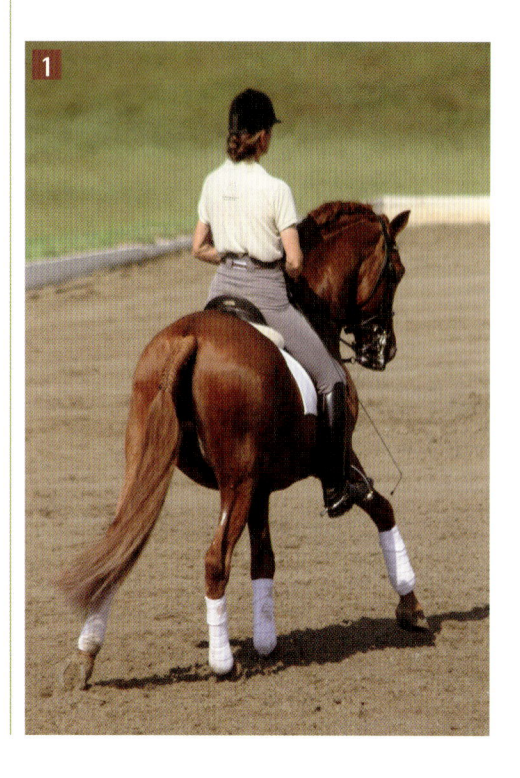

Putting Riding Theory into Practice—The Back-Friendly Way

much you can demand and expect from yourself and your horse. It depends on the situation at the time whether you should first practice an exercise in walk, take a break, or return to simpler preparatory exercises. Most important is to prevent the vicious cycle of rider strength versus horse tension as explained earlier (see p. 48).

A canter half-pass that looks this easy also feels good: The horse is "jumping" under the rider's weight and his movement is balanced and showing lightness.

3.8 Tools for Back-Friendly Collection 169

Lengthening and shortening the stride

If you have been practicing the exercise in which you are supposed to count steps and strides while riding on a circle (see p. 152), you have experienced how difficult it can be to continuously follow the circle line and keep the forelegs and hind legs on track. On straight lines, this challenge becomes even more obvious. Many horses, for example, tend to move their hindquarters to the inside when you ask for extended canter and they canter on two tracks. When shortening the stride after an extension the same difficulty can be encountered as many horses move their hindquarters sideways to avoid stepping correctly under the rider's weight.

In transitions from trot to walk, the outside hind leg often evades the increased collection by stepping to the outside. Preventing this common evasive action from occurring in the first place is much more useful than trying to retrain your horse later. In order to do this, you need to find out how best to support your horse—instead of just dwelling on his weaknesses.

Sitting straight during transitions is also very difficult for most riders. Every time you apply a half-halt, you are supposed to constantly check and reestablish the stability in your upper body. Only when you've achieved this can you support your horse and help him accomplish a fluent, balanced, and straight transition.

A useful exercise to help you achieve a goal of smooth transitions takes place in an alley fenced in with poles (see diagram). First, you ride through the poles in a constant rhythm. Next, trot into the alley, transition to walk for three to four strides, then trot on and ride out. The poles help your horse remain straight during both transitions. Focus straight ahead and learn to apply your aids in a way that interferes with the lateral balance of your horse as little as possible. You can vary this exercise in multiple ways. You can use it to practice the salute at the beginning of a dressage test, improve lengthening and shortening strides (also extending and collecting), or work on a simple canter change through the walk. The advantage of doing this while using a visual aid such as the alley is that your horse will instinctively understand what is demanded of him and react to subtler aids.*

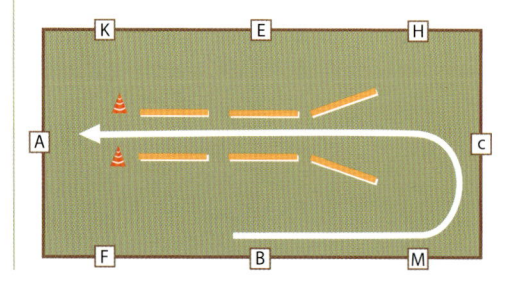

Crescendo, decrescendo, and a musical scale

Images based on music are very helpful for working on the *quality* of movement. It is helpful to think of a crescendo or decrescendo (gradually playing louder or softer), or going up and down a musical scale when you practice lengthening and shortening the strides. If you are counting along with the rhythm of the movement, you can assign each moment its own level of sound and imagine a scale, volume control, or a combination of both.

Extension and collection are supposed to make your horse (and you!) more flexible. Using the "playing musical scales" image to make transitions more smooth, start an extension in trot or canter on a low "note," go up the scale until you end on a high note. This high note then acts as the beginning of collection, and you gradually go down the scale to the next movement. By thinking to music and visualizing this way it becomes apparent that the extended trot is actually the preparation for the collected trot, and vice versa. Changing from extension to collection like this produces elasticity and activity in the hindquarters, avoiding overworking one specific chain of muscles. This kind of elasticity improves blood circulation, and strengthens and builds the deep back muscles in a way that is both intense and gentle.*

*Every form of riding based on subtle aids produces less wear and tear on your back.

Putting Riding Theory into Practice—The Back-Friendly Way

The decision about how many notes (strides) you want in your musical scale can vary and cater to the individual. The pace that is right for you and your horse—an active workout, the two of you can endure over a longer period of time with as little effort as possible—lies somewhere in the middle. At a working pace, you should always feel as if you have enough "space" at both ends (top and bottom) of your imaginary scale. When your horse shows a tendency to slow down in his extension, you can ask him to go for one or two notes further up the scale—that is, extend for a bit longer. When he starts to hurry, end the scale going up early so you can start going toward collection. In the end, your supple horse should be consistently "asking" you what the next note is in the mutual harmonious scale.*

This exercise not only improves the elasticity of your muscles, it also helps you maintain impulsion and the energy of the horse's movement in as effortless and harmonious way as possible.

As a matter of fact, your horse uses the same parts in his body for both extension and collection: The only difference is the amount of ground covered and the angle of the legs during motion. Collected movements are *elevated* and *shorter* in stride than extended ones where your horse *stretches out* (lengthens) his stride, thus covering more ground. In collection, energy is directed *upward*, while in extension, it travels *forward*. Collection is considered the highest achievement of training because it can only be developed by working directly against gravity.

All practical advice and tools necessary to achieve collection mentioned in Part 3 are the foundation of training both horse and rider. Every single exercise has been designed in such a way so that it fits into the six levels (building blocks) of the Classical Training Scale. A better understanding of the complex interplay of motion creates a basis for a way of riding that treats your back with care, protects, and strengthens it.**

*Extension and collection check and balance each other!

**When used correctly, classical riding theory provides the perfect training concept to sustain the health of both horse and rider.

Ready to collect more—or extend.

Extension and collection belong together.

3.8 Tools for Back-Friendly Collection

Acknowledgments

Our publisher, Siegmund Friedrich, patiently endured all of the changes, this project witnessed during its extensive production period (starting out as a small brochure that turned into the book you are holding now). And, he always trusted his authors. Without him, this book would not exist.

Special thanks to all involved in the English translation, especially to Caroline Robbins, publisher of Trafalgar Square Books, who put in endless hours and thought as she patiently helped to clear up all the many language difficulties!

A book is the never the work of its authors alone—many thoughtful minds and many helpful hands have contributed to make it happen and naming all of them is impossible in the space provided here.

First of all, we want to thank all the participants in front of—and behind—the cameras: all riders, trainers, horse owners and grooms at the state riding school of Rhineland (Langenfeld); the Mannheim Riding Club, in Beit Yannay (Israel); and at First Choice Farm (Maryland, USA). This book is indebted to them for the most important reason: vivid and real-life practical application. All of these people did their best for the photos, and did not shy away from exposing their weaknesses and flaws.

Mary McKenna, Barbara Schnell, Shira Yeger, Ricarda Mertens, and Jean Christen provided us with an abundance of more than 5,000 photos: We are sorry that we could not print all of their magnificent pictures.

"Our" graphic designers, Jeanne Kloepfer and Marianne Fietzeck, in their usual creative and professional way, brought order to the chaos of our ideas.

This book is a family endeavor through and through—not only in regard to the two cousins who wrote it together but also because of their families. Every production phase of a book is like a state of emergency, which many family members had to endure and support by being patient, giving their time, and taking over responsibilities.

A special thanks to professional horse trainer Felicitas von Neumann-Cosel, currently residing in the United States, who contributed to this book both theoretically and practically in her own special way. She turns riding into an art form and she delivered convincing proof of the fact that successful professional and effective riding can be harmonious, gentle, classical, and "back-friendly" at the same time.

Thank you, Felicitas!

173

Index

Age of rider, 35–36
Aids
    back-friendly program and, 106
    and circles, 152
    necessity of interplay between, 121
    rein, 67, 106
    and slalom on straight line, 161–162
Anatomy. *See also* Muscles of back
    horses' backs and, 12–13
    muscles of back, 5–7
    poll, 72–73
    spine, 2–4
    vertebrae, 4–5
Awareness, 7, 14, 25–29, 76–78.
    See also Senses/perception

Back-friendly training program
    contact and, 106–107
    creation of, 103–104
    impulsion and, 107
    rhythm and, 104
    straightness and, 107
    suppleness/relaxation in, 104–105
Back function
    back muscles and, 5–6
    dynamic stability and, 1
    individuals and, 7
    spine anatomy and, 2–4
    spine function, 2, 5
    subconscious motion of back and, 6–7
    vertebrae anatomy and, 4–5
Back pain. *See* Pain
Back strength
    for instructors, 61
    mounting/dismounting and, 60–61
    personal responsibility for, 57–59
    tack and, 58–61
Balance, 22–23
    back-friendly program and, 104
    collection and, 108
    as compensated by strength, 131
    as if riding bicycle, 81
    and motion during transitions, 120, 122–123
    motion pattern and, 53
    rising trot as exercise, 86–88
    and shortening the reins, 110
    and straightness, 148–149
    straightness and, 107
    and stretching/toning muscles, 140–141
Behind the motion, 123. *See also* Motion
Below-the-limit training, 99–101
    On the bit, 67
Body awareness, importance of, 14

Index

Canter
  after collection, 102
  canter - trot transitions, 126
  canter - walk transitions, 131
  circle and control of forehand (collection), 159
  counting corners (collection) and, 156
  footfall sequence of, 74–75
  half-pass at, 167, 169
  leg sequences of, 123–124
  rising trot - canter transitions, 122–123
  shoulder-in at, 165–166
  sitting trot - canter transitions, 123–125
  and straightness, 148–149
  walk - canter transitions, 130–131
  weight placement and, 44
Cervical vertebrae, 3–5, 66–67, 70–71
Collection
  advantages of, 120
  below-the-limit training and, 101
  on the bit, 67
  canter after, 102
  circle and control of forehand, 158–159
  circle as diamond/square, 157–158
  circles and counting, 152–153
  circles with cones as markers, 152
  corner as quarter of circle, 156–157
  counting corners, 155–156
  and influencing bend with seat, 160
  riding through corners (triangles), 153–155
  stretching to prevent muscle strain during, 100
  Training Scale and, 108
  weight placement and, 149–150
Communication. *See also* Senses/perception
  electronic systems during lessons, 18, 58
  feeling and, 19–21
  hearing and, 17–18
Compensation
  and eradication of bad habits, 45
  evasion patterns and, 49
  during riding, 42
Contact
  in back-friendly training program, 106–107
  biking exercise and, 142
  release during coordination of aids, 130
  and shortening the reins, 111

  and slalom on circle, 162
  Training Scale and, 108
Coordination and perception training, 14–15, 99
Coordination/dexterity and motion pattern, 54
Cresty neck, 13
Crooked, 147–148

Danger to back
  horse leaning on reins, 114–115
  horse with stiff back, 116–117
  lazy horse, 117
  unpredictable events, 117–118
Deep feeling, 19
Diagonals, 88, 127, 132. *See also* Trot
Dismounting, 61, 102
Dressage
  as basis, 62
  forward seat - dressage seat transition, 143–145
  mobility of hip/spine and, 89
  piaffe, 108
  walk of, 109
Dynamic stability
  back function and, 1
  back pain and, 33
  development of, 38–39
  and influencing bend with seat (collection), 160
  and patterns of evasion/compensation, 49

Equilibrium, inner ear and, 14
Eventing, three phases of, 7
Exercises
  awareness of self during riding, 76–78
  based on music, 170–171
  below-the-limit training and, 99–101
  circle and control of forehand (collection), 158–159
  circle as diamond/square (collection), 157–158
  circles and counting (collection), 152–153
  circles with cones as markers (collection), 152
  controlling forehand on circle, 163
  corner as quarter of circle (collection), 156–157
  counting corners (collection), 155–156
  counting strides during transitions, 131
  fitness/cross-training and, 50–51

Index

flexibility (diagonal patting), 90–91
flexibility (juggler), 93–94
flexibility (mobile/stable body parts game), 94–95
flexibility (mobility of shoulder girdle/neck/head), 95–97
flexibility (pelvis/shoulder girdle independence), 93
flexibility (spine rotation), 90
flexibility (stretching/turning combined), 92–93
flexibility (turn towards horse's rear end), 92
flexion/counter flexion on straight line, 164
half-pass, 166–169
hip joint relaxation, 79–80
as if riding bicycle, 81
importance of practice, 48
and influencing bend with seat (collection), 160
interval training, 101
interval trot - canter transitions, 132
mini biking, 142–143
and patterns of evasion/compensation, 49
reciprocal movement and, 47
before riding session, 57
riding through corners (triangles) (collection), 153–155
riding without stirrups, 142
rising high during trot, 119–120
rising trot as, 85–88
shortening the reins, 110–113
shoulder-in, 165–166
slalom on circle, 162
slalom on straight line, 161–162
stretching lower back, 82
stretching upper back, 83–84
stride lengthening/shortening, 170
taking up the reins, 109–110
thigh placement during, 80–81
upper body rotation during warm-up, 151
Extension, advantages of, 120

Facet joints, 5
Feeling, 14, 19–22
Fitness/cross-training
    importance of, 50–51
    motion pattern and, 54

Flexibility
    exercises, 90–97
    exercises (diagonal patting), 90–91
    exercises (juggler), 93–94
    exercises (mobile/stable body parts game), 94–95
    exercises (mobility of shoulder girdle/neck/head), 95–97
    exercises (pelvis/shoulder girdle independence), 93
    exercises (spine rotation), 90
    exercises (stretching/turning combined), 92–93
    exercises (turn towards horse's rear end), 92
    and forward seat - dressage seat transition, 145
Flexion
    of poll, 72–73
    and straight line, 164
Flight response of horses, 21
Forward seat, 62–63, 143–145

Gaits
    canter - trot transitions, 126
    canter - walk transitions, 131
    diagonals and, 88, 127, 132
    footfall sequence of, 74–75
    half-halt and, 103, 125, 131–133
    halt and, 134
    and intensity of aids, 45
    rising trot and transitions, 119–121
    rising trot - canter transitions, 122–123
    rising trot during walk - trot transitions, 127
    shifting weight and, 37–38
    and shortening intervals between transitions, 131–133
    and shortening the reins, 110
    sitting trot, 135–140
    sitting trot - canter transitions, 123–125
    sitting trot during walk - trot transitions, 128–130
    trot, 68–69
    walk - canter transitions, 130–131
    walk phase, 32
    walk - trot transitions, 121
    weight placement and, 44

177

Index

Hacking, back strength and, 64–65
Half-halt, 103, 125, 131–133
Half-pass, 166–169
Halt, 38, 134
Hand problems, 49
Hearing, 14, 17–19, 22
Helmet, 57–58
Horse
    choice of right, 103
    interaction between rider and, 69
    lazy, 117
    leaning on reins, 114–115
    signs of relaxation, 68
    spine during motion, 66–69
    with stiff back, 116–117
    swinging back of, 67–68
    unpredictable events and, 117–118
Horses
    as balance of reflexes/controlled movement, 21
    individuality of, 12–13
    movement of level of training of, 54
    salivary glands and, 15

Impulsion
    in back-friendly training program, 107
    Training Scale and, 108
Individuality
    awareness of self during riding, 76–78
    back function and, 7
    height/build and, 8
    of horses, 12–13
    and pain threshold/tolerance, 30
    and reference lines for proportion, 8–11
    of riders' bodies, 10–11
    and understanding motion, 52–55
Instructors. *See also* Lessons
    on back stability, 36–37
    and back strength, 61
    goal of, 29
    importance of, 50
    influence on horse of, 105
    as "medium" for perception, 26–27
    and returning to basic work, 43–44
    and taking up the reins, 109

    training sense of body motion, 41–42
Interval training, 101

Jumping
    back strength and, 63–64
    below-the-limit training and, 101

Lateral movements. *See also* Gaits
    diagonal/straight and, 166–169
    half-pass, 166–169
    renvers, 168
    shoulder-in, 163, 165–166
    travers, 163
Leg aids. *See* Aids
Lessons
    electronic communication systems during, 18
    and instructors as "medium" for perception, 26–27
    less-demanding movements during, 45–46
    longe lessons, 34
Long back, 12
Long neck, 13
Longe lessons, 34, 103. *See also* Exercises
    hand movement and, 140
Lumbar vertebrae, 3–5

Mental picture, 45–46
Mini biking, 142–143
Mobility/stability and motion pattern, 53–54
Motion. *See also* Gaits
    and balance during transitions, 120
    as balance of reflexes/controlled movement, 21
    behind the motion, 123
    control by rider, 72
    development of dynamic stability for, 38–39
    execution of movements, 39
    horse's spine and, 66–69
    interaction between horse/rider, 69
    and interplay of horse/rider, 54–55
    reciprocal movement, 47
    and sense of balance, 22–23
    shifting weight and, 37–38
    and shortening the reins, 110–112
    subconscious motion of back and, 6–7

Index

training sense of body motion, 41–42
understanding, 52–55
Mounting, 60–61
Movements. *See also* Motion
   planning of, 40–41
Muscle memory, 29
Muscles of back
   and abdominal muscles, 140–141
   below-the-limit training and, 100–101
   of horse, 67, 104–105
   intense training/recovery and, 101
   recovery phase for, 102
   of rider, 5–7, 99
   of rider after hiatus, 106–107
Music-based images, 170–171

Naturally crooked, 147–148
Neck
   of horse, 71
   of rider, 70–71

Overstraining back, 99
Overstretching horses, 66

Pain. *See also* Danger to back
   fear of, 103
   feeling/perception of, 30
   riding with, 31–33
Perception. *See* Senses/perception
Piaffe, 108
Pointy croup, 13
Poll, 72–73
Postures, 8–9. *See also* Riding
   improving incorrect, 42–44
Proprioceptors, 14, 21
Reciprocal movement, 47
Recovery phase for muscles, 102
Reference lines, proportion and, 8–9
Rein aids, 67, 106
Renvers, 168
Rhythm
   back-friendly training program and, 104
   and images based on music, 179–171
   motion pattern and, 53

rising trot - canter transitions and, 122–123
and shortening the reins, 110, 113
Training Scale and, 108
transitions and, 119
Rider
   height/build and, 8
   importance of knowing level of, 103
   muscles of back and relaxation of, 99
   and reference lines for proportion, 8–11
Riding. *See also* Gaits
   adolescents and, 51
   age and, 35–36
   awareness of self during, 76–78
   body awareness and seat corrections, 28–29
   circle and control of forehand (collection), 158–159
   circle as diamond/square (collection), 157–158
   circles and counting (collection), 152–153
   circles with cones as markers (collection), 152
   compensation during, 42
   concentration of one aspect at a time, 27
   corner as quarter of circle (collection), 156–157
   counting corners (collection), 155–156
   dynamic stability and, 38–39
   eradication of bad habits/compensations, 45
   evasion/compensation patterns in, 49
   exercises before, 57
   fitness/cross-training and, 50–51
   forward seat, 62–63
   hand problems, 49
   horse in a turn, 150–151
   and importance of back stability, 36–37
   importance of basics, 43–45
   importance of practice, 48
   and influencing bend with seat (collection), 160
   interaction between horse/rider, 69
   jumping, 63–64
   learning new movements, 45–47
   motion and, 34–35, 52–55
   movement execution and, 39–40
   movement planning and, 40–41
   posture improvement and, 42
   problem recognizance/analysis and, 43
   riding through corners (triangles) (collection), 153–155

179